MANAGING ACROSS BORDERS

MANAGING ACROSS BORDERS

The Transnational Solution

Christopher A. Bartlett

and

Sumantra Ghoshal

Harvard Business School Press

BOSTON, MASSACHUSETTS

To Barbara and Susmita
with love and appreciation

95   94   93   92   91   5   4   3   2   1

Library of Congress Cataloging-in-Publication Data

Bartlett, Christopher A., 1943–
    Managing across borders : the transnational solution / Christopher
A. Bartlett and Sumantra Ghoshal.
        p.   cm.
    "Originally published by the Harvard Business School Press in
1989"—T.p. verso.
    Includes bibliographical references and index.
    ISBN 0-87584-303-4 (pbk. : acid free paper) :
    1. International business enterprises—Management.   I. Ghoshal,
Sumantra.   II. Title.
[HD62.4.B36   1991]
658'.049—dc20   91-12792
                                                              CIP

CONTENTS

PREFACE TO PAPERBACK EDITION

In the two years since the publication of *Managing Across Borders*, the complexity of the international business environment has continued to increase. We have witnessed the beginning of an intricate transformation process within Eastern Europe, a broadening of the regionalization of trading blocs, an acceleration in the development and the diffusion of new technologies and innovative products worldwide, and an intensification of the battle among global competitors across a wide variety of industries.

Such developments have reinforced many of the imperatives for change we described. As their operating environment becomes more complex and multidimensional, managers around the world are concluding that they need to recognize and respond to that complexity, not minimize or deny it. To overcome the limitations of their historical strategic postures and structural configurations, they are striving to develop new organizational capabilities that will help them succeed in the charged competitive environment of the twenty-first century.

In this context, there are constantly reports in the business press of companies developing integrated worldwide structures linked by flexible management processes. The concept of transnational organization seems to be gaining a good deal of currency. IBM's announcement that it was transferring its important telecommunications business headquarters to London is only the latest in a long series of changes that confirm its objective of building an integrated worldwide network; Asea Brown Boveri, the European-based electrical engineering company, is deliberately and consciously trying to build a transnational organization through acquisition and integration of national companies around the globe; and Akio Morita, Sony's high-profile CEO, is committed to the transnational concept, describing it to his own organization as "glocalization"—the combination of global integration and local responsiveness.

Yet, as more and more companies make the transition to become transnationals, one conclusion has become crystal clear: it represents a major managerial challenge. Our hope is that by describing the new transnational model and a framework for thinking about it, we can give managers and students of management the tools to help them through the complex strategic and organizational tasks they face. But it is a framework, not a formula. Individual managers still must undertake the hard work of analyzing their company's particular environmental situation, understanding its unique administrative heritage, and developing the specific plan of action necessary to create the desired organizational capabilities. Those who succeed will have built a powerful and durable source of competitive advantage.

PREFACE

The 1980s have been a watershed for most large corporations worldwide. The era of "globalization" left most managers scrambling to understand the nature of the forces ·of change in their particular businesses, what responses were most appropriate, and, above all, how they could manage the more complex strategies and operations on an ongoing basis. This is the broad agenda we address in this book. Our objective is not only to report the core findings from a five-year study of nine of the world's largest corporations, but also to provide practicing managers with specific guidance and recommendations to help them prepare for the challenges that will confront them as they prepare for the twenty-first century.

Many of the findings presented here have their roots in research begun a decade ago in Christopher Bartlett's doctoral dissertation, and owe a great deal to the nurturing environment in which that effort began. The germination and initial nourishment of the ideas drew heavily on three important streams of research undertaken at the Harvard Business School in the 1970s—the strong business policy traditions pioneered by Kenneth Andrews and C. Roland Christensen, the major international business project led by Ray Vernon, and the influential organizational behavior research of Paul Lawrence and Jay Lorsch. Indeed, the gradual intersection of these streams of research influenced many of us who passed through the doctoral program in the 1970s, and the thesis findings and subsequent research of John Stopford, C. K. Prahalad, Yves Doz, and many others bear witness to the richness of the intellectual environment to which we were exposed during our training.

Although the roots of our current research were nourished in this intellectual soil, the real inspiration came from practicing managers. In developing case material for an MBA course in management of the multinational enterprise, we realized that managers in a wide variety of industries and from all parts of the world were having enormous difficulty responding to the transformation taking place in the international business environment. But the in-depth case studies of more than twenty large worldwide companies—as diverse as Corning Glass

ix

Works, EMI, Dominion Engineering Works, Komatsu, Merloni, and Kentucky Fried Chicken—led to an unexpected finding. Most managers seemed to understand very clearly the nature of the *strategic task* they faced; their main problem was developing and managing the *organizational capability* to implement the new and more complex global strategies.

In order to study this issue more systematically, we decided to undertake a clinical study of a group of leading companies that were trying to adapt to the changes we had observed. The research methodology, described in detail in the Appendix, centered on a study of a diverse group of companies in three distinctly different industries. During two and a half years of field work, we interviewed 236 managers in the worldwide operations of Procter & Gamble, Unilever, and Kao in the branded packaged goods business, General Electric, Philips, and Matsushita in consumer electronics, and ITT, Ericsson, and NEC in the telecommunications switching industry.

Our objective was to gain a rich understanding of the organizational and administrative tasks facing managers in companies with worldwide operations in a time of major environmental change. At the most basic level, we wanted to identify and conceptualize the forces of change and the strategic challenges they presented. More specifically, we hoped to reach some understanding of the organizational characteristics required to manage in the emerging environment. And, finally, we wanted to extract some guidance on how companies might develop and manage such characteristics.

As the project continued, the issues we were researching took on even greater urgency and importance. The signing of the historic U.S.-Canadian Trade Agreement, the growing effectiveness of the ASEAN trading block, and the evolution toward an integrated Europe in 1992 forced managers in many companies to reevaluate how they were managing their international operations. Even companies that were not seeking to expand abroad were confronted by the emerging challenges as the forces of internationalization reached out to embrace them. It became increasingly clear that the issues we were studying and the conclusions we were drawing were much broader than our original intention. The management of worldwide operations was the management of complexity, diversity, and change, and the same challenges faced all managers everywhere as the world's increasingly linked economies sped toward the twenty-first century. The transnational organization we describe, and the process we propose for building and managing it have lessons for managers in all large complex organizations.

While the book is written primarily for these managers, we hope that it will also be of value to our academic colleagues. In analyzing the clinical data and in developing conclusions, we have drawn on a diverse range of literature in the fields of organization theory, business policy, and international management. The Notes identify this literature and suggest how our arguments and findings relate to it.

While case research in nine companies constituted the core of our study and formed the basis of our observations and conclusions, we were also concerned with the broader validity and generality of these findings. Therefore, we carried out some intensive and extensive questionnaire surveys to complement the clinical studies. The detailed Appendix on research methodology describes the different approaches we adopted and also presents some of the more quantitative data and analysis that support the case study-based findings reported in the book.

ACKNOWLEDGMENTS

A major endeavor such as this would never have been completed without the support and guidance of many people and organizations. Our first and greatest debt of gratitude must be to the companies that cooperated in our study, and particularly to the 236 managers around the world who gave so generously of their time to us. It was through their patience and helpfulness that we gained whatever insights this book may contain, and the evidence of their direct contribution is scattered throughout the following pages in the form of quotes and references to their actions.

Next, we must thank the Harvard Business School for the funding and support it provided for our research. Under the successive guidance of Professors E. Raymond Corey and Jay Lorsch, the School's Division of Research has been unstinting in its belief in and commitment to the project. In addition, INSEAD's Research Department also backed the project and provided constant encouragement to our efforts.

A generous grant from the Rokkodai Foundation at Kobe University sponsored Christopher Bartlett during a one-month stay in Japan as a visiting professor at the university's Research Institute for Economics and Business. This extended visit provided an excellent opportunity to test and refine many of the ideas and concepts developed during the field work stage, and the foundation's support is gratefully acknowledged.

Among the many colleagues who contributed to this undertaking, two must be separated out for special recognition. Professors Hideki Yoshihara and Tadao Kogono of Kobe University were major collaborators from the earliest stages, and their counsel and advice added significantly to our understanding. Professor Yoshihara, in particular, spent many hours, not only educating us on the subtleties of Japanese management, but also in acting as translator in many meetings and interviews. To both, we offer our heartfelt thanks, and are delighted that they have become not just respected colleagues, but good friends.

Nitin Nohria, now on the faculty at Harvard Business School, also contributed significantly as a research associate, both in his analysis of questionnaire data, and his contribution to the overall conclusions. In particular, his broad knowledge of relevant literature was of enormous help in preparing the endnotes. We are pleased to count him as a valuable colleague in our ongoing research.

Many other colleagues also contributed to the project by challenging our ideas and critiquing our draft manuscript. Among them were Professors Kenneth Andrews, Joseph Bower, Jay Lorsch, Malcolm Salter, and Michael Yoshino, all of Harvard Business School, Yves Doz and Dominique Heau of INSEAD, Donald Lessard of MIT, John Stopford of London Business School, and Gunnar Hedlund of Stockholm School of Economics. Many others have provided valuable input at various stages by their criticism of papers, articles, and conference presentations. Specifically, we would like to thank the editors and reviewers at *Harvard Business Review*, *Sloan Management Review*, *California Management Review*, *Human Resource Management*, and *Journal of International Business Studies*, where earlier drafts of many of our ideas were refined with their help and critical challenge. Despite all the advice, guidance, and support, however, we must bear final responsibility for the conclusions, including the errors and omissions.

We would also like to express our thanks to the editors and staff at Harvard Business School Press—particularly Barbara Ankeny, Natalie Greenberg, and Nancy Jackson—for their most helpful suggestions and comments; the wonderfully supportive staff of the School's Word Processing Department, who remained remarkably cheerful and patient through an interminable succession of drafts; and our secretaries, Cathyjean Gustafson and Jill Huret, who somehow managed to hold the whole project together by constantly juggling travel schedules and deadlines. To all of you, we offer our warmest thanks.

We reserve the last acknowledgment for those who really made our research possible—our wives and families. To Barbara, Nicholas, Elizabeth, and Andrew, and to Susmita, Ananda, and Siddhartha, we owe the greatest debt. By providing a "safe haven" to which we could retreat after long field trips or tiring days of writing, they gave us the strength to see the project through. Their constant support and encouragement made it all worthwhile. To all of you, our thanks and our love.

Boston, Massachusetts   Christopher A. Bartlett
Fontainebleau, France   Sumantra Ghoshal
November 1988

PART I

THE TRANSNATIONAL CHALLENGE

1
ORGANIZATIONAL CAPABILITY: THE NEXT BATTLEGROUND

The world's largest companies are in flux. New pressures have transformed the global competitive game, forcing these companies to rethink their traditional worldwide strategic approaches.[1] The new strategies, in turn, have raised questions about the adequacy of organizational structures and processes used to manage worldwide operations.

Even within particular industries, worldwide companies have developed very different strategic and organizational responses to changes in their environment. While a few players have prospered by turning the environmental turmoil to their advantage, many more are merely surviving—struggling to adjust to complex, often contradictory demands. Some large well-established worldwide companies have been forced to take large losses or even to abandon businesses.

Our research has explored some provocative questions raised by the diverse experience of worldwide companies.

- How could Matsushita evolve in just two decades from a medium-size manufacturer of electrical products for the Japanese domestic market to a $20 billion global company, the undisputed leader in the consumer electronics industry? Of the companies it overtook, why has Philips found it so difficult to adjust to the industry changes? Yet how has it survived while General Electric was eventually forced to sell off its consumer electronics business?
- In branded packaged products like soaps and detergents, how has Unilever defended its dominant world position for more than half a century? How was Procter & Gamble (P&G) able to mount a major thrust into international markets in the postwar era? And why has the internationalization thrust of Kao, the dominant Japanese competitor in this industry, been stalled in the developing countries of East Asia, despite Kao's formidable technological capabilities, its highly efficient plants, and its demonstrated marketing muscle?

- How has Sweden's Ericsson enhanced its position as a leader in the dynamic telecommunications switching business? What is behind NEC's gains in this highly competitive global industry? Why was ITT, the most international of all telecommunications companies and second only to AT&T in size, forced to abandon its planned entry into the U.S. switching market, and then to sell its formidable European telecommunication business?

The disappointments and failures some of those companies have encountered in their international operations were not due primarily to inappropriate strategic analysis, but to organizational deficiencies. Throughout our five-year study, we were continually impressed by the fact that most managers of worldwide companies recognized *what* they had to do to enhance their global competitiveness. The challenge was *how* to develop the organizational capability to do it.

THE LAGGARDS AND LOSERS

Very few worldwide companies entered the 1980s with the kind of organization that could respond effectively to the changed business environment. During the course of our study, we saw traditional industry characteristics disrupted and reconfigured, and companies forced to modify their once effective organizational structures and relationships. But some companies found it particularly difficult to respond to the new pressures. The problems faced by GE, Kao, and ITT illustrate the new challenges a worldwide corporation now confronts.

Lost Competitiveness: The Case of GE

For General Electric, heir to Thomas Edison's innovative genius and one of the most admired companies in the world, a leading role in the global consumer electronics industry was once a cherished dream and a reasonable expectation. GE possessed the most advanced technological capabilities in the field, and its dominance in the electrical appliances industry provided a base on which to build a similar position in a related area. Yet, after decades of investment and effort, GE conceded defeat to the Japanese challenge and withdrew from the business.

GE's philosophy of internationalization was to build mini-GEs in each country that could draw on the vast technological and managerial resources of the parent company to internationalize successful American technologies and products. For some time, this strategy served GE's consumer electronics business well, and by the late 1960s the company had built strong, if somewhat scattered, positions in many national markets, particularly in Canada and in Central and South America.

By the early 1970s, as the Japanese challenge in radios and television sets intensified, GE saw that global competitiveness would require greater integration of its diverse worldwide operations. But an organizational mentality that considered foreign subsidiaries as appendages to a dominant domestic operation kept the company from recognizing the urgency of this strategic task. In the late 1970s, the Japanese threat finally forced GE to take stronger actions. Its "World Iron Project" was conceived as a pilot program for global integration. The project demonstrated that GE could achieve efficiencies through product and process innovations (redesign eliminated 40 percent of parts in a standard iron, and process changes reduced direct labor hours by 25 percent) and a massive shift in sourcing patterns (developing global-scale plants in Singapore, Mexico, and Brazil). But it was too little and too late. The Japanese competitors had already developed insurmountable leads, and GE's competitive position in many of its consumer products had been eroded beyond repair. The company's consumer electronics business withdrew to its home market, and in 1987 was sold to Thomson, a French company.

Forces for Global Integration: Need for Efficiency. GE's failure illustrates a problem that plagued American and European companies in a wide range of industries: the lack of *global efficiency*. According to Theodore Levitt, technological, social, and economic developments over the last two decades have combined to create a unified world marketplace in which companies must capture global-scale economies to remain competitive.[2] While Levitt's arguments are somewhat extreme and one-sided, he provides an insightful analysis of some of the forces of change that have recently reshaped markets around the world.

In some industries, a major technological innovation forced a fundamental realignment of industry economics and allowed companies to develop and manufacture products on a global basis, thereby taking advantage of the convergence of consumer preferences and needs worldwide.[3] A classic example is the impact of transistors and integrated circuits on the design and production of such products as radios, television, and tape recorders. Similarly, the introduction of quartz technology made watchmaking a scale-intensive global industry.

Even in industries that lacked such strong external forces of change, managers began to look for ways to achieve global economies. They rationalized their product lines, standardized parts design, and specialized their manufacturing operations.[4] Such internal restructuring triggered a second wave of globalization in industries as diverse as automobiles, office equipment, industrial bearings, construction equipment, and machine tools.

More recently, even some companies in classically local businesses have begun to examine the opportunities for capturing economies beyond their national borders. In Europe, where the branded packaged goods industry has traditionally responded to national differences in consumer tastes and market structures, companies are now achieving substantial scale economies by restructuring and specializing their plant configurations—even though that means standardizing product formulations, rationalizing pack sizes, and printing multilingual labels.[5]

Economics was not the only force driving companies to integrate their operations globally in this period. Consumer tastes and preferences, which once differed widely from one national market to the next, began homogenizing. Again, this influence has spread from businesses in which the worldwide standardization of products was relatively easy (watches, calculators, and cameras, for example) to others in which consumers' preferences and habits were only slowly converging. Again, major external discontinuities greatly facilitated the change. The oil shocks of the 1970s, for example, triggered a worldwide demand for smaller, more fuel-efficient automobiles. In some markets companies acted to influence changes in consumer preferences. Food tastes and eating habits were long thought to be the most culture bound of all consumer behaviors. Yet, as companies like Kellogg, McDonald's, and Coca-Cola have shown, in Eastern and Western countries alike, even these culturally linked preferences can be changed.[6]

Thus, the forces driving companies to integrate their operations worldwide spread from industries where external structural change or discontinuity dictated a global strategy to industries in which managers had to create the opportunity for global economies. A further force for globalization was a competitive strategy sometimes called "global chess." The game could only be played by companies managing their worldwide operations as interdependent units guided by a coordinated global strategy.[7] Whereas the traditional multinational approach assumed that each national market was unique and independent of others, this strategy emphasized the effect of financial interdependence. Regardless of consumer tastes or manufacturing scale economies, the corporation with worldwide operations was advantaged because it could use funds generated in one market to subsidize its position in another.[8]

In industry after industry, companies that operated their local companies as independent profit centers found themselves at a disadvantage to competitors playing global chess. Companies that found no economic, technological, or market reason to manage their businesses globally suddenly needed to do so for reasons of competitive strategy.

Thus, for a variety of reasons and in an ever-expanding number of industries, companies are being forced to manage their businesses in a more globally integrated manner in order to capture the benefits of efficiency. Some companies, like GE's consumer electronics business, were eventually overwhelmed by the challenge. Others, like Matsushita, found their principal source of competitive advantage in their ability to build an organization able to respond to these new demands.

Stalled Internationalization: The Case of Kao

Kao, Japan's leading producer of soaps, detergents, and personal care products, is both admired and feared by Procter & Gamble and Unilever as a potential global competitor. It has all the key elements of the Japanese juggernaut: a highly efficient centralized production system, an extremely strong position in its large home base, and a sophisticated process technology that has been gradually expanded through an extensive overseas licensing program. Acclaimed as one of the top ten in the ranks of "excellent" Japanese companies, Kao has continuously strengthened its position within Japan not only at the cost of other domestic competitors, but also by beating down the challenges of foreign competitors such as Procter & Gamble. For example, P&G was the first to introduce disposable diapers to the Japanese market and had developed a commanding 80 percent market share. Kao, a late comer to this product category, combined an innovation blitz with high-quality production to capture over 30 percent of the market. This effort, combined with two other local companies' disposable diaper launches, reduced P&G, at one point, to a low 8 percent share.

Kao has shown the same strategic commitment to globalization as many other Japanese companies. It first built up its offshore business in East Asian countries like Indonesia, Malaysia, Singapore, the Philippines, Thailand, and Hong Kong. Using this base to develop manufacturing scale and production technology, the company then attempted to enter the advanced markets in the United States and Europe. But, despite significant investments over several decades and a reputation for supplying high-quality technologically advanced products at relatively low cost, by the late 1980s Kao was still not a significant global player.

Historically Kao considered its foreign subsidiaries primarily as delivery pipelines for the company's standardized products and services. As a result, the entire system depended on strong headquarters functional capabilities. This organizational form worked well in small neighboring Asian markets, where market development and product technology often lagged behind Japan's, but represented a major impediment as the company approached the large sophisticated markets of Europe and North America.

In these markets, Kao found very different customer characteristics, habits, and expectations. For example, shampoo, deodorant, and bath soap developed for the Japanese did not always suit Western customer profiles. Neither did detergents developed for very different laundry practices in Japan. Product technologies that represented major advances in some Asian markets were often either commonplace or inappropriate in Europe and the United States. Furthermore, in channels of distribution, advertising media, and other aspects of the marketing infrastructure, these markets were highly sophisticated and quite different from those in which the company operated in Asia.

Kao's fundamental problem was not inappropriate products or marketing strategies, but its inability to understand the differences between markets and adapt appropriately. In the 1970s, it acquired industrial chemical companies in Spain and Mexico, and entered joint ventures with Colgate in the United States and Beyersdorf in Europe. But these steps did not provide the local sensitivity and market understanding the company needed, or the entrepreneurial capability to convert such understanding into appropriate product-market strategies.

Force for Local Differentiation: Need for Responsiveness. The fact that Kao's lack of *national responsiveness* to local needs has so far frustrated the company's efforts to build a global reach illustrates the limitations of Levitt's argument that "the world's needs and desires have been irrevocably homogenized" and that "the commonality of preferences leads inescapably to the standardization of products, manufacturing, and the institution of trade and commerce."[9] While these may indeed be long-term trends in many industries, there are important short- and medium-term impediments and countertrends that must be considered if companies are to operate successfully over the next decade, or two, or three, as the international economy jolts along— perhaps eventually toward Levitt's "global village."

Barriers and countertrends such as those experienced by Kao have forced managers of worldwide companies to be more sensitive to national differences and local interests in the host countries where they operate.[10] By the late 1970s, the impact of localizing forces was being felt with increasing urgency, particularly by many Japanese companies. Indeed, if the strategic implications of globalization have dominated management thinking in the West, localization has become the preoccupation of top-level executives in Japan.

The classic barrier to globalization has always been rooted in the differences in national market structures and consumer preferences. Clearly, as Levitt argues, international travel and communications have reduced those differences, yet worldwide tastes, habits, and preferences are far from homogeneous.

Many companies have exploited—and accelerated—the convergence of tastes and preferences by developing products that can be sold worldwide. However, even this trend toward standardized products has a flip side. In many industries, a large and growing group of consumers rejects homogenized product design and performance and wants to reassert its traditional preferences, thereby creating openings—often very profitable ones—for competitors willing to meet this need for locally differentiated products and services.

Other consumer and market trends also offset the forces of global standardization. In markets from telecommunications to office equipment to consumer electronics, customers are not buying individual products so much as selecting systems.[11] A typewriter is linked with an integrated office system; the television set is becoming an integral part of a home entertainment and information system, connected to the video cassette recorder, the hi-fi system, the home computer, and perhaps an on-line data bank and information network. This transformation is forcing companies to adapt their standard hardware-oriented products to more flexible and locally differentiated systems comprising hardware, software, and services. In such an environment, the company focused on achieving the most scale-efficient global operation may be at a disadvantage to one that develops the software and service to meet local requirements.

There are important impediments to the globalizing forces of scale economies. The benefits of scale economies are offset by the additional costs of supplying markets from a central point, and those costs go well beyond freight charges. In particular, the administrative costs of coordinating worldwide demand through global scale plants can be quite significant. For some products lead times are so short or market service requirements so high that scale economies may well be outweighed by other costs.

More significantly, recent developments in computer-aided design and manufacturing, robotics, and other advanced production technologies have made the concept of flexible manufacturing a reality. Companies that previously had to produce tens or hundreds of thousands of standardized products in a single plant to achieve minimum efficient scale now find they can distribute manufacturing among smaller national plants with little cost penalty. In this way they can respond to localized consumer preferences and national political constraints without compromising their economic efficiency.[12]

But the most important force for localization has been the reactions of national governments that see their markets flooded by the products of global producers.[13] If in the 1960s, worldwide companies could hold "sovereignty at bay," as one respected international researcher concluded, by the 1980s the balance had tipped in the other direction.[14] The rapidly growing power of global companies, particularly the Japanese, was seen as a threat by various national governments whose social and economic policies were upset by the rising import penetration. To stem the tide, many countries began bending or sidestepping trade agreements signed earlier. By the early 1980s, even the Republican-dominated U.S. government, traditionally one of the strongest advocates of free trade, began to negotiate a series of orderly marketing agreements and voluntary restraints on Japanese exports, while a variety of restrictions and sanctions were debated with increasing emotion in legislative chambers around the globe.

In many nations the new trade barriers were reinforced by increasingly sophisticated industrial policies, which thwarted such responses as the establishment of local plants to assemble knock-down kits exported from Japan. (Such "screwdriver plants" provided only limited low-skilled local employment, resulted in little local value added, and transferred minimal technology.) Foreign investment regulations soon defined necessary levels of local content, technology transfer, and a variety of other conditions from re-export commitments to plant location requirements.[15]

Thus companies in a variety of industries have been forced to become more sensitive to local market differences and host country pressures. As Kao found, failure to respond to local needs can undermine efforts toward international expansion.

Sale of the Crown Jewel: The Case of ITT

Founded in 1920 as a Puerto Rican telephone company, ITT based its worldwide expansion strategy on being attuned to local national interests and market needs. By 1980 it was the second-largest supplier of telecommunications equipment in the world. Under the influence of ITT founder and president, Colonel Sosthenes Behn, subsidiaries around the world strove to be seen as local entities rather than as parts of a global enterprise. All but the smallest national subsidiaries were set up as fully integrated, self-sufficient units, responsible for the development, manufacture, marketing, installation, and service of their products. So strong were these independent local entities that the subsidiaries could not only weather the protectionist pressures of the 1930s, but even continued their operations throughout World War II, providing telecommunications systems and services to Allied and Axis powers alike.

After the mid-1950s, the management style of the company changed markedly under the leadership of Harold Geneen, but the role of the national companies (or "systems houses") remained much the same. While Geneen replaced Behn's informal management with a strong emphasis on systems and formal management control, he allowed the subsidiaries to continue developing and implementing their local strategies independently.

These powerful, independent, and entrepreneurial national companies became the source of almost all major ITT innovations. But the products that resulted varied considerably across ITT's worldwide operations because the local units insisted on tailoring systems to local technological needs. Thus, while the French subsidiary led the development of the highly successful Pentaconta electromechanical switch, the subsidiaries in Britain, Germany, Italy, and Belgium each developed a very different version based on extensive local modifications. The story was the same with the Metaconta Stored Program Controlled (SPC) electronic switch. In both cases, the company tried but failed to integrate diverse product development efforts to standardize on a single global design. The systems houses would not give up the right to design and develop their own products, nor would they set aside traditional competitive rivalries and pool their capabilities or rely on the developments created in other national units. While this fragmentation led to some diseconomies, the company reaped political rewards for its ability to present a locally designed product to each national government.

In the late 1970s, two simultaneous developments challenged the strategic posture of ITT. First, with the emergence of digital switching technology, hundreds of millions of dollars were needed to develop and build a new switch; no one country unit could manage such a large investment. Second, a trend toward deregulation opened many national markets to global competitors, thereby reducing the rewards of local differentiation. As a result, integrating the technological capabilities of the national entities to design a standard global product became a strategic imperative.

Despite ITT's technological head start in researching digital signal processing (many of the original patents were held by ITT's British and French subsidiaries), the company failed to integrate its substantial but dispersed technical resources and knowledge. The large systems houses balked at cooperating with one another and resisted accepting common standards. Throughout the development of its System 12 switch, management struggled to overcome pervasive duplication of efforts and divergence of specifications; total development costs exceeded $1 billion.

The biggest problem appeared when the company decided, in response to the deregulatory moves of the early 1980s, to take System 12 to the U.S. market. In true ITT tradition, the U.S. group asserted its right to develop its own product and launched a major new R&D effort, despite appeals from the company's chief technological officer, who saw the effort as producing an ill-omened System 13. After years of effort and hundreds of millions of dollars in additional R&D costs, ITT acknowledged it was withdrawing from its home market because it had been unable to transfer and apply its leading-edge technology in a timely fashion. It was a failure that eventually led to further withdrawal from direct involvement in telecommunications worldwide.

Forces for Worldwide Innovation: The Need for Learning. ITT's failure illustrates the third strategic demand for competing in worldwide businesses—the need to develop and diffuse *worldwide innovations* internationally. As major global competitors achieve parity in the scale of their operations and their international market positions, the ability to link and leverage knowledge is increasingly the factor that differentiates the winners from the losers and survivors.[16]

The trends driving this shift in the competitive game derive from the globalizing and localizing forces we described earlier. The increasing cost of R&D, coupled with shortening life cycles for new technologies and the products they spawn, has driven companies to seek global volume in order to amortize the heavy investment as quickly as possible.

At the same time, even the most advanced technologies have diffused rapidly around the globe, partly in response to the demands of host governments seeking higher levels of national production and local content in the leading-edge products sold in their markets. But the high cost of product and process development has also encouraged companies to transfer new technologies voluntarily. Licensing has become an important source of funding, cross-licensing provides a means to fill technology gaps, and joint development programs and strategic alliances are emerging as a strategy for building global competitive advantage rapidly.[17]

Coupled with the convergence of consumer preferences worldwide, the diffusion of technology has significantly influenced both the pace and the locus of innovation. No longer can U.S-based companies assume, as they often did in the decades just after World War II, that their domestic environment provides them with the most sophisticated consumers and the most advanced technological capabilities, and thus the most innovative environment in the world. Today, the newest consumer trend or market need can emerge in Australia or Italy, and the latest technologies may be located in Japan or Sweden. Companies see that they can gain competitive advantage by sensing needs in one country, responding with capabilities located in a second, and diffusing the resulting innovation to markets around the globe.[18]

Another trend reinforces the need for a worldwide approach to innovation. A gradual shift from freestanding products to integrated systems has increased the importance of locally differentiated software nd market-responsive service in a number of industries. In view of the apid global diffusion of new products, the need to establish global tandards and specifications has become critical. The company that ets a globally accepted standard for computer software, video record-ng format, or even razor blade cartridge design can build a dominant ompetitive position that will be defensible for decades.[19] The rewards f moving first have increased substantially, encouraging companies to ocus attention not only on rapidly creating and diffusing innovations within their worldwide operations, but also on establishing the new oroduct as an industry standard.[20]

MULTINATIONAL, GLOBAL, AND INTERNATIONAL COMPANIES

GE, Kao, and ITT should not be regarded as examples of strategic in-competence or managerial ineptitude. Indeed, all three companies have frequently been cited as examples of corporate excellence. The prob-lems they faced were generic. In the 1980s, there were few clear win-ners in the game of global chess. Some, like these three companies, had fallen behind or had conceded the game to stronger opponents. Others, like Unilever and Procter & Gamble in the branded packaged products business, Philips and Matsushita in the consumer electronics industry, and Ericsson and NEC in the telecommunications switching industry, had survived but were battling to maintain viable competitive positions under new and different conditions. These nine companies—three los-ers or laggards and six survivors—constituted the core sample of our study, which is described in detail in the Appendix. These companies represented the leading American, European, and Japanese competi-tors in three worldwide businesses (see Table 1.1).

The businesses themselves had very different strategic characteris-tics. The need for global efficiency was particularly strong in consumer

Table 1.1
The Nine Companies

	Company		
Industry	American	European	Japanese
Consumer Electronics	General Electric (GE)	Philips	Matsushita
Branded Packaged Goods	Procter & Gamble (P&G)	Unilever	Kao
Telecommunications Switching	ITT	Ericsson	NEC

electronics. The branded packaged products business traditionally demanded a high degree of national responsiveness. In telecommunications switching, the ability to develop innovations and transfer them around the world was often the most vital requirement for success.

Within each business, the companies had very different strategic positions, organizational structures, and management processes, not necessarily reflecting the dominant industry characteristics. We found three distinct models represented in the nine companies we studied.

Some companies have developed a strategic posture and organizational capability that allows them to be very sensitive and responsive to differences in national environments around the world. In effect these corporations manage a portfolio of multiple national entities; hence we will call them *multinational companies*.

In consumer electronics, Philips has traditionally given its self-sufficient national organizations substantial strategic freedom and organizational autonomy; in branded packaged goods, Unilever has allowed its overseas companies to operate quite independently; and in telecommunications, ITT's commitment to building links to each host country's political infrastructure has led to the development of operations around the world that were almost always perceived as local companies.

In contrast, other companies (particularly the Japanese ones) have developed international operations that are much more driven by the need for global efficiency, and much more centralized in their strategic and operational decisions. Because these companies treat the world market as an integrated whole, we regard them as classic *global companies*. To these companies the global operating environment and worldwide consumer demand are the dominant units of analysis, not the nation-state or the local market. Products and strategies are developed to exploit an integrated unitary world market.

Like most other Japanese consumer electronic firms, Matsushita expanded overseas through an export-based strategy and has retained strong centralized product development, manufacturing operations, and marketing strategy. In telecommunications, because NEC's switching business grew by first exploiting the domestic market, it also tends to have strong centralized capabilities and a headquarters-based decision-making process. Expanding internationally by leveraging these home country assets, NEC developed a more globally coordinated strategy than its competitor, ITT. Even the soap and detergent company, Kao, exhibits a strong centralization bias to support its technology-driven strategy and its highly efficient domestic plants.

The strategy of a third group of companies is based primarily on transferring and adapting the parent company's knowledge or expertise

Table 1.2
Key Strategic Capabilities:
Multinational, Global, and International Companies

Multinational	Global	International
Building strong local presence through sensitivity and responsiveness to national differences	Building cost advantages through centralized global-scale operations	Exploiting parent company knowledge and capabilities through worldwide diffusion and adaptation

to foreign markets. The parent retains considerable influence and control, but less than in a classic global company; national units can adapt products and ideas coming from the center, but have less independence and autonomy than multinational subsidiaries. Because the strategies of these companies reflect the pattern of worldwide exploitation of knowledge described in the well-known international product cycle theory,[21] we call them *international companies.*

General Electric managed its international consumer electronics business by exploiting parent company technology and skills in various overseas markets. This strategic philosophy also characterized Procter & Gamble's internationalization strategy as it set up miniature replicas of the domestic organization to adapt P&G products without deviating from "the Procter way." Ericsson's worldwide network of local companies was much more sensitive and responsive than NEC's, and it retained much more central control and value added than ITT. But it too relied heavily on transferring and adapting technologies developed by the parent company as the basis for its international expansion.

Each of these nine companies had become a large worldwide corporation by exploiting its particular strategic capability. (Table 1.2 summarizes the key differences in the three strategic and organizational models.) Yet this very focus on a specific strategic approach was the crux of the problems each company faced in the mid-1980s. Environmental forces had dramatically changed the nature of the strategic demands in a wide range of businesses, and the traditional approaches of the multinational, global, and international companies could no longer yield an adequate response. The new challenges required a new solution—and herein begins our thesis. In this book we present a new approach to managing a company's worldwide operations—an approach we believe will be particularly effective in the highly competitive, volatile, and changing business environments of the present and the future.

THE TRANSNATIONAL SOLUTION

Unlike GE, Kao, and ITT, the other companies in our sample established and defended their positions as major worldwide players in the businesses we studied, and some even prospered. In the course of the study we developed some understanding of why the survivors could overcome the problems the others could not. We reached three major conclusions:

- In the past, each of the three businesses was characterized by a single dominant strategic demand. As a result, a company could compete effectively as long as its capability fit the strategic demand of the business. By the mid-1980s, however, the forces of global integration, local differentiation, and worldwide innovation had all become strong and compelling, and none could be ignored. To compete effectively, a company had to develop global competitiveness, multinational flexibility, and worldwide learning capability *simultaneously*.
- Building these multiple strategic competencies was primarily an *organizational* challenge, which required companies to break away from their traditional management modes and adopt a new organizational model. This model we call the transnational. As we shall describe here, this new management model has some distinct characteristics that differ from the traditional ways of managing worldwide operations. We believe that adoption of the transnational mode allowed companies like P&G, NEC, and Unilever to respond effectively to the new and complex demands of their international business environments. In contrast, the inability to develop such organizational capability was a major factor contributing to the strategic and competitive difficulties faced by companies such as ITT, GE, and Kao.
- Such organizational capability was not easily built and managed. The transition from a multinational, global, or international posture to the transnational mode of management required time and could be achieved only with a great deal of top management attention and effort. The challenge of building a learning and self-adaptive organization that was also competitive and flexible involved a range of tasks that we will describe and illustrate in this book.

The *transnational* solution we propose is based on what we learned from both the losers and the survivors. But the hypothetical organization we shall describe does not correspond to any specific company. None of the companies in our sample had attained all the attributes of the transnational. However, all the survivors were developing organizational characteristics and capabilities that moved them toward this idealized form.

In Part I of this book we consider the question "why the transnational?" Using evidence from the industries and companies we studied, we will show how existing organizational capabilities affected companies' ability to develop appropriate strategic responses to changing environmental forces. Our main objective here will be to develop the *conceptual* arguments linking environmental complexity, strategic demands, and organizational capability to show why the transnational organization is a feasible and perhaps necessary response to the changes in the international operating environment.

In Part II, we focus on the question "what is the transnational?" Here we are deliberately *descriptive*. These chapters illustrate in turn the three key attributes of the transnational—the characteristic configuration of assets and activities, the allocation of organizational roles and responsibilities, and the facilitation of multiple learning processes.

Part III moves on to "how to." Our primary purpose here is *prescriptive*—to suggest how managers can build and manage the transnational organization. These three chapters describe how to develop a balance among area, product, and functional management perspectives; how to build an array of coordination tools and use them flexibly in a variety of situations; and how to create an organizational context in which each individual manager can be co-opted into a specific role to support a shared organizational purpose.

The transnational is not a specific strategic posture or a particular organizational form. In essence, *the transnational is a new management mentality*. The most fundamental objective of this book, therefore, is to describe, illustrate, and advocate the transnational mentality: the one element of the transnational solution that we believe is necessary for every company that operates in an international environment. Without this mentality, none of our suggestions will produce the desired results, and some may prove to be counterproductive. Conversely, companies that adopt the transnational mentality will find many different ways to implement the broad management approach we propose.

2
NEW ORGANIZATIONAL CHALLENGE: BEYOND STRUCTURAL FIT

A s the turbulent international competitive environment of the 1970s boiled over into the decade of the 1980s, it unleashed a rash of studies, reports, and recommendations telling managers how to run their business more effectively in the new "global" environment. Some of the advice was thoughtful and sound, but like most fads, "globalization" soon became a term in search of a definition. And by the mid-1980s there was no shortage of contenders, as journalists, consultants, and academics jostled to bring fresh insight to the hot new topic. In the process, some simplistic solutions and dangerous overgeneralizations began to circulate.

Newsweek promised a neat prescription for managers struggling with the appropriate strategy and structure for their worldwide operations. Under the seductive headline "Rebuilding Corporate Empires: A New Global Formula," its correspondent wrote:

> It's a bit like the end of an empire, a colonial era coming to a close. Companies in the United States and Europe are reining in their far-flung foreign subsidiaries. . . . Executives are streamlining their divisions, trying to produce standardized global products, and pulling decision making power back to their home offices. . . . It's a formula that, not coincidentally, many Japanese companies have used for years.[1]

Yet, many managers were unconvinced by this neat formula of standardization, rationalization, and centralization. While it was true that many Japanese companies had succeeded using such an approach, others had not. Kao was a classic example of a first-rate Japanese company that had proven its ability by repeatedly blocking or taking share from P&G in Japan, yet it had been quite unsuccessful in leveraging its standardized, rationalized, and centralized capabilities in overseas markets. NEC was a telecommunications powerhouse in Japan, but its overseas expansion had been much slower and less spectacular than Matsushita's, for example. Furthermore, the more experience NEC obtained abroad, the further it seemed to be moving away from a strategy of standardized products and an organization based on centralized decision making. At the same time, companies like Unilever, Ericsson, and P&G could point with pride to highly successful international operations that did not conform to any "global formula."

Clearly the issues were much more complex than those discussed in the *Newsweek* article. The nature of the strategic task and the appropriate organization by which to manage it varied widely by industry, with branded packed food companies facing very different demands than those in the consumer electronics industry.

Equally important was the fact that a company's ability to respond to its industry demands was constrained by its internal strategic and organizational capability. A formula that imitated what Japanese companies were able to do was inappropriate for most American and European firms. Yet even managers who rejected a simplistic global formula were intrigued by the notion of "conditional fit." If a company could determine the key success factor in its industry and build the strategic and organizational capability to achieve it, the argument went, it should be able to succeed in the emerging competitive environment. The quest for a globalization formula was replaced by a search for fit.

THE SEARCH FOR FIT

Until fairly recently, most worldwide industries presented relatively unidimensional strategic requirements. In each industry, either responsiveness, or efficiency, or knowledge transfer was crucial, and companies that possessed the matching strategic competency were rewarded. In other words, company performance was based primarily on the *fit* between the dominant strategic requirement of the business and the firm's dominant strategic capability (see Figure 2.1).

Rewarding Responsiveness in Multinational Industries

Historically, branded packaged goods companies had to respond primarily to differing market needs. In laundry detergents, for example, there was little scope for standardizing products within Europe, let alone worldwide. As late as 1980, washing machine penetration ranged from less than 30 percent of households in the United Kingdom to over 85 percent in Germany. In northern European countries "boil washing" had long been standard, whereas hand washing in cold water represented an important demand segment in Mediterranean countries. Differences in water hardness, perfume preferences, fabric mix, and phos-

Figure 2.1

Industry Requirements and
Company Capabilities

Dominant Strategic
Requirements of
Industry

	Responsiveness (Multinational)	Efficiency (Global)	Transfer of Knowledge and Competencies (International)
Responsiveness (Branded Packaged Products)	Unilever	Kao	Procter & Gamble
Efficiency (Consumer Electronics)	Philips	Matsushita	General Electric
Transfer of Knowledge (Telecommunications Switching)	ITT	NEC	Ericsson

Dominant Strategic Capability of Company

phate legislation made product differentiation from country to country a strategic necessity.

Marketing strategies also had to address the different conditions in national markets. In 1985, five chains controlled 65 percent of the market in Germany, but no chain had even 2 percent of the retail market in Italy. Promotion opportunities and pricing flexibilities also varied. In Holland, for example, no brand could purchase more than a certain number of minutes of commerical air time each year; in Germany premium offers, coupon refunds, and similar forms of promotion were virtually blocked by local laws.[2]

Moreover, the detergent business offered few opportunities to build global-scale efficiencies. In R&D, consumer companies like Procter & Gamble and Unilever were involved only in formulating the final products, and most basic research for developing the ingredients was carried out by the manufacturers of the chemicals. Similarly, the relatively simple operations of soap making—sulphonation, mixing, spray drying, and packaging—could be carried out efficiently at such a small scale that it was feasible to operate separate plants for all but the smallest markets. In any case, with raw material purchases accounting for 40 percent to 50 percent of sales, and advertising and marketing costs another 20 percent, capital-related expenses were a small part of total costs.

In such businesses, the national industry structure was most relevant, because of the need for local differentiation in products and strategic approaches, and the underlying economics that allowed national companies to achieve minimum-scale efficiencies. This we refer to as a *multinational industry*—made up of multiple national structures only loosely connected across national boundaries.

However, companies in this industry adopted diverse strategic postures. As we saw in Chapter 1, Kao competed primarily on the basis of its highly efficient central plants and its centralized R&D facility, which developed technologically advanced products to be sold worldwide. Its *global* strategy sought to build competitive advantage by treating the world as a single, largely undifferentiated market—exploiting the economies associated with standardized product design, centralized global-scale manufacturing, and a strategy largely formulated and controlled by headquarters.

Procter & Gamble focused primarily on developing new products and processes in the United States, and moving overseas largely by transferring its strong technologies and well-developed marketing expertise. We describe this approach as an *international* strategy.

In an industry in which responsiveness was the dominant strategic task, Unilever's *multinational* strategy was a natural fit. The company had a long history of building strong national companies that were sensitive to local needs and opportunities, then allowing them the freedom to manage their local businesses entrepreneurially, with minimum direction from the headquarters. As a result, Unilever built and maintained a dominant worldwide business while P&G faced considerable initial difficulties when it tried to introduce Tide, Ivory, and other successful U.S. brands abroad, until it gradually learned to modify its classic international strategic posture. Kao's global strategy proved to be an even less appropriate fit, as we saw in Chapter 1.

Exploiting Efficiency in Global Industries

The development of the transistor by the Bell Laboratories in 1947 signaled a new era in consumer electronics. The replacement of vacuum tubes by transistors greatly expanded the efficient scale for production of key components, and the subsequent development of printed circuit boards made mass production feasible by reducing both the amount and skill level of labor required to assemble radios, TVs, tape recorders, and the like.

The introduction of integrated circuits in the late 1960s further reduced the number and cost of components and increased optimum manufacturing scale. The use of automated insertion machines allowed manufacturers to reduce costs and increase quality dramatically. On-line testing, materials handling, and final assembly and packaging were also automated. As a result, the efficient scale for production of color TVs rose from 50,000 sets per year in the early 1960s to 500,000 sets in the early 1980s.

Meanwhile, scale economies in R&D and marketing were also increasing. No single market could generate the revenues needed to fund the required state-of-the-art skills in micromechanics, micro-optics, and electronics. Similarly, the emergence of giant retail chains was changing the rules of marketing consumer electronics products.[3] Their bargaining power squeezed the margins available to manufacturers; at the same time, they had to be supported with a heavier advertising budget, since companies could no longer rely on knowledgeable store personnel to educate the consumer and communicate product benefits. Again, the effect was to raise break-even volumes. Given the new manufacturing, research, and marketing economies, some industry observers estimated that a total annual volume of 2.5 to 3 million sets was needed to remain viable as a global player in the color TV business—at least twenty times the volume required just two decades earlier.

Through the 1970s, the clear dominant trend in the consumer electronics industry was a progressive increase in the benefits of the world-scale economies, driven primarily by technical changes and reinforced by the homogenization of customer tastes and significant decline in trade barriers.[4] In our rather constrained use of the term, this was a classic *global industry*—one whose basic characteristics were defined by the need for global scale, relatively unimpeded by national differences.

Among the three consumer electronics companies we studied, only Matsushita built its strategy primarily on manufacturing scale economies. In 1980, over 90 percent of the company's production, valued at $13 billion, was concentrated in specialized, highly efficient plants in Japan, although foreign sales accounted for over 40 percent of total revenues. The 10 percent of production located abroad was largely assembly operations in countries such as Taiwan and Singapore. The company's overall strategy emphasized worldwide exports of fairly standard models produced in world-scale plants. In an industry dominated by the need for global-scale efficiency, Matsushita's *global* strategy represented an ideal fit.[5] Once a relatively minor player, the company catapulted to the number one position within less than two decades.

In the same business, Philips competed with a fundamentally *mul-*

tinational strategy.[6] With less than a quarter of its gross investments located in its home country, its key competitive asset was a portfolio of highly autonomous, self-sufficient national organizations, most of which carried out a complete range of activities from development to sales. They competed by adapting central products and strategies locally, in response to local market needs. In a sense, the company's worldwide strategy was the aggregate of the diverse strategies of its national organizations. Although Philips prospered in the postwar boom era, it began to experience problems as industry economics and global competitive conditions changed in the 1970s.

General Electric's consumer electronics group competed primarily with an *international* strategy focused on exploiting the parent company's vast array of products and technologies overseas. Eventually, GE found that this strategic approach represented a relative misfit in the consumer electronics business and led to the severe difficulties described in Chapter 1.

Leveraging Learning in International Industries

The telecommunications switching industry traditionally required a more multidimensional strategic capability than either consumer electronics or branded packaged goods. Monopoly purchasing in most countries by a government-owned post, telegraph, and telephone authority (PTT) created a demand for responsiveness—a demand enhanced by the strategic importance almost all governments accorded to developing local manufacturers of telecom equipment.[7] At the same time, global integration and coordination of activities were also required, because of significant scale economies in production and the need to arrange complex credit facilities for buyers through multinational lending agencies. However, the most critical task for switch manufacturers was the ability to develop and harness new technologies and to exploit them worldwide. This ability to learn and to appropriate the benefits of learning in multiple national markets differentiated the winners from the losers in this highly complex business.

The historical diffusion of telecommunications switching technologies followed the classic international product-cycle pattern. In most cases, new products were first developed in one of the advanced Western economies, most often in the United States, where the powerful research capabilities of Bell Labs were located. Next, they were adopted in other developed countries, typically first in Europe, followed by Japan. Once the technology was well understood and the product design was standardized, a company began to export to countries using early-generation products. Exports were usually replaced quickly by local manufacturing in response to host government demands. After the local subsidiary developed adequate understanding of the technology, it was allowed to develop and adapt the products to suit the local markets, or to help local vendors. By this time, the next new product—an augmented version based on the same technology, or one built on an altogether new technology—would be ready for transfer, and the same cycle would be repeated.

In such *international industries*, as we define them, the key to success lay in the ability to transfer knowledge to overseas units and to manage the product life cycle efficiently and flexibly. But companies competed in this industry with very different strategies. NEC had built a classic *global* strategy, developing products in collaboration with NTT, the Japanese post and telegraph authority, then building high-volume centralized production to supply both Japanese and export markets. ITT, as we described earlier, competed with a classic *multinational* strategy, built around the strength and sensitivity of its autonomous and entrepreneurial national systems houses.

Only Ericsson could be regarded as following the *international* strategy model. Recognizing that its small home market (Sweden) could not support the R&D efforts required to survive in this industry, Ericsson built its strategy around an ability to transfer and adapt its innovative product and process technologies to international markets. This sequential diffusion of innovations developed at home fit the industry requirements far better than the global strategy of NEC or the multinational strategy of ITT, and helped Ericsson build a strong position in the worldwide telecommunications switching business.

THE NEW STRATEGIC CHALLENGE: TRANSITION TO TRANSNATIONALITY

Our portrayal of these industries' strategic demands in the late 1970s is clearly oversimplified. Different tasks in the value-added chains of the businesses required different levels of efficiency, responsiveness, and learning capabilities. We have charted what appeared to be the "center of gravity" of these activities—the environmental forces that had the most significant impact on the industry's strategic task demands.

In the 1980s, each of these industries underwent major transitions. In all three, the earlier dominance of a single set of environmental forces was replaced by a much more complex set of environmental demands. Companies in these industries must now respond simultaneously to diverse and often conflicting strategic needs. Today, no firm can succeed with a relatively unidimensional strategic capability that emphasizes only efficiency, or responsiveness, or leveraging of parent company knowledge and competencies. To win, a company must now achieve all three goals at the same time. With their multidimensional strategic requirements, these businesses have become *transnational industries*.

Branded Packaged Goods

The last ten years have seen significant changes in the branded packaged goods industry. While national responsiveness and differentiation remain critically important, global efficiency and worldwide innovation have become increasingly feasible and necessary. Environmental changes have played a role. For example, the growing penetration of washing machines, together with the increasing standardization of machine design, has increased the opportunity for product standardization in the detergent business. The trend toward lower-temperature washing (spurred by widespread energy consciousness) and the increasing share of synthetics in clothing worldwide have helped narrow differences in washing practices across countries. But the greatest impetus toward globalization has come from the firms themselves. Some industries were born global, but branded packaged goods is being made global by the initiative of a handful of managers in P&G, Unilever, Henkel, and Colgate.

The dramatic rise in oil prices in the mid-1970s raised the consumer chemical companies' input prices significantly, while the simultaneous recession in demand made it impossible to pass those higher costs on to the customers. Searching for ways to reduce costs, the companies promoted standardization while retaining the variety of product attributes that diverse groups of customers desired. Such standardization made it possible to realize significant economies, primarily through standardization of packaging and economies of distribution, and also by developing common advertising and promotion approaches.

Innovations created jointly by the headquarters and a number of national organizations have proven to be an important instrument for creating multinational flexibility by allowing the development of relatively standardized products that were also able to meet the diverse demands of customers at acceptable levels of cost. In Chapter 7 we will describe how Procter & Gamble and Unilever exploited this approach to increase efficiency and innovative effectiveness simultaneously.

By the end of the 1980s, the strategic demands in the branded package goods business could no longer be regarded as dominated by the need for local differentiation. Global efficiency and the development and diffusion of innovations around the world were becoming equally important sources of competitive advantage.

Consumer Electronics

Competition in consumer electronics also became much more complex in the 1980s. One important trend has been driven by changes in the attitudes of national governments and shifts in customer tastes and preferences. Together, these forces have enhanced the need for national differentiation, requiring the major global competitors to become more responsive to local needs, while protecting their world-scale economies.

A variety of factors—antidumping suits by local manufacturers, government-imposed orderly marketing agreements, and political pressures prompted by unfavorable trade balances—have forced almost all manufacturers to set up local production in the United States. In Europe trade barriers, both explicit (local content requirements and formal quotas) and implicit (such as France's diversion of all VCR imports through the small inland port of Poitiers), have been going up steadily. Japanese manufacturers have been forced to fragment production by setting up local plants within the EEC. In many large developing countries, such as Brazil, Mexico, and India, local production has remained a precondition for market entry, and some smaller countries, formerly more open to imports, have been forced by deteriorating trade balances to minimize outflow of foreign exchange by insisting on local assembly.

Consumers have reacted to an overdose of standardized global products by showing a renewed preference for differentiated products that meet their unique tastes. The trend toward selling systems and services rather than freestanding products has reinforced this need for tailored products. The success of companies like Amstrad, the fast-growing British consumer electronics company that got its start by responding to such local consumer needs, has shown the importance of this trend. Companies like Matsushita have had to reverse their earlier bias toward standardized global designs; rather than address consumers en masse, they have begun to focus on target groups and respond to differences across markets. Matsushita had 30 models in its portable audio product range in 1985, up from 15 in 1980; it has also doubled the number of tape recorder models while sales per model declined 60 percent.

The forces for worldwide innovation have also been increasing over the past decade. A major industry shakeout since the late 1960s has left only a handful of viable competitors, all roughly equivalent in their potential to capture scale economies and develop responsive strategies. In an era of increasingly sophisticated markets worldwide, rapidly changing technology, and shortening product life cycles, a company's ability to develop and diffuse successful innovations is fast becoming a key strategic skill.

Consider the development of the video cassette recorder (VCR). Philips and Matsushita were among the pioneers in developing this new technology, and by the late 1970s both were trying to stake a claim on the consumer market that finally seemed ready to explode. To challenge Sony's Betamax format, Matsushita introduced VHS and Philips brought out its V2000 system. Although Sony had launched its Beta format two years ahead of its competitors and the Philips V2000 system was acknowledged to be technologically superior, by the mid-1980s the competitive battle had been won by Matsushita's VHS system.

Matsushita understood that the development and diffusion of innovation was closely tied to the pursuit of global efficiency and national responsiveness, and that it was becoming an equally important source of competitive advantage. The company sought to become the low-cost producer of VCRs by building volume as rapidly as possible. This required a sensitivity to market differences; in particular, U.S. consumers wanted to use their VCRs for "time shifting" (recording TV programs for later viewing), whereas Japanese buyers used VCRs primarily for viewing movies at home. The company defined the objective of a two-hour tape playing time to permit the recording of football games in the United States; it was equally sensitive to the need to sign up movie distributors in each country to provide a good backup of software for the new product. More important, Matsushita aggressively licensed its VHS format to other major manufacturers (e.g., Hitachi, Sharp, and Mitsubishi) and sought to become an OEM supplier to companies that chose not to manufacture (e.g., RCA and GE). As a result, in the seven years after the product's introduction in 1977, Matsushita's annual capacity increased from 200,000 units to 6.8 million units, and its prices decreased by 60 percent. By the mid-1980s Sony was struggling to keep its 5 percent market share, and Philips had withdrawn its V2000 system.

The introduction of the compact disk and the digital audio tape players reinforced the importance of innovation and learning as a source of competitive advantage—not only in developing a new technology, but being able to diffuse it rapidly worldwide, both inside and outside the company's own operations.

By the late 1980s, then, while efficiency was still a vital strategic requirement in consumer electronics, pressures for national responsiveness and effective worldwide innovation had also become key sources of competitive advantage. In this more complex environment, companies unwilling or unable to develop simultaneous global efficiency, local differentiation, and worldwide learning capabilities could no longer compete effectively.

Telecommunications Switching

The 1980s brought important changes that reshaped the dominant characteristics of the telecommunications switching industry and changed its strategic imperatives. With the simultaneous development of a new

generation of technology and the deregulation of the telecommunications industry in some of the world's largest markets, global-scale
efficiencies became both necessary and feasible. R&D costs for the new
electronic digital switching technology far exceeded those of the previous electromechanical generation. Some companies reported spending
up to $1 billion to develop their digital switching products, and such
cost levels clearly could only be supported by global scale.

At the same time, national governments recognized the growing
strategic importance of telecommunications. The convergence of computer and communications technologies placed the digital switch at the
core of a country's information infrastructure, making it vitally important for telecommunications companies to be highly sensitive to the
needs of national governments worldwide.

Thus, the strategic demands in this industry too became increasingly multidimensional during the 1980s. Companies that do not
achieve global-scale efficiency, national flexibility and responsiveness,
and an ability to develop and diffuse innovations worldwide will not
survive the shakeout now restructuring the industry. Even giant companies are vulnerable, and the price of failure can be very high, as ITT's
experience demonstrated.

The three industries we studied are not unique. Many other businesses, from heavy earth-moving equipment and automobiles to photo-
copiers and power tools, have confronted similar environmental
changes in the 1980s. Fewer and fewer industries are pure global, textbook multinational, or classic international. Instead, more and more
businesses are being driven by *simultaneous* demands for global
efficiency, national responsiveness, and worldwide leveraging of innovations and learning. These are the characteristics of a transnational
industry.

BEYOND STRUCTURAL FIT

Managers in many worldwide companies had long struggled with the
need to develop multiple strategic capabilities. Their search for solutions, however, most often turned into a quest for the right organizational structure. Influenced by the way in which the multidivisional
structure had facilitated diversification strategies, a generation of managers grew up believing that there was a structural solution to every
major strategic problem. Confronted with the growing complexities of
international expansion, they naturally looked for a solution in new
enabling structures.[8]

There were other reasons, too, for favoring reorganization. The
formal structure was recognized as a powerful tool through which management could redefine responsibilities and relationships. It allowed

Figure 2.2

Stopford and Wells's International Structural Stages Model

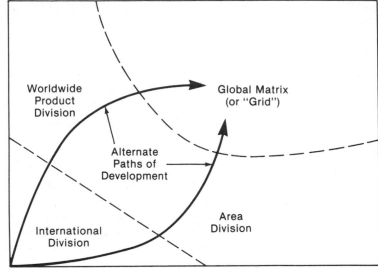

Foreign Sales
as Percentage of Total Sales

Source: Adapted from Stopford and Wells (1972).

top managers to make clear choices, have immediate impact, and send strong signals of change to all management levels.

Stopford and Wells's landmark study of the organizational structure of 187 large U.S.-based companies operating worldwide reflected and may have reinforced this belief. They proposed a "stages model" of international organizations that has become the benchmark for much subsequent research, consulting advice, and practice.[9]

The findings, summarized in Figure 2.2, suggest that worldwide corporations typically adopt different organizational structures at different stages of international expansion. They define two variables to capture strategic and administrative complexity: the number of products sold internationally ("foreign product diversity," shown on the vertical axis in Figure 2.2) and the importance of international sales to the company ("foreign sales as a percentage of total sales," shown on the horizontal axis).

Stopford and Wells suggest that worldwide companies typically manage their international operations through an international division at the early stage of foreign expansion, when both foreign sales and the diversity of products sold abroad are limited. Subsequently, some companies expand their sales abroad without significantly increasing foreign product diversity; they typically adopt an area structure. Other companies, facing substantial increases in foreign product diversity, tend to adopt the worldwide product division structure. Finally, when both foreign sales and foreign product diversity are high, companies resort to the global matrix.

Although these ideas were presented as a descriptive model, they were soon applied prescriptively by consultants, academics, and managers alike. For many companies, it seemed that structure followed fashion more than strategy. The debate was often reduced to simplistic choices between "centralization" and "decentralization," or to generalized discussions of the comparative value of product- and geography-based structures.

Confronted with the increasing complexity, diversity, and change in the 1980s, managers in many worldwide companies looked for ways to restructure. Received wisdom provided a ready solution: the global matrix. For most companies, the result was disappointing. The promised land of the global matrix turned out to be an organizational quagmire from which they were forced to retreat.

Failure of the Matrix

In theory, the solution should have worked. Having front-line managers report simultaneously to different management groups (such as area and business, area and function, or function and business) should have enabled the companies to maintain the balance among centralized efficiency, local responsiveness, and the building and leveraging of functional competencies. The multiple channels of communication and control provided the potential to nurture multiple management perspectives, with each building a particular strategic capability. Further, the ability to shift the balance of power within the matrix theoretically gave it great flexibility.[10] But the reality turned out to be otherwise, and the history of companies that followed the matrix route generally proved to be unhappy.

Dow Chemical, a pioneer of the global matrix organization, eventually returned to a more conventional structure with clear lines of responsibility being given to geographic managers. Citibank, once a textbook example of the global matrix, similarly discarded this mode of dual reporting relationships after a few years of highly publicized experimentation.[11]

Most companies that experimented with this structure encountered the same problems. The matrix amplified the differences in perspectives and interests by forcing all issues through the dual chains of command. Even a minor difference could become the subject of heated disagreement and debate. But the very design of the global matrix prevented the resolution of differences among managers with conflicting views and overlapping responsibilities. Barriers of distance, time, language, and culture impeded the vital process of confronting and resolving differences.

As a result, matrix companies developed a management process that was slow, acrimonious, and costly. Communications were routinely duplicated, approval processes were costly and time-consuming, and constant travel and frequent meetings raised the company's administrative costs dramatically.

Building Organizational Capability

The basic problem underlying companies' search for a structural fit was that it focused on only one organizational variable—formal structure—that could not capture the complexity of the strategic task facing the worldwide company. Structure defined a static set of roles, responsibilities, and relationships in a dynamic and rapidly evolving task environment. Worse, restructuring efforts often proved harmful, as organizations were bludgeoned into a major realignment of roles, responsibilities, and relationships overnight.

Companies like Procter & Gamble, Ericsson, Philips, Unilever, and NEC recognized that formal structure is a powerful but blunt weapon for effecting strategic change. To develop multidimensional strategic capabilities, they learned, a company must go beyond structure and expand its fundamental organizational capabilities. The key task was to reshape the core decision-making systems, and in doing so, the management processes of the company—the administrative systems, communication channels, and interpersonal relationships—often provided tools for managing such change that were more subtle but also more effective than formal structure. Moreover, given the complexity and volatility of environmental demands, structural fit was becoming both less relevant and harder to achieve. Success in coping with their multidimensional strategic task, they recognized, would depend on building strategic and organizational flexibility.

Philips and Matsushita showed remarkable flexibility as they strove to build the missing weapons in their strategic arsenal—for Philips, the efficiency to remain competitive with Matsushita; for Matsushita, the sensitivity and responsiveness to match the capabilities of Philips's national organizations. Similarly, in branded packaged products, Unilever and P&G both made major efforts during the 1980s to protect the creativity and drive of their national units while building more global integration into their operations and developing and diffusing innovations on a worldwide basis. And in telecom switching, both Ericsson and NEC were building the multidimensional capabilities of efficiency, responsiveness, and innovation that we have described as the hallmark of transnational strategies.

Clearly the strategic challenges facing companies in the branded packaged goods business are not the same as those confronting global competitors in the consumer electronics industry. Nor are these diverse companies adopting similar strategies. But while the nature, the strength, and the mix of the three broad strategic forces vary widely across industries, it is increasingly difficult in most businesses to defend a competitive position based on a single dominant capability. Recognition of this change has convinced many managers that their primary challenge is not to develop a strategic capability to fit the dominant industry demand, but to build multiple sources of competitive advantage that they can manage in a complementary and flexible manner.

The Role of Administrative Heritage

But if the companies we studied faced the same broad strategic goals, their specific implementation tasks and organization challenges were very different. In finding their way through the complex process of strategic change, all the companies have learned one fundamental lesson: a company's ability to build and manage the new strategic capabilities depends on its existing organizational attributes—its configuration of assets and capabilities, built up over the decades; its distribution of managerial responsibilities and influence, which cannot be shifted quickly; and an ongoing set of relationships that endure long after any structural change. Collectively, these attributes shape what we refer to as a company's administrative heritage. While strategic plans can be redrawn or scrapped overnight, it is more difficult to refocus a company's organizational capability. The administrative heritage can be one of the company's greatest assets—the underlying sources of its key competencies—and also one of its most significant liabilities, since it resists change and thereby prevents realignment or broadening of strategic capabilities.

For all the companies we studied, the key challenge in responding to the demands of the 1980s was not to define a strategy, but to overcome the unidimensional organizational capabilities and management biases that stood in the way of building a new, more complex, and dynamic transnational posture. They learned, often through trial and error, that these limitations and biases could not be overcome except in ways consistent with their own administrative heritages. Thus the companies needed to understand the nature of their administrative heritages and how their organizational capabilities could be used to better advantage.

3
ADMINISTRATIVE HERITAGE: ORGANIZATIONAL ASSET AND CONSTRAINT

In deciding how to manage their worldwide operations, most managers we studied focused intently on where they were going. They seldom asked themselves where they were coming from, although this question often turned out to be crucial. Companies had to respond to new environmental demands in the context of their existing organizational capabilities as shaped by various historical and structural factors. This administrative heritage represented both a major asset and a powerful impediment in the change process.[1]

COMPANIES AS CAPTIVES OF THEIR PAST

A company's ability to respond to the strategic task demands of today's international operating environment is constrained by its internal capabilities, which are shaped by the company's administrative heritage. Internal capability is developed over a long period of time and cannot be changed overnight or by management decree.[2] Instead, the first step for any company in adapting its organization to the emerging international environmental demands is to understand its corporate history, its "way of doing things." This analysis will reveal some characteristics that can be built on and leveraged, and others that must be adapted or surmounted. A comparison of the internationalization of Unilever and Procter & Gamble will illustrate how differences in administrative heritage shape strategic postures and constrain future direction.

Unilever's Independent Empire

Unilever's international organization began to take shape from the day William Lever established an export business. In the mid-1880s, Britain was already the center of the world soap trade, with abundant sea transport allowing shipments to Africa, India, the Far East, and South America at freight rates barely higher than the company's distribution costs within the U.K. market. Lever assigned a personal representative to each foreign market and expected him to build market share against other English exporters and local competitors.

By nature, Lever was a detail-oriented, hands-on manager who kept close tabs on all aspects of his business. Despite the growing number and dispersion of his overseas companies, he maintained a close personal contact with all of them through frequent overseas voyages. Having personally appointed the heads of the foreign companies (invariably expatriate Englishmen), Lever demanded their unswerving loyalty. As operations expanded, however, the aging patriarch was less and less able to keep up with all developments, and his decisions became increasingly erratic and ill-fated.

Over the years, concern had grown within the organization about Lever's centralized and highly personal management style. After his death in 1925, several important changes were made with respect to the management of the company's worldwide operations. The Overseas Committee (OSC) was established in 1926 to assume responsibility for managing the company's overseas businesses. The first chairman of the OSC, H. R. Greenhalgh, felt strongly that overseas managers should be given local autonomy. In his view, the role of the Overseas Committee was to provide guidance (not instruction), to approve the annual estimates of sales and profits, and to monitor the regular flow of financial data and correspondence from the field. A strong corporate norm resulted: the task in managing overseas companies was to develop and manage people rather than to analyze and resolve problems.

Other influences reinforced the trend toward decentralization of responsibility and reduced the power of the once strongly centralized system of management. The growing number and sophistication of local competitors forced Unilever to replace much of its huge export business with locally manufactured products. The rising trade barriers of the late 1920s and 1930s reinforced this trend, and soon most of Unilever's large national companies were fully integrated, self-sufficient operations. Also, the substantial country-to-country differences in consumer tastes, preferences, and practices, as well as in market structures, distribution channels, and local regulations, required subsidiaries to adapt products and marketing strategies more than ever before. Some national Unilever companies even developed their own totally local products; such operating independence reinforced the local units' managerial autonomy.

In the 1930s Unilever began what became known internally as the "ization" policy. Beginning in India, the company recognized the need to fill management and technical positions with citizens of the host country rather than expatriates. The "Indianization" precedent was replicated worldwide, particularly in the postwar years when many newly independent countries felt a strong surge of nationalism. This "ization" trend increased the independence of Unilever's national companies.

The outbreak of World War II quickly drove these changes home. When Rotterdam fell to the Nazis and communications with London became increasingly difficult, local companies were forced to operate independently. Decisions that once were referred to the center were made locally; reports from national companies were stripped down to basics; and manpower shortages virtually eliminated support from corporate-level staff.

The company emerged in the postwar era with a strongly held philosophy of management built around independent operating companies whose managers were given maximum responsibility and freedom. The clearly understood role of the board was to approve plans and budgets, control capital expenditure, and appoint and develop executives. At an operating level, local managers had great latitude to develop and implement strategies that reflected the opportunities and constraints of their particular environments. The watchwords that soon became corporate dogma in Unilever were "local initiative and decentralized control."[3]

P&G's Transfer of Knowledge

Approaching its 150th anniversary in 1987, Procter & Gamble looked back on a corporate history quite different from that of Unilever.[4] Like its European rival, P&G derived its culture from the strong and enduring values of its founders. The religious beliefs of William Procter and James Gamble left a legacy of hard work, thoroughness, self-discipline, high ethical standards, and respect for individuals.[5] Unlike Unilever, P&G did not pursue overseas markets vigorously until after World War II. Geographical and historical factors were at work: P&G's headquarters were in Cincinnati, hardly a crossroad of international trade, and the United States lacked the strong ready-made markets of the British Empire. Fundamentally, however, P&G focused on the domestic U.S. market because it was large and rich enough to provide extraordinary growth opportunities.

Before World War II, P&G had a very limited export activity, and its operations in Canada, Cuba, the Philippines, and Indonesia were regarded as appendages to the U.S. business. Even the important acquisition of the British company Thomas Hedley in 1930 was an isolated deal rather than part of a strategic plan to expand internationally.

After the war, P&G began to see overseas markets as an important source of growth and profit. Although some of its wartime efforts had been diverted to munitions production and its plants in the Philippines and Indonesia had been damaged, the company emerged from the war in better shape than Unilever. Its research into non-soap detergents in the 1930s gave it a technological lead that could provide the competitive advantage to open markets for it worldwide.

After a few failed attempts to transfer some of its most successful U.S. brands into foreign markets, P&G learned the lesson that Unilever had long since developed into a corporate credo—it had to adapt its products and marketing approaches on a country-by-country basis. The new learning was translated into policy by Walter Lingle, the head of P&G's international operations for two decades in the critical postwar period. He stated emphatically, "We cannot simply manufacture and sell products with United States formulas. They won't work. They won't be accepted."

However, P&G's international policies and practices fell far short of the almost total product development freedom that Unilever had built up over half a century. While local subsidiaries could modify products and adapt marketing approaches to suit local needs, innovations and overall strategies were directed by headquarters. Nonetheless, the new flexibility enabled most foreign subsidiary general managers to develop strong and reasonably independent local companies.

Unlike Unilever, P&G was already a well-established, mature company by the time it began its international thrust. As such, it had a strong tradition of products, policies, and practices that would inevitably influence the development of the fledgling international business. Indeed, while Lingle emphasized the need to modify products from country to country, he firmly believed that P&G's "way of doing things" represented the experience of a century of outstanding success, and that this wisdom should not be lost in overseas markets. Lingle stated this view forthrightly:

> We have decided that the best way to succeed in other countries is to build in each one as exact a replica of the United States Procter & Gamble organization as it is possible to build. We believe that exactly the same policies and procedures which have given our company success in the United States will be equally successful overseas.[6]

Thus P&G operations abroad were linked back to the parent company in two important respects. Not only did foreign subsidiaries depend on the parent for advanced technology and marketing expertise, but they were also structured to operate as replicas of the U.S. company, immersed in the same principles, guided by the same policies, and following the same practices.

There was another important influence on P&G's internationalization. Although many tariff barriers and market differences still existed, these impediments were eroding by the 1960s. The signing of the Treaty of Rome in 1958 created the European Economic Community (EEC), and the promise of an open European market gave P&G's subsidiaries new opportunities. Clearly, the company had less incentive to develop completely self-sufficient and independent local companies than Unilever had had. P&G built far fewer plants and developed more interdependency between operations than its largest European competitor. Its French company, for example, supplied perfumes to other units as well as active ingredients for Italian detergent manufacture; and when wildcat strikes closed the French plants in the late 1960s, the French market was supplied from Italy, Belgium, and Germany.[7]

In 1963 the European Technical Center (ETC) was established to serve common R&D needs of the company's European subsidiaries; although the local units had their own product development capabilities, the center, located in Brussels, provided a counterbalance to localization and fragmentation of the product line. Eventually, the role of ETC was broadened to that of a regional headquarters, coordinating and controlling all operations of the national companies.

Adaptation to New Challenges

With very different administrative heritages, Unilever and P&G responded differently to the industry changes that caused the highly differentiated national markets to converge during the late 1970s and early 1980s. Unilever recognized the challenge, but was more concerned about its newly established rival in these markets. Unencumbered by a long history of independent and autonomous subsidiary management, P&G seemed to transfer its formidable technologies and marketing capabilities to its subsidiaries quickly and painlessly. To gain similar strategic control over its national companies, in 1962 Unilever created the beginnings of a central product organization for each of its three major businesses—detergent, edible fats, and frozen products.

But a half-century of physical isolation and institutionalized autonomy gave Unilever's national companies a level of independence that was extremely hard to change. In keeping with the company's traditions, the new groups were designated "product coordinators" rather than managers. The "coordinations" as they became known within Unilever, were expected to advise not direct, to persuade rather than dictate to the national companies. And the powerful subsidiary managers did all in their power to defend their independence. Even after twenty years, Unilever's ability to develop and implement a coordinated worldwide strategy was limited to some modest successes in Europe. Coordination on a global basis was still a long way off.

Although managers in P&G talked about the operating independence of their national subsidiaries, they were far less autonomous
than Unilever's national companies. Not only were the P&G subsidiaries constrained by the parent company's structure and its strong
policies and practices, but they had hardly begun to exercise their
freedom when senior management started imposing various means of
coordination and control. In the late 1970s, ETC worked actively to
rationalize manufacturing, centralize research, and even coordinate
marketing programs on a European basis. P&G was able to gain strategic control of its operations much more quickly, and painlessly than
Unilever.

Administrative heritage was an important influence in all the companies we studied. An organization's strategic capabilities are built up
over time and cannot be easily undone or changed. Like Unilever,
Philips developed as a loosely linked network of highly autonomous
national subsidiaries, while Matsushita retained much of the decision-
making authority and concentrated more of its organizational resources
at the center. Similarly, at ITT the management process was dominated
by tight administrative and financial controls, although the national
units had considerable strategic and operating freedom. Ericsson took
almost an opposite approach: it retained firm central control over key
strategic and operating matters, but used relatively simple planning
systems and financial controls.

The importance of administrative heritage is now well understood
at Philips. Almost twenty years ago, the company's board of management became concerned about the ability of a management system built
around a "world federation of national organizations" to respond to
economic, political, and technological forces that were "permitting
non-European competitors to operate in Europe on the same scale as
they did in their home markets." The committee appointed to examine
the situation published its report (widely known within Philips as
"The Yellow Booklet") in 1972. In clear and concise terms it stated that
it was "imperative for Philips to increase the scale of its activities,
resulting in a decrease in the number of product types marketed, a
concentration of production, [and] an increasing flow of goods between
national organizations."

Despite a very clear recognition of its strategic task, Philips
struggled over the next decade and a half to implement the necessary
changes. The decisions to rationalize the network of local plants to
achieve global scale, to standardize diverse product lines, and to coordinate activities and policies across national boundaries had important
organizational implications. The organizational challenge was the major hurdle for Philips to clear. The company's rich administrative heritage had built and reinforced an organizational structure and a management process that could not be changed overnight.

SHAPERS OF ADMINISTRATIVE HERITAGE

Many forces shape a company's configuration of assets, distribution of responsibilities, dominant management style, and ingrained organizational values. But those that seemed most influential in the companies we studied were the impact of leadership on corporate norms and priorities, the influence of home country culture on underlying values and practices, and the powerful influence of organizational history.

The Role of Leaders

Asked what has shaped their company's norms, values, and "way of doing things," managers often cite the influence of the company's founder or another key executive.[8] In some companies, the leader has had an enduring impact on strategic direction. Such is clearly the case at NEC, where in January 1969 the newly named president, Koji Kobayashi, charted a strategic course tied to his vision of the merging of computer and communications technologies. The "C&C philosophy," as he termed it, dominated all strategic decisions in NEC over the next two decades. By the late 1980s, Kobayashi's C&C vision had become a firmly established part of the company's administrative heritage.

In other companies, the leader's influence is felt primarily in the organization structure. At Philips, the enduring (but often harmful) management practice of balancing technical and commercial interests in key decisions can be traced back to the relationship between the entrepreneurial founders—Gerard Philips, a technologically oriented engineer, and his brother Anton, a consummate salesman. Their relationship was institutionalized in the practice of giving divisions and national organizations dual-headed management, an organizational norm that shaped all key decisions in Philips for over ninety years. Only in the 1980s did the company begin to replace dual-headed structures with single-headed management, to speed up decision making. But management behavior still reflected the competition between technical and commercial groups, and negotiated decision making.

Harold Geneen had an important impact on ITT's organization and management processes. While his successors have refocused the company's strategy and reshaped its organization, Geneen's influence is still felt in the discipline he instilled through his famous management systems and review meetings.

The company in which we were the most clearly conscious of the potential power of a leader's influence was Matsushita. There, any employee will be able to tell you how the company's objectives and philosophy come directly from the teachings or practices of Konosuke Matsushita, or K.M. as he is universally known within the company.

On May 5, 1932, the fourteenth anniversary of the company's founding, K.M. announced his business philosophy and a 250-year plan for the company, broken up into ten 25-year segments. The business philosophy, which has become institutionalized through "cultural and spiritual" training programs and forms the basis of the morning assembly ritual held in facilities worldwide, defines the fundamental goals of the company and describes how they are to be achieved. The philosophy proposes that "the purpose of an enterprise is to contribute to society by supplying goods of high quality at low prices in ample quantity," and that "profit comes in compensation for contribution to society." It is encapsulated in the Seven Spirits of Matsushita: service through industry, fairness, harmony and cooperation, struggle for progress, courtesy and humility, adjustment and assimilation, and gratitude. Within Matsushita these values are regarded as more than platitudes. Managers refer to them constantly and use them to help make even the most basic operating decisions.[9]

The founder's enduring influence is also felt in the current organization structure. Concerned about his poor health, K.M. felt he needed to delegate more than was normal in traditional Japanese companies. Thus in 1933 Matsushita became one of the first companies in the world to adopt a divisionalized structure. K.M. gave each division full responsibility for its strategy, product development, financing, and operations, and held it accountable for meeting stringent growth and revenue objectives. Under the "one product–one division" system, he was able to maintain the small business environment and entrepreneurial spirit that had driven the company's early growth, while developing managers able to fulfill the next phase of the 250-year plan. In vision, values, and management practices, Konosuke Matsushita has had a profound and lasting influence on Matsushita's administrative heritage.[10]

Although Matsushita represents an extreme case, the powerful influence of individual leaders is not unusual. Most companies have been irreversibly influenced by the beliefs and decisions of a handful of key individuals. Attempts to change such strongly held beliefs and values have often been frustrated, in part because the values are tied to larger-than-life figures in company folklore.

The Impact of National Culture

The influence of a nation's history, infrastructure, and culture permeates all aspects of life within the country, including the norms, values, and behaviors of managers in its national companies. Nationally influenced behavioral characteristics become an ingrained part of each company's "way of doing things" and shape its international organization structure and processes.[11]

Business historian Alfred Chandler has traced the influence of the cultural values and social structures on British management practice.[12] For reasons related to Britain's unique geography, political economy, legal structure, social history, and educational system, companies developed under a system of family management that emphasized personal relationships more than formal structures, and relied more on broad-gauged financial controls than on coordination of technical or operational details. Until World War II, according to Chandler, the management processes in most large British companies were dominated by "family capitalism." As these companies expanded abroad, family members or hand-picked "trusted company servants" were often sent to manage offshore operations. Control was achieved largely through the bond of family membership or the personal loyalty of appointees. The family patriarch might take an annual voyage to visit key foreign holdings, and would perhaps also correspond with the appointed heads of those operations. Apart from such contacts, however, the overseas businesses were often treated as a portfolio of investments rather than an integrated worldwide business.

Such cultural influences were very evident in Lever Brothers and later Unilever, where the important overseas operations were managed by an inner circle of trusted managers who reported directly to William Lever. After his death, the Overseas Committee became the institutional embodiment of this paternalistic oversight role. Philips too conformed to this model: the Philips family dominated the company's top management until well after World War II. Overseas operations were managed by a group of trusted appointees (known internally as the "Dutch Mafia"), whose understanding of Philips technology, commercial objectives, and overall strategy provided the major link between the parent company and its dispersed national organizations.

The cultural forces influencing management of U.S. companies were completely different, marked by the pioneering spirit and sense of limitless opportunity that pervaded American society in the late nineteenth and early twentieth centuries. The United States had emerged as an egalitarian society, without the European concentration of wealth and power in a small socio-economic class. Such an environment was less tolerant of the elitism and paternalism found in large, family-dominated companies in Britain. A corporate meritocracy emerged that fostered the development of a new class of professional managers, to whom owners delegated the authority of running the business. Chandler described this management culture as "managerial capitalism."[13]

Owners' delegation of responsibility to professional managers established a corporate norm that was then carried down through the organization. The product diversification trend that began in the United States in the 1920s required still greater delegation of responsibility to managers of diverse businesses. Such delegation could succeed only if top management retained access to information as a means of control.

Thus developed the classic American management processes built around divisionalized structures, which were transferred worldwide as U.S. companies expanded abroad. This combination of delegation of responsibility to professional management and coordination and control through sophisticated management systems proved immensely powerful. To Jean-Jacques Servan-Schreiber, U.S.-based companies' enormous international success was due to "something quite new and considerably more serious [than financial or technological strength]—the extension to Europe of an *organization* that is still a mystery to us."[14]

We saw the influence of sophisticated systems and controls in all three of the American companies we studied. GE's use of strategic planning systems became the model for companies worldwide, as did Procter & Gamble's use of clear policies and practices (the Procter way) and one-page memos as a means of control. But ITT best illustrated this delegation of responsibility and counterbalancing management control. Harold Geneen's influence combined with culturally shaped norms to make this company an archetype (some would say a caricature) of a systems-dominated, control-oriented American company.[15]

In contrast to European family capitalism and American managerial capitalism, the Japanese cultural heritage fostered a form of management Chandler called "group capitalism." As many observers have noted, the homogeneity of Japanese society, its isolationism during the Tokugawa period, and the influence of Eastern religions and philosophies have reinforced strong Japanese cultural norms that emphasized group behavior and valued interpersonal harmony. Such values carried over into the country's commercial organizations and helped shape distinctive management styles and organizational practices.[16]

At a corporate level, the group-oriented values were reflected in the *zaibatsu* and other enterprise groups, which paternalistically watched over their affiliated companies. Within the organization, such values were evident in the widespread norm of lifetime employment commitments—by both employer and employee—and such managerial practices as *nemawashi* or *ringi*, which institutionalized information sharing and joint decision making.[17]

These influences bound managers and corporations together into a very culturally dependent system, which many companies found an impediment as they expanded internationally. Management systems were so communications intensive and relationship dependent that they did not function well when operating units were separated by substantial time and distance barriers. In addition, language and cultural barriers made it difficult to integrate non-Japanese into the ongoing management process. And lifetime employment commitments and the need to promote employees within the organization further encouraged Japanese companies to expand operations at home while reaching foreign markets through zaibatsu-linked trading companies or offshore sales affiliates. The net effect was to encourage Japanese companies to retain decision making and control at the center, where they could be managed by those who understood the subtleties of the system.

Kao's international expansion was impaired by such a culturally influenced management philosophy, and while less of a handicap, the administrative heritage in both NEC and Matsushita was also strongly influenced by the Japanese culture. In Japan, Matsushita was well known for its decentralized management style. Yet, even into the 1980s, its overseas operations were highly dependent on the parent company for products (over 90 percent of manufacturing was concentrated in Japan); and all technology and new product development came from headquarters. The delegation of responsibility and authority was more constrained than at either Philips or General Electric, and was usually achieved only when Matsushita could extend its culturally linked system abroad. Then Japanese managers in foreign locations engaged in nemawashi and ringi by intensive telephonc contact and frequent exchanges of visits between headquarters in Japan and the overseas units.

The Influence of Organizational History

The context in which management decides to expand operations abroad and the environment in which it executes that decision also have an enduring influence. Early choices about products, markets, and modes of operation are locked in through decisions about asset configuration and organization structure, constraining future options. The influence of historical context is particularly important in the international business environment, which is shaped by diverse, often volatile, economic, political, and social forces.

Although strategic forces vary widely by industry, as we described in Chapter 2, one can make some generalizations about the influences on worldwide companies expanding in different eras.[18] In the earliest decades of the century, many companies, particularly in Europe and North America, had learned that their very survival depended on capturing the scale economies made possible by mass production, cheap reliable distribution, and mass merchandising. It was only natural that managers would look to overseas markets for additional scale potential.

Some companies quickly developed what today would be called

classic global strategies. Singer, for example, built a mass production operation in Scotland with sufficient capacity to serve all of Europe and export sewing machines to Asia, Africa, and even back to the United States. John D. Rockefeller captured a quarter of the world's kerosene production in Standard Oil's three highly efficient refineries, which exported two-thirds of their 20,000 barrel-a-day capacity. And Henry Ford dominated the world market for low-priced automobiles by exporting from his highly efficient Highland Park plant—a classic global strategy replicated by the Japanese 50 years later.

But for most companies, the barriers to such global integration were too high—and even these three companies were soon forced to modify their pure global posture. For a wide variety of products, well-established national preferences differentiated one country's consumer demand from another's. Equally important in the early part of the century were the logistical barriers that separated national markets. The delays and cost of shipping products internationally completely offset the economies of global mass production for all but a limited range of products. And local competitors soon sprang up. As worldwide companies' exports were challenged by local companies in foreign markets, it often seemed preferable to set up a fully integrated local company that could respond in a more direct and timely fashion.

In these years, companies from European countries, particularly those with extensive overseas empires, dominated the expansion of investment abroad.[19] In 1914, for example, the United Kingdom accounted for half of the stock of foreign investment held abroad, with France, Germany, and the Netherlands responsible for an additional 43 percent. The United States' share at this time was 6 percent.[20]

In the 1930s and 1940s, politics dominated the international business environment. Protectionist pressures, which had been developing since the late 1920s, peaked in the mid-1930s with the passage of the Smoot-Hawley legislation in the United States and similar laws around the world. Even the most dedicated seekers of global-scale economies were often forced to set up manufacturing facilities behind tariff walls. National subsidiary companies typically used their fully integrated local capabilities to modify products and even manufacturing processes to meet local needs. Their dependence on headquarters declined, as did the ability of managers in the corporate office to control them.

The coming of the war further isolated overseas companies from their parent organizations, particularly those located in Europe. For example, the fear of German confiscation led Philips to spin off its companies in England and the United States and restructure them as legally independent companies owned by trusts.

The postwar international environment was very different. Demand boomed worldwide as consumers caught up on purchases postponed by the war. In producer goods, the economies of Europe were undergoing major postwar reconstruction, while new international financing agencies helped fund massive development projects in many developing countries.

For several reasons, U.S.-based companies were in the best position to take advantage of the worldwide postwar boom. Many of their European rivals were preoccupied with reconstruction of their domestic operations, whereas most American firms had emerged unscathed from the war. More important, many U.S. firms had new technologies and capabilities that boosted their competitive advantage. American technological hegemony was unquestioned, and many U.S.-based companies were pulled into foreign markets by unsolicited export orders and licensing opportunities. By 1960, the United States was responsible for 59 percent of the stock of foreign investment held abroad, far outstripping the four previously dominant European countries, whose share had dropped to 33 percent.[21]

The companies that internationalized in this period faced less pressure to be responsive to national differences. The international trading environment had become less restrictive, reducing the need for autonomous local operations, and massive troop movements and the postwar shortages had a homogenizing effect on local preferences. An even more powerful influence was companies' recognition that they could capitalize on knowledge developed in the home market, by managing its transfer to less advanced overseas environments. Indeed, this pattern of overseas expansion became so common, particularly for American-based companies, that it was used by Harvard researcher Raymond Vernon as the basis for his product cycle model of the internationalization process.[22]

The phased international transfer of knowledge applied not only to technological innovation, but also to marketing skills and managerial capabilities. The American marketing system was changed dramatically by the arrival of television as a medium of mass communication; the revolution in distribution brought about by the growth of supermarkets, discount outlets, and suburban shopping malls; and the new emphasis on convenience in products and packaging. Because these trends emerged first in the United States, American-based companies like Procter & Gamble developed marketing knowledge and capabilities that could be transferred sequentially around the world as similar changes came about in other countries.

By the 1960s and 1970s, new forces were shaping the international environment and influencing the operations of companies expanding abroad. The protectionist trend of earlier decades was reversed as successive negotiations and agreements under the General Agreements on Tariffs and Trade (GATT) created an environment with fewer tariff and nontariff barriers than the international economy had seen since early in the century.

The more open trade environment made global sourcing possible, and other forces reshaped its economic viability. Transport costs were drastically restructured with the coming of containerization and super-tonnage cargo ships. New product and process technologies increased the opportunity (and often the need) for scale economies. The switch from electromechanical to electronic technologies revolutionized the economics of many industries.

Meanwhile, the dramatic increase of international travel and communication in this period gradually eroded the differences in consumer tastes that were once an important barrier to globalization. In several industries, products could be standardized for international consumption, and in many others, worldwide demand could be met with a basic design that was slightly modified for particular markets. In either case, the need for unique local products in each national market was all but eliminated.[23]

Many Japanese companies were now expanding abroad. In response to prevailing conditions, they developed a strategic thrust and organizational capability very different from those of companies that internationalized earlier. Matsushita, for example, was ideally positioned to develop standardized global products, manufacture them at a central location, and export them worldwide, while Philips developed, manufactured, and marketed products on a "local-for-local" basis, and GE based its international strategy on the ability to transfer its U.S. technology and innovations overseas.

Because most Japanese companies' overseas business experience had been limited to neighboring Asian countries, they often felt they could not match the large sophisticated national facilities and capabilities of their European and American competitors. Besides, the well-established Japanese trading companies often provided them with an easier means of access to new markets. Many companies, too, recognized that their new, efficient, scale-intensive plants gave them a competitive advantage in the upstream end of the value-added chain that could offset competitors' downstream strengths. So they favored export-based strategies emphasizing the global-scale cost advantages and high-level quality benefits achieved through tight central control of product development, procurement, and manufacturing.

ADMINISTRATIVE HERITAGE: THE STRATEGIC AND ORGANIZATIONAL CONSEQUENCES

In Chapter 2 we described how environmental forces acted on industry characteristics to shape the strategic profile of businesses. We sketched the characteristics of multinational, global, and international businesses.

Similarly, a company's administrative heritage influences its organizational form and capabilities. We observed three very different organizational models, each characterized by distinct structural configurations, administrative processes, and management mentalities. The first and perhaps most widespread type is one we term the *multinational organization model*. This was the classic organizational pattern adopted by companies expanding in the prewar period. We have described how economic, political, and social forces encouraged these companies to decentralize their organizational assets and capabilities to allow foreign operations to respond to the differences that distinguished national markets. The resulting configuration of distributed resources and delegated responsibilities can be described as a *decentralized federation*.

This structure was particularly well suited to the management norms of many European companies that expanded abroad in that era. Because of the enduring influence of family ownership, organizational processes were built on personal relationships and informal contacts rather than formal structures and systems. Such management processes reinforced the tendency to delegate operating independence to trusted appointees sent to manage offshore subsidiaries. Control and coordination were achieved primarily through the personal relationship between top corporate management and subsidiary managers. This social control process was normally supplemented by some simple financial systems to allow accounting consolidation and to manage the capital outflows and dividend repatriation. In such organizations, the dominant management mentality viewed the company's strategy as developing positions in key markets worldwide and managing offshore operations as a portfolio of independent businesses. The approach was literally multinational—each national unit was managed as an independent entity whose strategic objective was to optimize its situation in the local environment.

The multinational organization is defined by these characteristics: a decentralized federation of assets and responsibilities, a management process defined by simple financial control systems overlaid on informal personal coordination, and a dominant strategic mentality that viewed the company's worldwide operations as a portfolio of national businesses. (See Figure 3.1.)

The second basic type we identified is the *international organization model*. This organization structure and process became predominant in the early postwar decades. The key task for companies that internationalized then was to transfer knowledge and expertise to overseas environments that were less advanced in technology or market

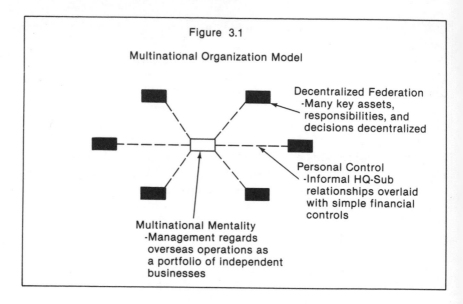

Figure 3.1

Multinational Organization Model

Decentralized Federation
-Many key assets,
responsibilities, and
decisions decentralized

Personal Control
-Informal HQ-Sub
relationships overlaid
with simple financial
controls

Multinational Mentality
-Management regards
overseas operations as
a portfolio of independent
businesses

development. While local subsidiaries were often free to adapt the new products or strategies (market differences and international barriers were eroding in this period, but only slowly), their dependence on the parent company for new products, processes, or ideas dictated a great deal more coordination and control by headquarters than in the classic multinational organization. The structural configuration can be described as a *coordinated federation*.

The managerial culture of U.S.-based companies fit this structure well. These companies had built a reputation for professional management that implied a willingness to delegate responsibility, while retaining overall control through sophisticated management systems and the specialist corporate staffs. The systems provided channels for a regular flow of information, to be interpreted by the central staffs. Holding the managerial reins, top management could control the free-running team of independent subsidiaries and guide the direction in which they were headed.

Parent company management was often somewhat superior and parochial in its attitude toward international operations, perhaps because of the assumption that new ideas and developments all came from the parent. Despite corporate management's increased understanding of its overseas markets, it often seemed to view foreign operations as appendages whose principal purpose was to leverage the capabilities and resources developed in the home market.

While the structure of the international organization resembled the

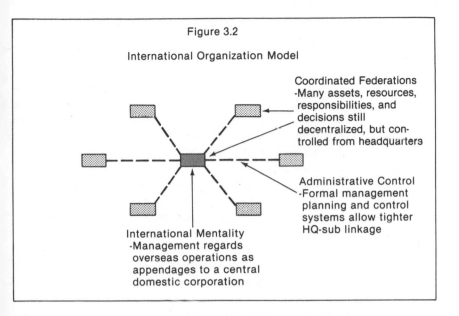

Figure 3.2

International Organization Model

Coordinated Federations
-Many assets, resources, responsibilities, and decisions still decentralized, but controlled from headquarters

Administrative Control
-Formal management planning and control systems allow tighter HQ-sub linkage

International Mentality
-Management regards overseas operations as appendages to a central domestic corporation

multinational form, the international's subsidiaries were more dependent on the center for the transfer of knowledge and information. Furthermore, the parent company made greater use of formal systems and controls in the headquarters-subsidiary link. (See Figure 3.2 for a diagrammatic representation of the international organization model.)

Our third organization type is the classic *global organization model*. This was one of the earliest corporate forms, adopted by such pioneers of internationalization as Henry Ford and John D. Rockefeller as they built global-scale facilities to produce standard products shipped worldwide under a tightly controlled central strategy. And it was this organizational form that underlay the much-studied Japanese model of worldwide competition in the 1970s and early 1980s.

The global configuration is based on a centralization of assets, resources, and responsibilities; overseas operations are used to reach foreign markets in order to build global scale. The role of offshore subsidiaries is limited to sales and service, although local assembly plants may be dictated by economic or, more often, political pressures. The role of the local units is to assemble and sell products and to implement plans and policies developed at headquarters. Compared with subsidiaries in multinational or international organizations, they have much less freedom to create new products or strategies or even to modify existing ones. This structural configuration can be described as a *centralized hub*.

This configuration suited the managerial norms and processes in

Japanese companies. With centralized decision making and control, these companies could retain their culturally dependent management system based on group-oriented behavior. Because the management process required intensive communication and a complex system of personal interdependencies and commitments, it was very difficult to transfer abroad. It worked very effectively, however, if decisions were centralized in the Japanese headquarters. Overseas subsidiaries depended on the center for resources and direction. Headquarters managers kept tight control on subsidiary operations, and the flow of goods, knowledge, and support was one-way.

Managers in global organizations focused more on world markets than did their counterparts in multinational and international organizations. But because national subsidiaries had little independence, global managers had less understanding of local environmental differences. The dominant management perspective was that the world could, and should, be treated as a single integrated market in which similarities were more important than differences. The entire globe was the prime unit of analyses.

The combination of a centralized hub configuration, dependent and tightly controlled subsidiaries, and a management mentality that saw the world as a single economic entity thus define the classic global organization. (See Figure 3.3.)

Clearly, the three organization models, shaped by historical, cul-

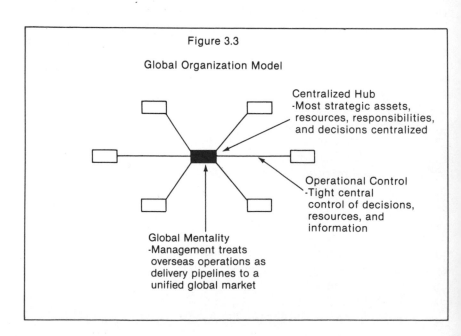

Figure 3.3

Global Organization Model

Centralized Hub
-Most strategic assets, resources, responsibilities, and decisions centralized

Operational Control
-Tight central control of decisions, resources, and information

Global Mentality
-Management treats overseas operations as delivery pipelines to a unified global market

tural, and personal influences, have very different strategic capabilities. The multinational model allows companies to be extremely sensitive and responsive to local market differences and national political demands; the international model provides an effective means for companies to transfer knowledge and skills from the parent company, and adapt them to local needs; and the global organization is most likely to facilitate the development of coordinated strategies and to capture global-scale efficiencies.

COMPANY PERFORMANCE: THE ENVIRONMENT-STRATEGY-STRUCTURE LINKAGE

The environment-strategy-structure paradigm provides a powerful way to understand differences in corporate performance. Simply put, the model suggests that superior performance comes from a good fit between corporate strategy and environmental demands, and between organization structure and strategy.

In Chapter 2, we focused on the environment-strategy link and showed that the best performers were companies whose strategy fit the industry demands (e.g., by pursuing a global strategy in the global consumer electronics industry, Matsushita outdistanced Philips with its multinational strategy and GE with its international posture). As industry demands have become more complex, however, unidimensional concepts of strategic fit are being replaced by a more dynamic form of strategic flexibility.

In this chapter, we have emphasized the strategy-structure link, and especially the effect of a company's administrative heritage on its structure and management mentality. Many managers in the companies we studied were more concerned about the strategy-environment interface than about the implications of their planned strategic overhauls for the organization, or the possibility that the organization might constrain or even completely block their plans.

In Chapter 2 we described some of the initial actions taken by corporate managers of Philips and Unilever to respond to changes in their businesses. Both companies' efforts to centralize product development failed because of deeply entrenched norms of strategic and operational decentralization. Changes in those norms, and in the management processes that reflected them, were necessary before the structural or strategic changes could become effective.

Similarly, Matsushita's divisionalized structure is now creating problems for the company. In a period of low growth, its profitability-oriented measurement system causes divisional managers to emphasize short-term results and to avoid risky development investments. Competition among divisions impedes the sharing of people, resources, and information. As products become more and more multifunctional systems rather than stand-alone equipment, these impediments have increasingly serious consequences for the company's ability to create new products that require cooperation by different product groups. Matsushita is finding it difficult to address these problems because of the deeply rooted philosophy and values embodied in the divisional system.

Some researchers imply that firms can change their strategy or their formal organizational structure to regain fit. Our findings, however, suggest that such changes are extremely difficult to achieve, since both strategy and structure are products of a company's unique and ingrained administrative heritage.

We do not imply that companies cannot change. Indeed, the purpose of this book is to emphasize that change is possible, to describe how some companies adapted to their new strategic challenges, and to suggest how managers can learn to manage change in their own organizations. But change in competitive strategy or in formal organizational structure is difficult to implement and rarely effective unless it is accompanied by matching changes in the company's values and management processes. In short, any change must begin with a clear understanding of the assets and the constraints of the particular company's administrative heritage.

TRANSITION TO THE TRANSNATIONAL

In Chapter 2 we advanced the hypothesis that many worldwide industries have been transformed in the 1980s from traditional global, multinational, or international forms toward a transnational form. Instead of demanding efficiency, or responsiveness, or learning as the key capability for success, these businesses now require participating firms to achieve all three strengths simultaneously to remain competitive. As a result, most companies face challenging problems of adaptation. Even those that were once successful because their administrative heritage matched the unidimensional strategic requirement of their businesses now must develop new capabilities.

Companies differ in their perception of the problem; Matsushita, Unilever, and Ericsson, whose historical strategic postures were well suited to industry demands, see the challenge as one of adaptation to changing industry requirements. Other companies, such as Philips, Kao, and NEC, believe they must develop a fit with the dominant strategic need. In essence, the problem is similar for both groups: to protect the particular competence they possess, and develop those capabilities they currently lack. Yet each group's perceptions put a distinctive spin on the problem. Companies that have been relatively successful may find change difficult because of the very success of their past strategies. Those that have lagged behind, on the other hand, feel a need for total strategic reorientation, and may fail to protect those capabilities that were less critical in the past but are now becoming increasingly important.

In conceptual terms, we have described industries as gradually evolving to a similar transnational form. In operative terms, however, companies face very different specific challenges. Similarly, differences in administrative heritages make the adaptation process very different, even for those companies competing in the same business.

Over time, through trial and error, the companies are developing certain similarities. Fundamentally, they are evolving a common vision about managing across borders. This vision recognizes the importance of administrative heritage both as an asset to protect and as a constraint to overcome. Another central belief is that the first step toward developing the multidimensional strategic competencies needed in transnational businesses is to build organizational capabilities. Such a management mentality, more than any particular organizational form or strategic posture, is at the heart of what we call the transnational organization. Chapter 4 describes this organization; the rest of the book suggests how such a company can be built and managed.

4
THE TRANSNATIONAL: THE EMERGING ORGANIZATION MODEL

As we have described in Chapter 2, managers in most worldwide companies recognize the need for simultaneously achieving global efficiency, national responsiveness, and the ability to develop and exploit knowledge on a worldwide basis. Some, however, regard the goal as inherently unattainable. Perceiving irreconcilable contradictions among the three objectives, they opt to focus on one of them, at least temporarily. The transnational company is one that overcomes these contradictions.[1]

We begin this chapter with a brief discussion of why traditional management modes cannot effectively respond to the multidimensional and dynamic demands of today's transnational industries. Next we highlight some key attributes that allow the transnational organization to overcome the contradictions among various strategic demands. The chapter concludes with a brief discussion of the main management tasks involved in building and managing a transnational organization. Subsequent chapters will flesh out this sketch in greater detail. Our primary objective here is to provide a conceptual summary and a road map for the second and third parts of the book.

Our account of the transnational describes an idealized organization type rather than any specific company. Such an organizational form is not easy to develop and manage. Even while we were conducting our research, two of the nine companies we studied in detail quit the business on which we were focusing. In both cases, the decision was due in part—we would suggest in large part—to the difficulty of evolving toward the kind of transnational organization that could prosper in the changing businesses. The remaining companies in the study all shared one common characteristic: top management recognized the need to build and manage a very different kind of worldwide organization. It made strong and consistent efforts to develop the organizational capabilities characteristic of the transnational company.

Table 4.1
Organizational Characteristics of Multinational, Global,
and International Companies

Organizational Characteristic	Multinational	Global	International
Configuration of assets and capabilities	Decentralized and nationally self-sufficient	Centralized and globally scaled	Sources of core competencies centralized, others decentralized
Role of overseas operations	Sensing and exploiting local opportunities	Implementing parent company strategies	Adapting and leveraging parent company competencies
Development and diffusion of knowledge	Knowledge developed and retained within each unit	Knowledge developed and retained at the center	Knowledge developed at the center and transferred to overseas units

DILEMMAS AND TRADE-OFFS

All nine companies we studied had implicitly recognized the need to manage efficiency, responsiveness, and knowledge simultaneously. However, as we have shown, all of them found the challenge a difficult one—some more so than others. The ways in which they traditionally approached different strategic tasks led to dilemmas that prevented them from achieving any one objective without sacrificing, or at least seriously compromising, the others.[2] These dilemmas arose from the ways in which companies configured their assets and capabilities, assigned roles to their overseas units, and diffused knowledge within the company (see Table 4.1).

With its resources and capabilities consolidated at the center, the global company achieves efficiency primarily by exploiting potential scale economies in all its activities. Such a configuration of assets, however, also implies that national subsidiaries are managed without any slack resources and thus have neither the motivation nor the ability to respond to local market needs. Similarly, centralization of knowledge and skills allows the global company to be highly efficient in managing innovations. It can create new products and processes at relatively low cost and high speed. Yet the central groups responsible for innovation often lack adequate understanding of the market needs and production realities outside of the home market. Even when diverse local needs are understood, the central responses can be inappropriate because of either overspecification that tries to satisfy all the demands, or a grand compromise that satisfies none. Limited resources and the narrow implementation role of its overseas units prevent the company from tapping into learning opportunities outside its home environment. These are problems that a global organization cannot overcome without jeopardizing its trump card of global efficiency.

With dispersed resources and decentralized decision making, subsidiaries of the multinational company can respond to local needs, but the fragmentation of activities inevitably carries efficiency penalties. Learning also suffers, because knowledge is not consolidated and does not flow among the various parts of the company. Local innovations often represent little more than the efforts of subsidiary management to protect its turf and autonomy, or reinventions of the wheel caused by blocked communication or the not-invented-here (NIH) syndrome.

In contrast, the international company is better able to leverage the knowledge and capabilities of the parent company. But its resource configuration and operating systems make it less efficient than the global company, and less responsive than the multinational company.

ATTRIBUTES OF THE TRANSNATIONAL

The transnational company redefines the problem in very different terms. It seeks efficiency not for its own sake, but as a means to achieve global *competitiveness*. It acknowledges the importance of local responsiveness, but as a tool for achieving *flexibility* in international operations. Innovations are regarded as an outcome of a larger process of organizational *learning* that encompasses every member of the company. This redefinition of the issues allows managers of the transnational company to develop a broader perspective and leads to very different criteria for making choices.

The Integrated Network Configuration

Beneath each of the traditional models of worldwide management lie some implicit assumptions about how best to build global competitive positions. The global company assumes that scale and the resulting cost leadership are the key sources of competitive advantage; the multinational company sees differentiation as the primary way to enhance performance; and the international company expects to use innovations, created at headquarters, to reduce costs, increase revenues, or both.

The transnational recognizes that each approach is partially true and has its own merits, but none represents the whole truth. To achieve global competitive advantage, costs and revenues have to be managed simultaneously, efficiency and innovation are both important, and innovations can arise in many different parts of the organization. Therefore, instead of centralizing or decentralizing assets, the transnational makes selective decisions.

Certain resources and capabilities are best centralized within the home country operation, not only to realize scale economies, but also to protect certain core competencies and to provide the necessary supervision of corporate management. Basic research is often viewed as such a capability, best kept at home. The same is true, to a lesser extent, of the treasury function or international management development.

Certain other resources are also centralized by the transnational, but not necessarily at home. World-scale production plants for labor-intensive products may be built in a low-wage country such as Mexico or Singapore. The advanced state of a particular technology may demand centralization of relevant resources and activities in Japan, Germany, or the United States. Such flexible centralization complements the benefits of scale economies with the advantages of low input costs or ready access to scarce resources.

Some other resources may be best decentralized, on a local-for-local basis, either because potential economies of scale are small compared with the benefits of differentiation, or because of the need to create flexibility and to avoid exclusive dependence on a single facility. Local-for-local facilities may protect against exchange rate shifts, strikes, natural disasters, and other disruptions, and may also reduce the need for coordination. In addition, such facilities may help build the organizational capability of national subsidiaries, making small efficiency sacrifices worthwhile.

The transnational centralizes some resources at home, some abroad, and distributes yet others among its many national operations. The result is a complex configuration of assets and capabilities that are distributed, yet specialized.[3] Furthermore, the company integrates the dispersed resources through strong interdependencies. The world-scale production plant in Singapore may depend on world-scale component plants in Australia, Mexico, and Germany; major sales subsidiaries worldwide may in turn depend on Singapore for their finished products. Such interdependencies may be reciprocal rather than sequential.[4] The British subsidiary may depend on France for one range of products, while the French depend on the British for others. Some of these interdependencies are automatic outcomes of the specialized and distributed configuration of assets and resources. Frequently, however, they are specifically designed to build self-enforcing cooperation among interdependent units.

As discussed in Chapter 2, global competitiveness increasingly requires the simultaneous optimization of scale, scope, and factor cost economies, along with the flexibility to cope with unforeseen changes in exchange rates, tastes, and technologies. The transnational's complex configuration of organizational assets and capabilities more closely approximates this optimization than the traditional organization's centralization or decentralization.

In Chapter 3, we described three organizational models—the centralized hub, the decentralized federation, and the coordinated federation—as stylized representations of the configurations typically associated with global, multinational, and international companies. The distribution of the transnational's assets and resources is best represented as an *integrated network*. This term emphasizes the very significant flows of components, products, resources, people, and information that must be managed in the transnational.[5] Beyond the rationalization of physical facilities, the company must integrate tasks and perspectives; rich and complex communication linkages, work interdependencies, and formal and informal systems are the true hallmarks of the transnational.[6] In Chapter 5, we shall illustrate this organizational model and suggest how such a configuration can be built and managed.

Differentiated Organizational Roles and Responsibilities

In the global organization, the cost and quality advantages of global efficiency are expected to provide sufficient value that customers will eschew idiosyncratic differences in preferences and accept standard products. In the multinational organization, it is assumed that tailoring products and strategies to individual national markets will offset the higher costs that may result. The international organization settles on a middle path, allowing local operations to choose from a menu of products and processes, perhaps modifying them in minor ways to suit local conditions.

All these organizations, however, make a common assumption: the subsidiary's role is local, limited to activities within its own environment; the headquarters plays a global role, deciding on issues that affect the company's operations in multiple environments.

We argued in Chapter 2 that in transnational industries the need for responsiveness is complex. Customers demand differentiated products, but with the same high quality and low cost as standard global products. In such an environment, the local-for-local responsiveness of the multinational organization is decreasingly viable economically, while the center-for-global insensitivity of the global organization is increasingly vulnerable to more nationally responsive competitors.

The challenge of responsiveness is exacerbated by the unpredictable and frequent changes in economic, technological, political, and social environments. The real challenge is not to be responsive today, but to build the capability to remain responsive as tastes, technologies, regulations, exchange rates, and relative prices change. Flexibility in sourcing, pricing, product design, and overall strategies is now the key for maintaining "requisite differentiation."[7] Both the centralized and the dispersed organizational forms are too inflexible to meet the challenge.

The transnational develops responsiveness by building multinational flexibility in many ways. It designs some slack into its production facilities and adopts flexible automation to respond to unforeseen shifts in demand or in supply. It creates products with modular structures so that features and styling can be differentiated by market while basic components and core design are standardized. Most important, the transnational builds systematic differentiation of roles and responsibilities into different parts of its organization.[8]

Recognizing that differentiation is not necessary in all markets, only in some, the transnational varies the roles of its national operations. In some markets, national subsidiaries adopt standard global products, and their role is limited to effective and efficient implementation of central decisions. Other subsidiaries are encouraged to differentiate. Often the latter category creates products that other subsidiaries adopt. In such cases, headquarters relinquishes its lead role to the subsidiary—a key attribute of the transnational that contrasts sharply with the uniformity of organizational roles in more traditional companies.

In addition to customer tastes, government regulations, the availability of leading-edge technologies, and the position of global competitors are all considered in determining subsidiary roles in the transnational. Subsidiaries in highly regulated countries may be given an autonomous role and managed in a decentralized federation mode, while subsidiaries in more open economies are managed in an integrated, interdependent mode. Subsidiaries in the home countries of global competitors, or in centers of technological excellence, may be assigned roles and resources that help them disrupt the competitor's cash flow, or exploit the technology for the transnational's worldwide use. The subsidiaries' internal resources and capabilities may also be a factor in determining their roles and responsibilities.[9] A subsidiary in a strategically important location may not have the resources required to play a global role, while subsidiary in a noncritical environment may be resource-rich. Their roles may be adjusted accordingly.

In Chapter 6, we describe how some companies are building such a differentiated system and suggest how other companies could develop similar capabilities. Differentiation in subsidiaries' roles, however, is only one aspect of a broader system of internal differentiation in the transnational. Businesses, products, and functions are all managed differently, with an eye to industry structures, competitive positions, and the nature of the strategic tasks. This system of internal differentiation implies an overall management mentality very different from those of the global, multinational, and international traditions. In the absence of such a transnational mentality, a mechanical adoption of our framework (or any other system of differentiation) cannot become effective. On the contrary, it can be severely dysfunctional, destroying internal norms of equity, creating enormous ambiguity, and increasing complexity with few compensating benefits. But in a company that adopts the transnational mentality, such a system of differentiation becomes a dynamic and self-regulating process through which the firm can build flexibility in its worldwide operations and achieve responsiveness with a minimum sacrifice of efficiency, and often with considerable enhancement of its competitiveness.

Managing Multiple Organizational Processes

Most large companies with worldwide operations have recognized that managing innovations is a key strategic capability. As structural changes in many industries forced out weaker competitors, the survivors often found that they had comparable scale and differentiation capability. Thus, competition often shifted to companies' ability to sense emerging trends, to develop creative responses, and to diffuse their innovations worldwide—their capability for *worldwide learning*.[10] This has certainly been the case in the telecommunications industry. Learning is also rapidly becoming the central game in consumer electronics and is emerging as a key competitive capability in branded packaged goods.

Traditionally, both global and international companies have depended on a *central* process for creating and exploiting innovations: sensing a new opportunity in the home country, using the centralized development resources of the parent company to create a new product or process, and then adopting the innovation in appropriate locations around the world. Multinational companies, on the other hand, relied heavily on *local* innovations: their autonomous, self-contained national subsidiaries used their own resources to create new products or processes that met the needs of their local environments. Earlier in this chapter we described some of the limitations of these traditional innovation processes.

Managers of transnational companies approach the management of innovations and learning very differently. They recognize that environmental demands and opportunities vary widely from country to country. Some markets have more sophisticated consumers; in some countries, key competitors are more active; and in some environments, certain technologies are more advanced than others. Furthermore, the home country may be the most critical environment for some businesses and activities, but not necessarily for all.

These managers also recognize that different parts of the company possess different capabilities. Often, key physical and organizational assets of the company are located overseas, developed there in response to local demands (or simply by chance). A worldwide company's exposure to a range of environmental stimuli represents an important potential advantage over a national company. The broader range of customer preferences, competitor behavior, government demands, and technological stimuli can trigger learning and innovation within the organization.[11] Transnational managers see no reason to prevent resources outside the home environment from benefiting the entire corporation. Instead, they foster the development of such organizational assets, and ensure that the whole firm has access to them.

Centrally designed products and processes still play an important global role in the transnational. But innovations are created by the subsidiaries as well. Often, instead of finding a central solution to an emerging global opportunity (as in a global or international organization) or different local solutions in each environment (as in a multinational), the transnational will pool the resources of central facilities and many national subsidiaries to develop a worldwide solution for its dispersed organization. Efficient local plants may be converted into international production centers; innovative national or regional development labs may be designated as "worldwide centers of excellence" for specific product or process development; and creative subsidiary marketing groups may be given lead roles in developing worldwide strategies for certain products or businesses.

Such transnational innovation processes support and complement the traditional central and local processes. The task of worldwide learning requires that the company nurture all possible ways of developing innovative products and processes. The issue of worldwide learning will be the main topic of Chapter 7. There, we will review a number of specific innovation cases in different companies, and will offer some general guidelines on how managers can enhance the efficiency and effectiveness of these processes.

An Internally Consistent Organizational System

Table 4.2 recapitulates the key organizational attributes of the multinational, global, and international companies (from Table 4.1) and adds those of the transnational company. The attributes of the transnational are internally consistent and mutually reinforcing. The integrated net-

Table 4.2
Organizational Characteristics of the Transnational

Organizational Characteristics	Multinational	Global	International	Transnational
Configuration of assets and capabilities	Decentralized and nationally self-sufficient	Centralized and globally scaled	Sources of core competencies centralized, others decentralized	Dispersed, interdependent, and specialized
Role of overseas operations	Sensing and exploiting local opportunities	Implementing parent company strategies	Adapting and leveraging parent company competencies	Differentiated contributions by national units to integrated worldwide operations
Development and diffusion of knowledge	Knowledge developed and retained within each unit	Knowledge developed and retained at the center	Knowledge developed at the center and transferred to overseas units	Knowledge developed jointly and shared worldwide

work configuration; the differentiation of subsidiary roles and responsibilities; and the simultaneous management of multiple innovation processes collectively constitute an integrated and viable organizational system.

The integrated network configuration of resources is essential for developing transnational innovations, as well as the more complex and flexible responsiveness we have described. The differentiated and specialized capabilities of organizational units make mutual cooperation necessary in creating new products and processes; the reciprocal interdependency among units allows such cooperation to be self-sustaining.

At the same time, the differentiation of organizational roles leads certain parts of the company to develop specialized resources and capabilities, which in turn allow them to play unique roles in the various innovation processes. The very existence of such processes also creates the need for differentiated roles and dedicated resources. All three attributes of the transnational are intertwined into a complex organizational system. It is this complex organizational system, rather than a particular structure or even a specific "way of doing things," that characterizes the transnational organization.

BUILDING AND MANAGING THE TRANSNATIONAL

The strengths of the transnational are also the source of its problems. The distributed and specialized configuration of assets, the diversity of organizational roles and responsibilities, and the multiplicity of innovation and learning processes can lead to internal fragmentation and dissipation. To make such an organization work, management needs to marshal equally powerful forces of integration and unification.[12] Otherwise, the organization can easily become too dispersed to be competitive, too interdependent to be flexible, and too complex to develop or leverage its learning capability.

To build and manage the transnational as an effective strategic entity, management faces several administrative challenges (see Table 4.3). First, it must be able to balance the diversity of perspectives and capabilities within the organization and ensure that no single management group dominates others. Second, given the differences in the roles and responsibilities of organizational units, management must build a set of flexible coordination processes so that each unit and task is managed in the most appropriate manner. But, while appropriate systems and management processes are essential, in themselves they cannot counteract the enormous centrifugal force in such organizations. Therefore, the most crucial task of transnational managers is to encourage a shared vision and personal commitment to integrate the organization at the fundamental level of individual members.

Table 4.3
Building and Managing the Transnational

Strategic Capability	Organizational Characteristics	Management Tasks
Global competitiveness	Dispersed and interdependent assets and resources	Legitimizing diverse perspectives and capabilities
Multinational flexibility	Differentiated and specialized subsidiary roles	Developing multiple and flexible coordination processes
Worldwide learning	Joint development and worldwide sharing of knowledge	Building shared vision and individual commitment

Balancing Perspectives and Capabilities

In Chapters 2 and 3 we have seen some of the pitfalls that await companies trying to respond to the changing strategic demands in their businesses. Over time, most companies develop somewhat biased (and in some cases, highly skewed) organizational capabilities and management perspectives. Unilever's early international success was due to its sensitivity to national market structures and local consumer preferences. As a result, the company developed a strategy based on multinational responsiveness and paid less attention to global efficiency and worldwide learning. In contrast, Matsushita owed its early success to the cost advantage it gained from its global-scale R&D and manufacturing operations in Japan, while Procter & Gamble leveraged its strong domestic technology and marketing expertise worldwide. Like Unilever, both companies focused on a single dominant source of competitive advantage, and their management perspectives and capabilities became biased.

Strong unidimensional strategic biases were reinforced by the organizational difficulties the companies faced. The very act of going international multiplies organizational complexity. Typically, a third dimension must be added to the existing business- and functionally oriented management structure of domestic operations. The trauma of integrating a geographic dimension into the management process strains managerial relationships. For most companies it was a difficult enough challenge to create product divisions while maintaining the effectiveness and legitimacy of corporate staffs whose functional expertise and access to information gave them an important counterbalancing role.[13] The thought of adding geographically oriented management and maintaining a three-way balance of perspectives and capabilities was intimidating to most managers. Their task was to resolve tensions among operating units divided by distance and time, and managers separated by culture and language.

In many companies, the group that responds to the most critical strategic tasks gains organizational power.[14] By enabling the company to sense and respond to the needs of national markets, the *geographic* managers in Unilever became the dominant group, since their contribution was crucial to achieving the dispersed *responsiveness* central to Unilever's multinational strategy. In Matsushita, managers in the powerful product divisions dominated most decision making, since strong business management was key to the company's dependence on global-scale efficiency. Not surprisingly, Procter & Gamble's historically strong functional groups retained their influence through many reorganizations, since managers with specialized technical and marketing knowledge were vital to the company's strategy of building and transferring its core competencies—a capability vital to worldwide learning.[15]

The transnational company, however, must develop a multidimensional organization that maintains the viability and effectiveness of each organizational group. Any bias that favors a particular business, function, or area management must be eliminated, and the company must adopt a decision process in which each perspective is represented, albeit with a differing level of influence.[16]

As the experience of ITT, Kao, and GE illustrates, it is no small task to move from unidimensional to multidimensional management, and to maintain a balance among competing perspectives. In Chapter 8, we will describe how some companies, such as Procter & Gamble and Ericsson, have created such balance in their organizations. We will contrast their experiences with those of companies that failed to overcome their unidimensional biases, drawing some broad conclusions on how managers can build the multidimensional organizational capability needed in a transnational company.

Developing Flexible Coordination Processes

Changes in structure and relationships influence a company's management processes. As companies develop more multidimensional capabilities, the differences in tasks and roles amplify the diversity of management perspectives. In most companies, such diversity cannot be effectively integrated through existing management processes. The growing interdependencies of the various organizational units further strain available control systems and emphasize the need for more sophisticated coordination capabilities.

The volatility of the external environment compounds the need for flexible coordination processes. Since consumer needs, technologies, political forces, and competitive strategies are in constant flux, any company with a static view of coordination needs, or an inflexible approach to problems will face significant difficulties, not unlike those of ITT.

Most companies tend to concentrate on one primary mechanism for coordination and control—one "way of doing things." At ITT, for example, it was "the system"—Harold Geneen's sophisticated control mechanisms, which were highly formalized and institutionalized throughout the organization. At Kao, coordination and control were achieved primarily through centralization of decision making; corporate management was directly involved in most strategic and even operational tasks. Unilever relied primarily on socialization—an intricate process of instilling a common culture and a shared perspective in all managers—to hold the organization together and integrate managers responsible for different areas and functions. But no single mechanism can deal with the complex coordination needs that arise in worldwide companies.

The transnational requires highly flexible coordination processes to cope with both short-term shifts in specific role assignments and long-term realignments of basic responsibilities and reporting relationships. Furthermore, it must be capable of modifying roles and relationships on a decision-by-decision basis. The company must develop multiple means of coordination and allocate its scarce coordinating resources on the basis of a careful assessment of specific task demands.[17]

The very nature of the transnational organization dramatically expands the number of issues that have to be integrated. But three flows are crucial. First, the company has to coordinate the flow of parts, components, and finished goods. Second, it must manage the flow of funds, skills, and other scarce resources among units. Third, it must link the flow of intelligence, ideas, and knowledge that are central to its innovation and learning capabilities.

The transnational company builds a portfolio of coordinating processes that includes *centralization* (substantive decision making by senior management), *formalization* (institutionalization of systems and procedures to guide choices), and *socialization* (building a context of common purpose, values, and perspectives among managers to influence their judgments).[18] It uses the entire portfolio, rather than just one process, to achieve a richer and more differentiated kind of coordination. The flow of parts, components, and products is often managed through systems; the flow of resources is usually directed through more substantive involvement of top management; and the flow of information and knowledge may be facilitated primarily through mechanisms that lead to normative integration of managers and to a common culture and unifying vision. Similarly, different parts of the organization may be managed differently: some businesses, functions, and areas may require more direction and centralization, while formalization or socialization may be the primary integrative process in others.

Chapter 9 will examine how the transnational develops and deploys its diverse coordination tools. We will draw on the experiences of Philips, Unilever, and Ericsson to illustrate the process of differentiation in coordinative processes and to explain the choice of different tools for different tasks. We shall also describe how such companies use both the visible hand of managed integration and the invisible hand of coordination through internal market mechanisms to build powerful centripetal forces and counterbalance the pressures of fragmentation that are unavoidable in the transnational mode of operation.[19]

Unifying the Organization Through Vision and Co-option

Transnational management processes differ from those of more traditional organizations in two significant ways. First, the reliance on control tends to erode as unidimensional systems and practices are supplemented by new coordination mechanisms. Second, the processes are managed in a differentiated fashion, not only from issue to issue, but across businesses and organizational units.

Internal differentiation in organizational roles and management processes can lead to severe conflict within a company. To maintain morale and to provide a sense of unity at every level of the company, the transnational has to move beyond restructuring assets and remolding management processes. Top management must obtain the personal commitment of every individual in the firm to the overall corporate agenda. We call this process co-option. Its integrative effects often prove to be more powerful than those of any structure or system, however sophisticated.[20]

To develop such commitment, each individual must understand and share the company's purposes and values, must identify with the broader goals and objectives, and must accept and internalize its key strategies. In essence, the company must build on an overall management mentality that sees beyond the organization's specific economic purposes to a larger mission that deserves to be supported and cherished. In Chapter 10, we will describe how such a mentality can be embedded and nurtured.

In any complex organization, the main difficulty in obtaining individual commitment to an overall purpose is the limited perspectives and parochial interests of managers in key positions. Neither organization structure nor coordination systems can fully neutralize the typical hierarchy of managerial loyalties, which place local above global interests. Therefore, a fundamental prerequisite for the normative integration a transnational seeks is a sophisticated human resource management system. The transnational uses systems of recruitment, training and development, and career path management to help individuals cope with its diversity and complexity.[21]

These then are the broad characteristics of the transnational—the organization model that is becoming increasingly necessary for companies operating in today's international competitive environment. In the next part of the book we will describe in more detail the transnational characteristics and capabilities that we observed several of our sample companies creating.

PART II

CHARACTERISTICS OF THE TRANSNATIONAL

5
BUILDING COMPETITIVENESS:
THE INTEGRATED NETWORK

An observer of the largest worldwide consumer electronics companies in the early 1970s probably would have had difficulty recognizing the same firms fifteen years later. Philips, for example, had over 500 factories in forty-five countries in the early 1970s. Its practice had long been to immerse itself in the culture and economy of the host country and to produce for the local market as many products as possible from its broad portfolio of businesses. The company's national organizations (NOs) operated with great autonomy, and many had their own product development capabilities. The company's range of locally tailored products was immense. Fifteen years later, Philips was sourcing major products from efficient global-scale international production centers (IPCs), developing new products and technologies through a global R&D network that had integrated research laboratories and product development facilities, and managing its overall product strategy through a powerful product-division organization that had worldwide profit responsibility.

During the same period Matsushita had undergone an equally impressive transformation. In the early 1970s, it was still essentially a Japanese company with a fast-growing export business concentrated in consumer electronics. Although government pressures in developing countries had encouraged local production, its few overseas plants (the oldest established only a decade earlier) were little more than embryonic satellite operations, almost totally dependent on headquarters for technology, material, and management direction. Yet, by the late 1980s, Matsushita had over fifty manufacturing companies in twenty-six countries; several were manufacturing products adapted for their markets using locally sourced materials and equipment. The company president's commitment to localization was reflected in an ambitious objective of increasing the capacity of Matsushita's offshore manufacturing operations from 10 to 25 percent of the company's total within a decade.

Perhaps most surprising has been the transformation of General

Electric's consumer electronics business over the same fifteen-year period. In the early 1970s, GE was in the midst of a major internationalization process, establishing self-sufficient, market responsive, national subsidiaries around the globe. Fifteen years later, after several strategic reorientations, the company was out of the consumer electronics business altogether.

Such changes were not unique to the consumer electronics industry. Every company we studied had recently undergone or was in the midst of a major reconfiguration of worldwide assets and resources. In the branded package goods industry, the changes occurred relatively gradually, while the telecommunications switching companies, faced with a technological revolution and a worldwide trend toward deregulation, took more dramatic and urgent action. Each firm was torn, to some extent, between an analytical ideal of achieving strategic "fit" through restructuring assets and resources, and a managerial reality of adapting its existing organization within the constraints of its administrative heritage.

ANALYTICAL IDEAL: FIT THROUGH RECONFIGURATION

Proposals for reconfiguring assets and resources are most often broached during a crisis that threatens a company's short-term profitability or perhaps raises doubts about its longer-term international viability.[1] Philips made its first moves in 1971 after an alarming drop in profits, which declined by 16 percent in 1970 and a further 21 percent the following year. The board of management established a top-level review committee whose report set the structural changes in motion; momentum for the changes that followed was provided by the continuing problem of uncompetitiveness against the Japanese in global markets.

While Philips rethought its highly dispersed and relatively uncoordinated configuration, a different set of forces challenged Matsushita's highly centralized organization. In the early 1970s, American manufacturers filed an antidumping suit with the U.S. Department of Justice against Japanese color TV exporters. Over the next decade, such political pressures spread in the developed world, particularly in Europe, where protectionist sentiments intensified as Japanese-made VCRs flooded the market in the 1980s. But if Matsushita's structural crisis was triggered by political pressure, it was reinforced by the emergence of new lower-cost competitors from Korea and Taiwan, and by the rising value of the yen, which reduced the company's worldwide sales by an estimated $500 million in 1986 alone.[2]

GE's consumer electronics business had also been beset by a series of problems: its loss of domestic market share to Japanese imports in the 1960s, the recognition of the limited transferability of its technology in the 1970s, and the profit crises of the 1980s, triggered by a continued inability to achieve global-scale manufacturing efficiencies. GE responded to each problem by adapting the company's structural configuration.

In all three companies, managers tended to attack major problems—of whatever nature—by reconfiguring assets, reallocating resources, and redefining tasks and responsibilities. The bias toward restructuring is understandable since it is a concrete response with quantifiable potential impact and sends a clear signal to the organization of the need for change. Furthermore, such action was supported by many academic theories and consulting advice of the time. As the forces of globalization became more clearly defined and widespread, conventional wisdom focused increasingly on a search for "fit" between environmental characteristics and corporate capability.

Macroeconomists suggested investing abroad to exploit the factor cost differences (particularly in labor costs) that were at the root of the theory of comparative advantage;[3] industrial organization researchers argued that vertical integration across international boundaries could be a source of competitive advantage;[4] and international management theorists developed a model of internalization of resources and knowledge to explain the viability of multinational enterprise.[5]

Then consultants and applied researchers translated many of these concepts into managerial terms through the concept of the value chain. Breaking down complex operations into a series of value-added elements, they analyzed the source of one company's competitive advantage vis-à-vis another in terms of each element. The analyses dramatically demonstrated that a company's competitive position depended on such decisions as which activities it would perform itself, how concentrated such activities would be, where they would be located, and how they would be linked.[6]

Using this approach, many managers began to look at their company's international operations in a completely different way. Overseas operations, for example, were no longer regarded as simply a means of reaching incremental markets; instead they might be the key to low-cost manufacturing. Managers saw global success inexorably linked to building the appropriate worldwide infrastructure of assets and resources. Despite the constant turmoil in factor costs, exchange rates, and host country environments, which made any such "ideal configuration" a highly elusive concept, some companies seemed to be highly focused on this goal.[7] The experiences of General Electric in the consumer electronics business provide a good example.

GE's Search for Global Efficiency

Of the companies we studied in the consumer electronics business, General Electric had perhaps the most solid foundation. It enjoyed a large position in the U.S. market, plentiful capital and management resources, and a solid technological heritage. Yet its approach to the international market was surprisingly inconsistent and even erratic. Again and again, GE tried to redefine its source of competitive advantage to fit shifting industry demands, and with each change in strategic direction, it restructured.

Having established some important overseas investments before World War II (particularly joint ventures and licensing with equity participation with companies such as AEG, Thomson, and Toshiba), GE was obliged to disengage from its international alliances and de-emphasize its overseas operations because of antitrust pressures in the United States. Only in the 1960s, with the advent of the EEC and the Kennedy Round of GATT negotiations, did the company reassess its domestic market emphasis. In 1964, GE's new chairman, Fred Borsch, established a study group to recommend how the company should expand into rapidly developing and more open world markets. Its findings, known as the "Borsch directive," urged GE to "go international."

The Borsch directive emphasized the need to maintain a market orientation, confirmed the commitment to decentralization, and prescribed a more aggressive approach to worldwide expansion based on serving customer needs. This clear focus on the downstream end of the value chain coupled with a new commitment of resources to overseas expansion triggered a major effort across all businesses to establish new foreign operations. The idea was to establish so-called mini-GEs, which could leverage the parent company's technological assets and adapt them to local market needs. This, after all, was similar to the approach that GE's Dutch competitor, Philips, had followed to become the leading international consumer electronics company of the period. Greenfield investments were made in local plants and facilities, and nationally sponsored acquisitions and joint ventures were undertaken throughout the world.

As exports from the parent company were replaced by local production, and distributors were replaced by GE sales companies, the number of employees abroad increased 150 percent in the decade after 1965—from 40,000 to over 100,000. (In the same period the domestic work force grew only 15 percent.) International sales in this period grew at an annual rate of 18 percent, compared with 7.8 percent for domestic sales.

But GE encountered problems in implementing such a dramatic shift in its international value-added configuration. There were several abortive initiatives, such as the thrust to establish a TV set business in Europe by acquiring a German television manufacturer. The central problem was that GE did not know enough about the local markets in which it suddenly found itself. New plants, transferred technology, and assigned-from-home managers did not compensate for the failure to understand local distribution, competition, regulations, and consumer preferences.

Furthermore, the company's technical expertise remained firmly in the hands of the domestic division managers, who had little interest in the offshore operations. At top management's urging they would ship off domestic product or process information, but made scant effort to adapt it for other needs. When overseas subsidiaries required a different technology (as Brazil did when color TV was introduced using the PAL transmission system rather than the American NTSC standard), the parent company was unable to help. Since the mini-GE concept was new, most local subsidiaries had not had the time to develop the self-sufficiency of the typical Philips national organization. As a consequence, when GE's home country products and processes did not fit the local environment, the business failed. In Brazil, the company withdrew from the television market in 1967, the year color television was introduced locally.

By the early 1970s, under Reginald Jones's leadership, GE appropriately identified the emerging competitive threat of Japan as a major strategic issue for its worldwide operations. The company's newly created strategic business units (SBUs) were given responsibility for their operations on a worldwide basis. The era of mini-GEs faded into the past, replaced by a philosophy of "direct connect" global business management. As described in the company policy bulletin, the central SBU was required to "provide direction to the planning and operating functions and assume responsibility for the investment and results of its business in the country, including results of day-to-day management."

Again, the company restructured its international operations, this time closing down national plants that did not fit the strategic priorities or could not leverage the company's technology. Recognizing the tremendous cost advantage available to producers located in the Far East, the company began giving more attention to the upstream activities in its value chain. Under severe pressure from low-priced Japanese competitors, the audio products division established a production source in Singapore, to draw on the low-cost labor necessary to stay competitive in the business. Several GE divisions began sourcing components and subassemblies from low-cost suppliers rather than manufacturing them internally in plants located in high-wage-rate countries, with outdated manufacturing technology and less than minimum efficient scale.

But again, GE's restructuring did not achieve the intended results. Host country officials were angry at the plant closings and the increase in imported products that replaced their output, and often curbed GE's new approach through import restrictions. Internally, country subsidiary managers were discouraged by their loss of autonomy and local responsibility; those who did not leave often operated in a resentful and even adversarial relationship with central SBU managers, who (they felt) gave directions without understanding the local business. By the early 1980s, most of GE's consumer electronics managers felt that the company had done too little too late, and that further major restructuring would be required to make the business viable.

In 1981, Jack Welch became GE's new chief executive. Concerned about the dramatically changing international competitive environment, Welch decided to focus the company's resources on fewer businesses. Soon after taking control, he clustered GE's diverse business in three broad groups—core businesses (such as lighting, appliances, and motors), high technology (including medical systems, aircraft engines, and engineered materials), and services (such as GE's credit, information, and construction companies). Managers were told that if they could not make their business one of the top two players in their league, they would be sold off or shut down.

When he drew his famous three circles around the main businesses that represented GE's future, many in the audio and video divisions were shocked to learn that their businesses were excluded from the core. Given the cost positions, the technology base, and the market penetration of the Japanese, Welch doubted that GE could become the number-one or number-two consumer electronics competitor worldwide.

Soon after, the company closed its remaining international television operations, primarily in Mexico and Canada, and for a while focused on trying to make its U.S. plants competitive. Eventually, however, it decided to source televisions from its Japanese competitors. The company would simply leverage its well-known brand name and concentrate on providing downstream value elements such as sales and service.

The final chapter of the story occurred after GE's acquisition of RCA in 1985. Although Welch stated that consumer electronics "wasn't even part of the analysis" that motivated the purchase, within a year the company had decided to make one more attempt to recapture the upstream part of the television value-added stream. The sourcing agreements with its Japanese suppliers were terminated, and responsibility for annual production of 500,000 GE sets was transferred to RCA's Bloomington, Indiana, plant. The consumer electronics manager convinced Welch that this plant, which was operating with technology two generations behind the state-of-the-art, could be automated for $20 million, and that the projected 20 to 30 percent cost savings would allow the company to defend against Japanese manufacturers in the United States, as well as the new South Korean exporters who had begun flooding the market.

Welch's commitment to this business was not strong, however, and a few months later he negotiated a deal with Thomson, the French electronics company, trading GE's consumer electronics operations for Thomson's medical electronics business. A Matsushita official said, "It was unexpected because it seems to show a lack of self-confidence. GE wanted to start making TVs again [in the United States], but when it looked like it might not be easy, they just gave up."

The history of GE's consumer electronics business shows a company trying to build and defend its competitive position through almost continuous restructuring of its asset configuration to fit the fast-changing environmental demands. Over two decades, GE shifted from building locally self-sufficient assets and capabilities, to offshore global sources in low-cost countries, to outsourcing, and finally to centralized scale-intensive facilities driven by advanced manufacturing technology. Restructuring failed to build the competitiveness the company so desperately wanted; in fact, many observers felt, the turmoil it created was the main barrier to GE's success.[8]

MANAGERIAL REALITY: RESTRAINED RESTRUCTURING

Through much of the 1970s and early 1980s, academics and consultants offered increasingly precise and forceful prescriptions for reconfiguration. Some enthusiasts even suggested that for any particular company, an idealized value-added chain might well be designed by computer, using a linear program loaded with relevant data on comparative factor costs by country, scale efficiency at various output levels, logistical costs to and from various locations, and so on.

But few operating managers were convinced by such high-certainty economic approaches. They recognized the internal organizational forces that constrained any change effort. Unlike the linear program, the manager cannot ignore the political difficulty of closing inefficient plants, the time-consuming process of developing new interorganizational relationships, or the human constraint of relocating individuals with particular knowledge or skills to facilities in a distant country. These are elements of a company's administrative heritage, and they must be considered on equal terms with the economic, political, and other external pressures in decisions on configuration.

As the GE example illustrated, managers who attempted to bring about change through drastic reconfiguration, with little consideration for the existing organization, found the exercise frustratingly unsuccessful. Although companies like Philips and Matsushita experienced great difficulty in reconciling external demands with the reality of their administrative heritage, their more subtle, gradual, and consistent changes in structure were more successful.

Philips, Matsushita, and most other companies in our sample took a more restrained approach to restructuring than the theorists might have prescribed, and showed a far more pragmatic sense of the time required to bring about change. They followed two fairly simple principles:

- First, they concentrated at least as much on defending and reinforcing their existing assets and capabilities as on developing the new ones. They recognized the folly of zero-base organization planning, as if the company was to be created from scratch, and were determined not to compromise their traditional competitive advantage by trying to transform it into something else.

- Second, to the extent that they needed to create new capabilities, these companies looked first for ways to compensate for their deficiency or approximate a competitor's source of advantage, rather than imitate its physical structure or organization process.

Building on Existing Capabilities

Compared with the theorists of restructuring, managers in most of the companies we studied were a conservative group. They seemed much more concerned that a major realignment of the company's infrastructure might destroy their current sources of competitive advantage or compromise their existing strategic capabilities. Their approach tended to be one of building on—and eventually modifying—the existing organizational structure and the capabilities it embodied rather than radically reconfiguring to create new and different competencies.[9]

In its 1972 Yellow Booklet, Philips's board-appointed organization committee confirmed top management's growing concern when it emphasized the need to concentrate production and increase the scale of its activities. Rather than urge a dramatic reconfiguration of assets, resources, and responsibilities, however, the report described how the *existing* infrastructure and the *existing* management responsibilities might be modified to provide the desired strategic capabilities without major organizational disruption. Indeed, the report stressed that "[t]he essential point herewith is the possibility to adapt the structure in each individual case to changing external and internal circumstances without disturbing current operations." Management understood that many of the company's strengths had been developed in its national organizations and concluded that "continued local control based on local knowledge of the local market [is] essential to obtain optimal operational results . . . [and] a positive factor for the motivation of the individual workers and of the organization as a whole."

While recognizing the need for greater coordination of the national organizations, the company's gradual approach built on its strengths rather than put them at risk through precipitous restructuring. For example, manufacturing efficiency was developed by designating the company's most efficient plants as international production centers (IPCs). But while the central product divisions took over factory loading and distribution of finished goods, the national organization retained responsibility for the overall operation of the plant—managing the labor force, controlling the inventory, and executing the other tasks for which it had built up local competence over decades.

Similar arrangements were established for new product and process development to ensure that the company made good use of its historically creative and entrepreneurial local R&D facilities. The product divisions were assigned primary responsibility for establishing strategic world plans and worldwide product policy, but the report stressed they were to hold "intensive consultations with the NOs." It would be especially important to capture the knowledge and expertise in key NOs, "those from which innovation or market leadership may emerge, or those with significant possibilities for development, production, sales or profit." Managers from these national organizations were asked to join task forces and committees responsible for developing product policy and formulating worldwide strategic plans—a very different approach from GE's "direct connect" concept, which many country managers felt subjugated them to domestic control virtually overnight.

Equally important, once Philips had determined the nature and direction of the required change, it followed that overall thrust for many years. Whereas GE managers had to deal with structural turmoil for twenty years, Philips managers saw the Yellow Booklet not as a crash program to fix a short-term problem, but as an overall blueprint for change based on a long-term vision of the company's desired organizational capabilities. As Philips's chairman, Dr. Wisse Dekker, explained in 1986, "Rationalization has taken the company twenty years already, and the process will continue for another fifteen or twenty years."

Although top management continually reminds security analysts that 63 plants in Europe and another twenty operations worldwide have been closed or sold off, the reality is that Philips still operates over 200 plants in Europe and another 200 elsewhere. Despite the success of the manufacturing program, the company is still fundamentally organized around its historical configuration of distributed assets and resources. Rather than regard restructuring as a matter of reconfiguring assets and redistributing resources, management has seen its task as one of protecting, building on, and leveraging its existing organizational capabilities and managerial competencies to refocus them on a changed operating environment.

Nonetheless, Philips's configuration at the end of the 1980s was very different from that of the early 1970s. The company was producing almost twice the volume of a very different product mix at fewer plants. Moreover, most of the remaining national plants had become highly efficient operations, using the most advanced manufacturing processes and technologies to produce a focused product range for global markets. These international production centers represented the core of the new rationalized manufacturing system. At the same time, investments in the manufacturing facilities in Taiwan and Singapore were increased to take advantage of the availability of highly productive and low-cost labor forces, and build these national organizations into the company's major source of more mature products like black and white TVs and radios.

It took Philips fifteen years to reshape its decentralized federation of assets and resources into an efficient integrated network—a period that seemed interminable to most insiders and to many outside critics as well. Perhaps the company could have moved faster, but it is more difficult to redirect existing operations than to build new facilities from base zero. Philips management was sophisticated enough to recognize that the latter course was neither politically feasible nor organizationally desirable. Today the company has a viable worldwide operation, which has achieved global competitiveness without sacrificing the substantial assets, resources, and capabilities of its national organization base.

Matsushita also underwent a quiet revolution as management tried to reconfigure the company's assets and resources without seriously compromising its core capabilities. Building on its established export base, Matsushita opened its first overseas manufacturing facility in Thailand in 1961. During the 1960s and early 1970s, host governments and its own local distributors pressed the company to establish more local operations, particularly in the developing countries of East Asia and South America, where its initial overseas expansion had been focused. Unlike GE, Matsushita was not tempted to follow the Philips model and build self-sufficient independent national organizations. It remained committed to its founder's goal, "to contribute to society by supplying goods of high quality at low prices in ample quantity." Shifting production to local plants, in management's view, would threaten the quality and the cost of Matsushita's products.

But the host country requests were not ignored. Indeed, Konosuke Matsushita believed equally that corporations had an obligation to contribute to the welfare of the communities in which they operated, telling company managers that "profit comes in compensation for contribution to society." Thus, a top manager noted:

> Unlike the subsidiaries of American and European multinationals, our overseas affiliates were not established in conformity with a well-defined worldwide strategy. Their principal objective is to serve the host country by making contributions to the improvement of social welfare and the national economy by providing employment opportunities, technical and management training, and products that can help raise the local standard of living.

In doing so, the company was also careful to protect its competitive advantage by manufacturing all new and sophisticated products and all key components and subassemblies in Japan. Local operations were almost always assembly plants that imported knockdown kits of mature products from central plants that produced at global-scale efficiency and to world quality standards.

By 1973, Matsushita had twenty-five overseas manufacturing plants, of which thirteen were in Southeast Asia; five in Central and South America; three in Africa, the Middle East, and Oceania; and only two each in the company's major export markets, North America and Europe. But by this time, Matsushita was beginning to feel political pressures in developed countries as well. As Japanese color TV sets flooded the U.S. market, capturing a 29 percent share in 1969, the Electronics Industry Association filed an antidumping suit with the U.S. Treasury Department. As in Malaysia, Brazil, and many other countries, Matsushita responded by committing itself to manufacture locally, in this case by acquiring Motorola's operations. In response to Canadian government pressure, it established a manufacturing facility in Toronto; in Europe, it built a TV plant in Cardiff, Wales.

These highly politicized moves masked the fact that the basic configuration of Matsushita had changed little since the 1950s; it continued to depend on highly concentrated specialized plants manufacturing high-quality products at low cost. Although by 1980 it had established thirty-nine manufacturing companies in twenty-three countries, over 90 percent of the company's production still came from domestic plants. Moreover, because the overseas plants operated with equipment designed by the parent company, using procedures directed from the center and materials supplied from Japan, they were far from self-sufficient.

For a company that gained half of its sales in overseas markets, this position became increasingly untenable in a period of rising protectionism. In both internal speeches and public statements, Toshihiko Yamashita, Matsushita's president since 1977, stressed the issue of achieving a better mix among Japanese exports, overseas production, and exports from overseas plants. Unsatisfied with progress, in 1982 he announced a localization program to increase overseas production to 25 percent of the company total by 1990.

Matsushita intends to effect this transformation through the concurrent and interdependent localization of capital, personnel, technology, and materials. Rather than pursue a crash program to establish new greenfield operations, the company will upgrade and reinforce established local units, allowing them to take on greater responsibility and manufacture a broader range of products. Matsushita sees its overseas operations as evolving through three phases. Phase I companies are almost completely dependent on the parent for equipment, supplies, and direction, while those in Phase II have achieved some flexibility in sourcing local equipment and materials. Phase III operations are self-sufficient in equipment and supplies, can modify corporate processes and techniques to local conditions, and have the management capability to authorize their own quality performance.

Even the most independent of these local companies remain closely tied to the parent company's traditional sources of strength. The highly competent Taiwan color TV plant—regarded as a Phase III operation by product division managers in Osaka—still depends on the parent company for 35 percent of materials, and that figure includes most key components. Although it now has the technical freedom to design for local aesthetics, the basic chassis and components are still developed in Japan. And despite the increasing self-sufficiency in personnel, in 1986 there were still four Japanese managers in the TV department, acting as advisers and consulting with the parent company on key decisions. In building greater localization, Matsushita is determined to leverage its core strength, not abandon it.

By the late 1980s, both Philips and Matsushita had significantly modified the structures in place in the early 1970s, yet neither company had abandoned its roots. Philips's network of efficient international production centers and its integrated centers of R&D excellence were built on the company's traditional decentralized federation of national organizations. Matsushita's emerging structure, on the other hand, still bore the clear imprint of a centralized hub on its newly dispersed assets and resources. Both companies were consciously using existing structural bases as platforms on which to build.

Restrained Restructuring

In Chapter 2 we argued that the strategic challenge for the transnational corporation is the simultaneous achievement of efficiency, flexible responsiveness, and worldwide learning and innovation. Many companies found, unfortunately, that their existing configurations constrained their ability to develop the strategic capabilities they lacked. For example, Philips's classic decentralized federation hurt its efficiency, while Matsushita's centralized hub limited its responsiveness to national markets. As companies evolved toward transnational organization forms, they soon found that the ideal configuration of assets, resources, and responsibilities involved trade-offs among objectives that often had contradictory organizational implications.

Most managers in the companies we studied were realists and pragmatists. They recognized the difficulty of creating the new organizational capabilities they needed, and understood that it could not be built simply by imitating a competitor's assets and resources. The best they could hope to do was compensate in some way for their deficiencies, not remove them entirely.

Even this modest goal required managers to broaden their perspective on competitive advantage. Some discovered, for example, that there were many other routes to efficiency besides imitating the global companies' centralized hub configurations; others learned that their company could be sensitive, flexible, and responsive even without a decentralized federation structure.

In their search for global-scale efficiency, managers in Philips found a potential source of efficiency that the company had long underutilized: the fact that the cost of labor, capital, materials, and other inputs varied widely across the countries in which its national organizations were located. By adapting roles, shifting emphasis, and building on capabilities in its existing configuration, Philips began to concentrate activities in the countries that had the least cost for each activity's primary input factor. It expanded its small operations in Singapore and Taiwan, where labor costs were low, by transferring labor-intensive production items to those plants; and it exploited the fact that it had R&D facilities in the United Kingdom, which had a rich technology base and relatively low-cost scientists and technicians.

In the late 1970s and early 1980s, some Philips managers sensed that the scale economies that had encouraged concentration of activities were approaching their limits. It seemed that the diseconomies of managing larger and larger operations had begun to burden some of their competitors, while the basic potential to realize scale economies was undermined by the rise in protectionist sentiment and the growing consumer disaffection with homogenized products. But the most revolutionary development was the advent of flexible manufacturing processes. The use of computer-aided design (CAD) and manufacturing (CAM), robotics and other technologies reduced the scale sensitivity of many manufacturing processes; the minimum efficient scale for most products was now much less than global volumes.[10]

Given these changes, Philips believed it could match the efficiencies of its competitors' global-scaled plants by investing heavily in manufacturing technology in its regional or even national facilities. By the early 1980s, Philips had decided to bet on "the factory of the future" and created policy committees at the board level to develop a corporatewide approach to the use of the new manufacturing technologies. As company president Cor van der Klugt said, "The debate about global products will be short-lived when flexible automation becomes the dominant production methodology. Basic models that achieve the requisite scale economics will easily be able to be translated into more individualized products."[11]

The conversion of the company's international production centers produced impressive results. By introducing more robots and computer-aided manufacturing equipment in its big television factory in Monza, Italy, for example, Philips reduced the number of employees by 500 to 1,200. The change in production technology (as well as the ever present shadow of Japanese competitors) helped Philips renegotiate work rules with local unions, winning some important concessions that greatly increased worker productivity. As a result, the plant doubled its output over four years and achieved lower costs than the company's Taiwan plant, which was previously the cost leader.

Whereas Matsushita's competitiveness was based on global scale, Philips pursued global efficiency in its own way, focusing on different sources of economic advantage. After doing what it could through plant consolidation and rationalization, the company turned to fine-tuning its network of operations to exploit factor cost differentials. Then, by investing in technology rather than the redistribution of assets, Philips made its existing configuration more efficient.

At the same time, Matsushita was trying to overcome the limitations of its highly centralized structure, which tended to insulate the company from local market differences. Much as it envied the ability of Philips's national organizations to respond to host government demands and local consumer needs, Matsushita knew that imitating such a structure would undermine the centralized operations that were the source of its phenomenal success. As we will describe in Chapter 7, Matsushita took actions that converted local sales subsidiaries into sensitive and responsive national companies. The structural change was gradual and incremental, and built on the company's basic centralized hub structure.

Thus, both Philips and Matsushita developed the strategic capabilities they lacked, not by imitating their most effective competitors, but by compensating for the impediments in their existing organizations. Although the imprint of each company's earlier organization remained clearly visible, there was some convergence in the emerging configura-

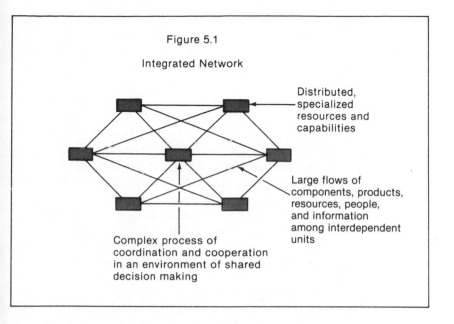

Figure 5.1

Integrated Network

Distributed, specialized resources and capabilities

Large flows of components, products, resources, people, and information among interdependent units

Complex process of coordination and cooperation in an environment of shared decision making

tions. Both companies were evolving into a structure based on dispersed, specialized, and interdependent units: the configuration we described briefly in Chapter 4 as an integrated network.

INTEGRATED NETWORK: STRUCTURAL FRAMEWORK OF THE TRANSNATIONAL

The gradual redistribution of assets and resources at Philips and Matsushita was typical of transformations we saw in most companies we studied. From vastly different structural bases, they were converging toward a common configuration, in which increasingly specialized units worldwide were linked into an integrated network of operations that enabled them to achieve their multidimensional strategic objectives of efficiency, responsiveness, and innovation. (See Figure 5.1.) The strength of this configuration springs from its fundamental characteristics: dispersion, specialization, and interdependence.

Dispersed Assets

Historically companies dispersed their assets and resources in order to respond better to highly differentiated local market needs. With gradually converging consumer needs and preferences, however, this motivation has become less important.

The ability to sense diverse market needs, technological trends, and competitive actions remains crucial, however, because such stimuli represent an important source of innovation.[12] Today new consumer trends, technological advances, and competitive strategies can emerge anywhere in the world. As we will describe in greater detail in Chapter 7, the ability to sense and respond to these widely scattered stimuli represents a major source of competitive advantage.

A dispersed configuration also allows worldwide companies to capitalize on factor cost differentials. They not only have access to low-cost labor and materials, but can tap into an international pool of increasingly scarce technological and managerial resources.[13] Ericsson, for example, recruits most of the engineering graduates from Stockholm universities and technical schools, but still cannot meet its huge developmental needs at home. Particularly for software engineers, the company relies increasingly on personnel in its U.K. and U.S. operations.

Finally, dispersed operations are vital in an international environment where concentration of assets exposes companies to intolerable political and economic risk. Given widespread political sanctions and wildly gyrating currencies, companies feel they must spread their operations to reduce their exposure.[14] When government agencies in the United States and Europe restricted Japanese imports during the 1970s and early 1980s, companies that had established viable offshore production sites could often circumvent the sanctions, while those whose assets were concentrated centrally could not. Later, when the Japanese yen appreciated 40 percent against the U.S. dollar, companies with centralized sourcing facilities were again hit hard; Matsushita's loss of $500 million in 1986 sales served to reinforce the company's commitment to shift more of its value added offshore.[15]

Specialized Operations

As Philips painfully learned, a configuration of fully integrated, self-contained national organizations can mean a significant disadvantage in efficiency. But by specializing such operations and giving them a broader mandate, companies can capture minimum-scale efficiencies yet retain a dispersed structure.

The viability of this approach has been greatly enhanced by the latest generation of manufacturing technologies. In the past, specialization and dedicated assets tended to create a rigidity that was particularly risky in an environment of shortening product life cycles and increasing volatility in costs, technologies, and tastes. By using new flexible manufacturing technologies, however, specialized operations can overcome the scale-flexibility dilemma.[16] Thus Philips's plants specialize in particular parts of its product line. In TVs, for example, the United Kingdom is the lead country for the teletext line, while Belgium has primary responsibility for development and manufacture of stereo sets. As mature product lines begin segmenting, the ability to specialize operations can have enormous economic benefit.

The available scale economies, and thus the need to specialize, vary by product and by task. In most cases, the optimum plant size for component production tends to be larger than the efficient capacity for final assembly. In consumer electronics, the optimum capacity of assembly facilities is determined by the efficient scale of computer-aided testing, which is much larger than the efficient scale of the actual assembly process. The introduction of this technology was one factor in Philips's decision to consolidate its worldwide television production, and these concentration and specialization trends will continue, particularly as Europe moves toward its 1992 objective of market integration.

The benefits of specialization are not confined to manufacturing. For most companies, the base of relevant technologies is becoming so broad and changing so rapidly that the R&D task is increasingly difficult to manage. Unilever, P&G, and Kao not only continue research in basic oils and fats chemistry, but also are now involved in polymer chemistry, surface science, organic chemistry, flavor and fragrance research, and other specialties, many of which hardly existed a decade ago. New materials science has revolutionized products and packaging, and new process technologies have fundamentally changed the industry's economics.

In such an environment, many companies have found it increasingly awkward to rely on a large central research laboratory. Smaller, more specialized facilities, focusing on a single research area or a range of related technologies, are better able to deal with the new environmental demands.[17]

Since the late 1970s, Philips has pursued a policy of developing special competencies in its eight research labs, located in Holland, Germany (two), the United States (two), the United Kingdom, France, and Belgium. The central laboratory in Eindhoven, which employs 2,500 scientists and engineers, has been given the broadest mandate, working on state-of-the-art developments in basic disciplines like physics, chemistry, and mathematics, as well as numerous applied fields from electronic optics to integrated circuit design and materials science. Other labs are more specialized. The Redhill facility in the United Kingdom focuses on a few specific areas such as solid-state electronics for discrete components in silicon and gallium arsenide, and software design for artificial intelligence. The Paris laboratory built its expertise in technologies supported by the French government, such as microprocessor and VLSI architecture and digital signal processing.

By the late 1980s, the head of the Eindhoven laboratory claimed that overlap and duplication in research, previously a major problem, had been significantly reduced. Furthermore, a sense of collegiality across laboratories had replaced the earlier feeling of competition and protectiveness.

Specialization need not mean monopolization of a particular scarce resource or asset. In many companies, management deliberately ensures duplication of specific skills and capabilities, which not only allows the company to develop alternative approaches to difficult research problems, but can be managed to create a healthy sense of internal competition. For example, by allowing its European Technical Center to work on a liquid laundry detergent even though the parent company's R&D group had already come up with such a product, P&G developed several breakthrough technologies that were then incorporated into the American product. The improved performance helped it achieve market leadership. Similarly, Ericsson was glad its Australian subsidiary had been pursuing its own approach to the development of a new fully electronic central switch when the parent's focus on an analog technology proved to be out of step with market developments. It saved a great deal of time and expense by picking up the Australian work in digital switching.

Interdependent Relationships

In traditional organization structures, the relationship between units has typically been either clear-cut dependence (as in the case of the centralized hub) or strong independence (as exemplified by the overseas subsidiaries in a decentralized federation structure). As we have seen, however, changes in the international operating environment have made both simple interunit relationships inappropriate. Independent units can be overcome by competitors whose coordinated global approach gives them the strategic advantages that come with global-scale operations and the ability to cross-subsidize the losses from battles in one market with funds generated in others. On the other hand, foreign operations totally dependent on a central unit may be unable to exploit local market opportunities or respond effectively to strong national competitors. Today's worldwide competitive environment demands collaborative information sharing and problem solving, cooperative resource sharing, and collective implementation—in short, a relationship built on interdependence.

But it is not easy to change relationships of dependence or independence that have been built up over a long history. Many companies have tried to foster greater cooperation by adding layers of administration. Top managers have extolled the virtues of teamwork and have even created special departments to audit management response to the need. In most cases, these efforts have been disappointing. Independent units have feigned compliance while fiercely protecting their autonomy. Dependent units have found that the new cooperative spirit implies little more than the right to agree with those on whom they depend.

Some companies, however, have gradually developed the capability to build what one author calls an "integrative organization."[18] Of the companies we studied, the most successful did so not by creating new units, but by forging genuinely interdependent relationships among product, functional, and geographic management groups. In essence, they made integration and collaboration self-enforcing by requiring each group to cooperate in order to achieve its own interests.

For example, during the 1970s, Procter & Gamble's subsidiary companies in Europe were gradually becoming more and more independent, and by the early 1980s, most were fairly self-sufficient operations. They had not only local sales and marketing capabilities, but also (except for the smallest countries) their own product development and manufacturing facilities. More important, the local general managers had sole authority to decide which products should be launched in their countries and how those products should be marketed. Such independence made the company vulnerable to competitors. P&G found that both local and global competitors could exploit gaps in its national subsidiaries' product market positions—often by imitating successful products or marketing strategies of P&G companies in other countries. Yet it was hard to get the subsidiaries to cooperate on product development, manufacturing, or market strategies. Each unit was self-sufficient and autonomous, and was held responsible for performance in its own country. Any proposal that would reduce their independence or compromise their sales and profit figures was treated with great wariness.

The opportunity to bring about change came with the introduction of the company's so-called Euro Brands. Frustrated by costly duplications in product development, inefficient manufacturing scale, and uncoordinated marketing strategy, the European vice president initiated a program that would require subsidiaries to collaborate in developing and executing Europewide product market strategies. Rather than impose coordination on them from headquarters, however, he delegated the responsibility to Euro Brand Teams composed primarily of subsidiary personnel. "This, after all, is where the expertise and entrepreneurship is located," he said.

Each team was headed by the general manager of a subsidiary that had a particularly well-developed competence in that business. It also included product and advertising managers from the other subsidiaries and functional managers from P&G's European headquarters.

Historically, the company's subsidiaries had had little incentive to cooperate. Now, however, the success of each team—and the reputation of the general manager heading it—depended on the support of other subsidiaries; this made cooperation self-enforcing. Each general manager knew that the level of support he could expect from the other members of the Euro Brand Team depended on the contribution product managers from his subsidiary provided to the other teams. The result was cross-subsidiary teamwork driven by individual interests.

Such relationships are significantly different from the usual interdependencies in multiunit organizations. Worldwide companies have traditionally attempted to use so-called pooled interdependence to make unit managers responsive to global rather than local interests. Before the Euro Team approach, for instance, P&G's European vice president often tried to convince independent-minded subsidiary managers to transfer surplus-generated funds to other more needy subsidiaries, in the overall corporate interest. "Someday when you need help," he argued, "they might be able to fund a major product launch for you."

Pooled interdependence is often too broad and amorphous to affect day-to-day management behavior. The interdependencies in the Euro Brand Teams are more clearly reciprocal and are thus better able to expand the company's organizational capabilities.[19]

New Challenges: Managing Differentiated Roles

No company in our sample had built an integrated network that included its entire organization, nor is a comprehensive network necessary, as we will discuss in Chapter 6. Our research, however, suggests that this configuration is becoming the basic framework around which more and more companies will build their worldwide operations.

We now turn to the roles and responsibilities of units in the network, and ways to ensure flexibility and responsiveness to local situations.

6
DEVELOPING FLEXIBILITY: SPECIALIZED ROLES AND RESPONSIBILITIES

L ike many other companies we studied, Unilever built its international operations under an implicit assumption of organizational symmetry. Managers of local operating companies in products ranging from packaged foods to chemicals and detergents reported to strongly independent national managers, who in turn reported through regional directors to the board. After World War II, the company supplemented this geographically dominated structure by establishing several product-coordination groups at the corporate center, to capture potential economies and to transfer learning across national boundaries. But all businesses were similarly managed, and the number of coordination groups grew from three in 1962 to six in 1969 and to ten by 1977.

By the mid-1970s, however, Unilever's organizational symmetry was being threatened. Global economic disruption caused by the oil crisis highlighted the differences in the company's businesses and markets and forced management to differentiate its organizational structures and administrative processes. While standardization, coordination, and integration paid high dividends in the chemicals and detergent businesses, for example, important differences in local tastes and national cultures worked against coordination in foods.[1] As a result, the roles, responsibilities, and powers of the central product coordination groups began to diverge.

But even in those businesses it decided to manage in a more globally coordinated manner, Unilever had to decide *what* to coordinate. Most of its national subsidiaries were fully integrated, self-sufficient operations. While they were free to draw on product technology, manufacturing capabilities, and marketing expertise developed at the center, they were never required to do so, and most units developed, manufactured, and marketed their own products. Thus functions too tended to be managed symmetrically.

Over time, it became clear that the decentralization of all functional responsibilities was making it difficult for the company to respond effectively to competitive threats. In particular, competition in the European detergent business had intensified in the 1970s. When Procter & Gamble's subsidiaries were launching new laundry detergents based on the company's rape seed formula (developed in the United States), Unilever companies were forced to respond individually. The result was thirteen different products and formulas, developed at tremendous cost, yet none as good as P&G's.

Having their own product development capability also made the local detergent companies strongly resistant to ideas developed in the central R&D labs. A new low-temperature bleach developed by corporate R&D in the early 1960s was offered to local companies. Under some pressure, five countries agreed to test it in their markets, but after brief trials, all rejected the formulation. Scores of similar incidents convinced Unilever's top management that it needed to manage its R&D differently from its marketing. In 1975, it began centralizing the product development function in Europe, closing down product development facilities in some countries, and coordinating and controlling more closely the activities in others.

Corporate managers soon realized that they needed to do more than decide which functions should be delegated to the local level. Within each functional area of responsibility, some tasks need to be coordinated by central management more than others. Thus, the company's decision to manage its detergent products' R&D in a more centralized fashion while leaving the marketing function more decentralized emerged as a general solution that was gradually modified to clarify responsibilities on a task basis. In detergents marketing, for example, product policy was managed directly by the center; pricing decisions and advertising strategy were delegated but coordinated from the center; and sales, distribution, and promotional tasks were kept largely local.

Figure 6.1 shows graphically the varying needs for global integration and national differentiation in Unilever's business strategies, functional responsibilities, and tasks.[2] As the diagram on the left shows, the detergent business occupies an intermediate position among the company's activities, requiring less coordination by corporate managers than the chemicals business, but more than personal products. Within detergents (center diagram), research is controlled by the headquarters, but marketing decisions are significantly influenced by subsidiary managers. Among marketing tasks (right-hand diagram), the headquarters is more involved in product policy, while local promotion decisions are left almost entirely to the discretion of subsidiary managers.

Such differentiation in management processes is not unique to Unilever; we observed similar phenomena in most companies we

Figure 6.1

Integration and Differentiation Needs at Unilever

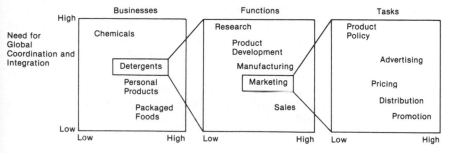

Need for National Differentiation and Responsiveness

studied. For example, Philips's consumer electronics division has begun to differentiate its organization by product life-cycle stages. High-technology products such as compact disk players that require intensive marketing support are managed with strategies, structures, and processes different from those for stable, high-volume products like color television sets, which in turn are managed differently from mature and declining products like portable radios and audio tape recorders.

Yet, long after they had differentiated their management approach by business, product, function, and even individual tasks, many companies still regarded their overseas subsidiaries as a homogeneous group. Informally, differences among subsidiaries were often recognized, but the formal structures and systems tended to be uniform. Typically all foreign subsidiaries reported through identical organization structures, were assigned the same broad roles and responsibilities, and operated under the same planning, control, and information systems.[3]

No clear process for differentiating roles, responsibilities, and relationships by national entity had been developed. Businesses or products could be differentiated on the basis of their ripeness for global strategic approaches; functional tasks could be differentiated by their potential need for or benefit from coordination or control; but the basis for differentiating the management of country units was rarely clearly defined.

Yet our observations suggest that the uniform treatment of foreign subsidiaries is a major impediment in building the flexibility a worldwide company requires today. Such uniformity locks management into simplistic and often dichotomous choices (as reflected, for example, in the unresolvable centralization versus decentralization debate) and pre-empts the more subtle options available both within the worldwide company and in its various businesses and markets.

The rest of this chapter will focus on this particular aspect of differentiation—the task of building specialization in the roles and responsibilities of national subsidiaries. First we illustrate the need for such differentiation. Next we present a conceptual framework defining four generic roles that subsidiaries play in the transnational organization. Finally we conclude with a brief discussion of how such roles can be allocated, legitimized, and integrated into a viable organizational system.

ROLE OF NATIONAL SUBSIDIARIES

Among the earliest motivations for overseas investment was the need to secure key supplies, especially of minerals, energy, and scarce raw materials. Aluminum producers needed bauxite, tire companies developed rubber plantations, and oil companies opened up new fields in Canada, the Middle East, and Venezuela. By the early part of this century, Standard Oil, British Petroleum, Anaconda Copper, and International Nickel were among the largest of the emerging worldwide companies.[4]

Another motive for internationalization was the search for new markets, particularly by companies that had some intrinsic advantages, typically related to their technology or brand recognition. Many companies eventually realized that these additional sales allowed them to exploit economies of scale and synergy, thereby reducing costs and leveraging existing assets and capabilities. Market expansion induced many manufacturing companies to venture abroad, first building a sales and distribution organization, then manufacturing plants.[5] Philips went abroad to find new markets for its electric lamps; Unilever expanded into the British colonies to restore profits hurt by intense competition from local firms in the United Kingdom.

Factor cost differences also prompted internationalization. Particularly as tariff barriers declined in the 1960s, many companies for whom labor was a major cost found they were at a competitive disadvantage to imports. Firms in the clothing, electronics, watchmaking, and similar industries began to explore the possibility of establishing offshore sourcing locations for components and even whole product lines.[6]

These three objectives—the search for resources, markets, and cheap labor—had motivated the overseas expansion of most worldwide companies and shaped the attitudes of their managers. A significant further influence on attitudes, as described in Chapter 3, was the companies' administrative heritages, which reflected the conditions under which they first expanded abroad. Characteristic global, multinational, and international mentalities evolved, which had an important impact on companies' organization and management of their worldwide operations.[7]

The Multinational and Global Mentalities

Particularly in the late 1950s and early 1960s, when many worldwide companies accelerated their overseas investment, it became managerially fashionable to develop a better understanding of and adopt a more flexible approach to overseas markets. Many companies emphasized the need to modify their products, their strategies, and even their management practices country by country. Catering to unique local requirements was "the price of admission to the market," to quote one manager we interviewed. Typically under the protective umbrella of an international division organization, these companies followed a multinational strategic approach: their worldwide strategy was the sum of the multiple national subsidiaries' needs.

Managers with a global mentality, in contrast, focused on creating products for a world market and manufacturing them on a global scale in a few highly efficient central plants. They assumed that national tastes and preferences were more similar than different, or that they could be made so. These managers tailored products or strategies to national markets only reluctantly.[8] Overall they felt that the diversity of international environments was an inconvenience, to be minimized or isolated.

As we reviewed in Chapter 3, these two approaches led to different configurations of organizational assets and different organizational systems and processes. Yet both global and multinational managers shared two organizational assumptions, we found. We termed these well-ingrained beliefs the "UN Model Assumption" and the "Headquarters Hierarchy Syndrome."

The UN Model Assumption. The assumption that all foreign subsidiaries should be treated as equals was described by one manager as the UN model of multinational management.[9] The same assumption is reflected in the family metaphor that describes foreign subsidiaries as the children of a watchful parent company. By implication, the parent should not play favorites—a norm that inhibits differentiated treatment of subsidiaries.[10]

For most worldwide companies, operations in major markets such as Germany, Japan, or the United States, are substantially more important than those in Latin America, East Asia, or Africa. Yet typically information and control systems are applied uniformly systemwide, subsidiary roles and responsibilities are expressed in generalized terms, and all country managers are involved to the same degree in the planning process and are evaluated against standardized criteria.

When the various national subsidiaries are operationally self-sufficient and strategically independent, the UN model appropriately reinforces the need for each to develop strategies for dealing with its local environments. Similarly, when all organizational resources and competencies are centralized and the subsidiaries are expected primarily to implement standardized "global" strategies, the model reflects the actual homogeneity of subsidiaries' roles. Thus managers find the simplicity, clarity, and uniformity of the UN model immensely appealing.

The Headquarters Hierarchy Syndrome.   The other common organizational assumption is captured in the "headquarters-subsidiary" terminology, which implies a clear superior-subordinate relationship. The metaphor of headquarters as parent and subsidiaries as children reinforces the norm of decision making and resource concentration at the center.

The headquarters hierarchy syndrome and the UN model assumption are mutually reinforcing. Managers are encouraged to think of the company in terms of two roles—one for headquarters; another for national subsidiaries. In the last two decades, as companies have responded to the strengthening forces of globalization, it was natural for the headquarters to take responsibility for coordinating and controlling the key decisions and global resources, and for the national organizations to implement and adapt the global strategy in their local environments.

As the globalization strategy is implemented, country managers struggle to retain their freedom, while their counterparts at the center work to establish their control and legitimacy as managers of a global strategy. In the midst of this process, it is not surprising that relationships between the center and the subsidiaries tend to become strained or even adversarial.

Limitations of the Symmetrical Hierarchy Organization

The combined effect of these two assumptions has substantially limited the organizational capability of many worldwide companies' international operations. Those companies operate in a diverse and changeable environment with an undifferentiated structure and an inflexible management process—an organizational form we have termed the *symmetrical hierarchy.*

Three problems are particularly important. First, the symmetrical hierarchy leads management to underestimate the differences in the strategic importance of various national environments. Symmetrical treatment tends to overcompensate the needs of smaller, relatively unimportant markets, while shortchanging key countries where new market trends usually emerge and competitive strategies are often shaped. Strategic responses move toward the lowest common denominator or the grand compromise.

Second, the symmetrical hierarchy breaks down complex strategic demands into simplistic national and central components. Thus, many companies typically delegate responsibilities for downstream activities such as sales, service, and perhaps manufacturing assembly to the national organizations on a local-for-local basis, while the center controls upstream elements such as R&D and component production, and support activities such as global sourcing and human resource development. By casting the national organizations as local implementers and adapters of global directives, management risks grossly underutilizing their physical assets and organizational capabilities. Regardless of interest or capacity, the focus of the national organizations in the symmetry hierarchy is limited by their geographic identities.

Finally, these assumptions have an important motivational effect. As more and more responsibilities are controlled by corporate headquarters, managers at the national level may feel deprived of outlets for their skills and creative energies. The very managers who often had been the company's entrepreneurial spark plugs become discouraged and even disenfranchised.[11] The resultant management system might be compared to a computer system in which the central processing unit (CPU) is linked to a network of input/output terminals. As the functionality of the CPU increases, the need for distributed computing capability decreases. The risk is that as the roles of the national units shrink, their ability to sense and respond to the changing environment may atrophy, so that they become nothing more than "dumb terminals."

ROLE OF NATIONAL ORGANIZATIONS IN THE TRANSNATIONAL

Most companies internationalized gradually, in an incremental process that was usually linked to their home market strategic objectives. International units might have been established to secure supplies for domestic operations or as a means of lowering costs to improve competitive positions vis-à-vis domestic rivals.

However, once international sales and production operations had been established, the perceptions and strategic motivations of managers often changed. Initially most saw foreign subsidiaries as strategic and organizational appendages to the domestic business. As they began to think about strategy in a more integrated worldwide fashion, they typically developed a new approach that recognized the different advantages of operating internationally. In our terms, they matured from a multinational or global mentality to a transnational mentality.

The Transnational Mentality

Fundamental to the new transnational mentality is a different set of motivations and assumptions about the role of the company's international operations. In the transnational view, the national subsidiaries become strategic partners whose knowledge and capabilities are vital to the corporation's ability to maintain a long-term global competitive advantage.

New motivations are drawing companies offshore today. Among the most important is the quest for scarce information or new knowledge. Many companies have recognized the important competitive advantage represented by the global scanning capability of their international operations. For example, a company originally drawn offshore to secure raw materials is more likely to become aware of alternative low-cost production sources around the globe; a company that sought market opportunities is often exposed to new technologies or market needs that stimulate innovative product development. Worldwide presence conveys a huge information advantage that can translate into more efficient sources or more advanced product or process technology.

The value of global scanning is illustrated by the gradual erosion of the competitive position of Dominion Engineering Works (DEW), the Canadian manufacturer of paper-making machinery.[12] Formed during World War I, when European suppliers were unable to serve Canada's paper mills and power companies, DEW grew and was profitable until the mid-1970s. In 1962, it was acquired by the Canadian subsidiary of General Electric; constrained by the company's philosophy of operating each international unit as a mini-GE, DEW remained focused on its lucrative domestic market and ignored the opportunities to expand or even to source from abroad.

DEW's major international competitors, such as the U.S.-based Beloit Corporation and Germany's Voith, expanded abroad energetically. By the mid-1970s, Beloit's worldwide operations included five plants in the United States, manufacturing facilities in the United Kingdom, Brazil, Canada, Spain, and Italy, and licensees in Japan, India, and Poland. Voith had built a plant in Brazil and had acquired the existing plants of competitors in the United States.

In the mid-1970s, the paper machinery industry entered a long recession. Squeezed by both rapidly declining demand for paper (and hence for paper machinery) and rising costs of pulp and energy (which could not be passed on to customers because of industry overcapacity and severe price competition), profit margins narrowed substantially and the industrywide return on investment fell well below the average for all manufacturers.

Under these difficult conditions, companies such as Beloit and Voith not only retained their above-average profitability, but expanded their global market shares. One of their key advantages was the ability to use very different inputs for manufacturing paper. Operating in Latin America, Asia, and Eastern Europe, they had been exposed to new technologies that were emerging in the southern hemisphere for manufacturing paper out of hardwoods and even nonwood fibers such as bagasse, grass, reed, and straw pulp, and had adapted their machines to handle the new materials. As a result, when the demand for paper machinery declined in the developed Western markets, the companies had strong competitive positions in the developing country markets where demand continued to grow. DEW, in contrast, had not been exposed to the alternative technologies and became uncompetitive because of its dependency on the extreme swings of a single market, and its inability to compensate by picking up contracts in the fast-growing markets.

Another new motivation of the transnational is to use its diverse geographic portfolio of assets to play increasingly sophisticated competitive games that require national units to adopt different strategic roles on a global competitive chessboard. Here the potential advantages include global-scale economies, global-scanning capabilities, and cross-subsidization of markets.[13]

For example, Bic, the European manufacturer of ballpoint pens, developed a dominant global position by conquering one market at a time and by using the established strong cash flows to support its entry into new markets. It first developed a near monopoly in France and leveraged that position to enter and compete aggressively in Britain. Having captured a majority share in the U.K. market, it then proceeded to build up its position in the United States. It could sustain very low margins here because of attractive profitability in its existing European strongholds. In each market, Bic's rivals—purely domestic companies dependent entirely on the local markets—could do little to prevent the landslide except to defend as long as they could their existing markets with unsustainable prices.[14]

Companies with such complex motivations and justifications for international operations develop distinctive assumptions about the nature of worldwide organizations. The first is that exposure to a wider and more diverse range of environmental stimuli represents a key potential advantage over national companies. The broader range of customer preferences, competitor behavior, government demands, and sources of technology represent potential triggers for innovation and are major sources of learning for the company. To realize this potential advantage, management must build an organization sensitive and responsive to the diverse stimuli, and be able to transfer the learning that results.[15]

The second belief fundamental to the transnational mentality relates to the distribution of the company's resources and capabilities. In some worldwide companies, important physical and organizational resources and abilities that are developed outside of the home environment do not benefit the entire firm. In the transnational corporations, one of top management's key tasks is to foster the development of such organizational assets and to ensure that the entire corporation has access to the developed capabilities.

National Organizations in the Transnational: Differentiated Roles and Dispersed Responsibilities

Once managers adopt this transnational mentality, they begin to question the underlying assumptions of the symmetrical hierarchy mode of operations. Once the stark differences in environmental demands and opportunities are recognized, the UN model seems untenable. Similarly, the headquarters hierarchy appears unjustified when the resources and capabilities of subsidiaries vary widely, and often independently of challenges and complexities of their local environments. Discomfort with the traditional organizing norms has led some companies to experiment with a new organizational form in which the roles of the national subsidiaries are differentiated and responsibilities for global tasks are dispersed.

Clearly, national markets differ widely in their importance to the company's global strategy. Some markets have more advanced and sophisticated customers, in some countries key competitors are more active, and in some environments certain technologies are more advanced. Instead of treating all national organizations equally, managers with the transnational mentality see their task as tailoring the roles and responsibilities of the local organizations to reflect the strategic importance of the local environments. This implies consciously building an organization with differentiated capabilities, tasks, and resources.

The company's formal administrative systems are also modified. Subsidiaries are allocated different degrees of influence in various decision processes, and subsidiary management is measured and rewarded differently, to reflect the differences in its roles and tasks. Resource allocation systems are differentiated, as are coordination processes and the nature of information flows between the subsidiary and the rest of the global organization.

Transnational managers also recognize the influence of an organization's administrative heritage. Past priorities and resource allocation decisions, idiosyncratic events, internal power structures, and logical or illogical incrementalism all affect the national organization's skills and competencies.[16] As a result, the company's capabilities in a given national operation may not match the environmental demands it faces there.

Transnational managers see no reason to limit the application of organizational assets arbitrarily to particular local environments. They believe that the capabilities of a creative marketer, a flexible manufacturing facility, or an innovative development group must be used for the benefit of the entire organization. In several companies, we saw managers who were breaking out of the headquarters hierarchy syndrome, and striving to create an organizational context in which the national units would be co-opted into a global strategy that benefits the corporation as a whole.

DIFFERENTIATION OF SUBSIDIARY ROLES AND RESPONSIBILITIES: A CONCEPTUAL FRAMEWORK

In Chapter 4 we described how some companies have begun to differentiate the roles and responsibilities of their national subsidiaries. None had developed a well-defined basis for assigning roles and allocating tasks. Yet our research suggests a vague but consistent pattern in their actions. Figure 6.2 represents a somewhat oversimplified conceptualization of the pattern. The intersection of strategic and organizational considerations defines four generic roles that country organizations can play in fulfilling the global objectives of the transnational organization.

The principal strategic consideration is the overall importance of national environments to the firm's global strategy. A very large market is obviously important, but so is a competitor's home market, or a market that is highly sophisticated or technologically advanced. The major organizational consideration is the national subsidiary's competence—in technology, production, marketing, or another area. Depending on its positions along these dimensions, a national organization may function as a strategic leader, contributor, implementer, or black hole.[17]

Strategic Leader

National organizations with high internal competence located in strategically important markets must be legitimate partners with the headquarters in developing and implementing broad strategic thrusts. In addition to detecting early warning signals for change, they must par-

Figure 6.2

Generic Roles of National Organizations

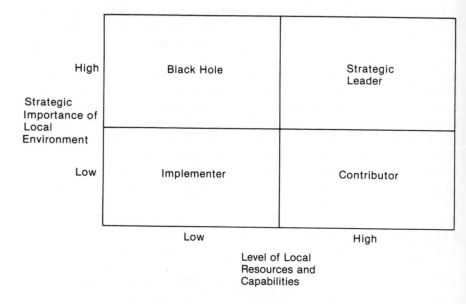

ticipate fully in analyzing the resulting threats and opportunities and developing appropriate organizational responses.

For example, Philips's U.K. subsidiary played a key role in developing the company's strong leadership position in the teletext TV business. Of the 625 lines that make up the transmission in a television broadcast, only 575 are used to transmit the pictures that appear on the TV screen. In the early 1970s, the BBC and ITV (an independent British TV franchise) simultaneously undertook projects to exploit the transmission capacity of the 50 unused lines to broadcast text and simple diagrams. This was the birth of teletext, a major new information technology product.

Teletext, however, required a different type of TV receiver. For manufacturers of TV sets, this was a new opportunity, but one that required significant investment in R&D and production facilities. In the early 1970s the commercial possibilities of teletext were far from certain, and most TV manufacturers decided against making those investments. Even within Philips, many managers considered teletext a typical British toy—quite fancy, but not very useful—and doubted consumers would ever pay a substantial premium just to read text on their TV screens.

The U.K. subsidiary of Philips, however, was convinced of the future of teletext and decided to pursue its own development plans. Subsidiary managers persuaded Mullard, Philips's component manufacturing subsidiary, to design and produce the integrated circuit chip for receiving teletext. Next, despite less than enthusiastic support from some key headquarters managers in the initial stage, the development group at Croyden developed a teletext decoder. Finally, in 1976, they introduced the new teletext TV set in the British market. At first, sluggish demand seemed to vindicate the skepticism of the corporate group. In 1977, four years after the service was first announced, only 1,000 teletext sets were sold; the following year, sales increased to only 5,000.

But the U.K. subsidiary did not give up. It fully supported the British government in developing and implementing a coordinated strategy for promoting teletext. A senior manager was assigned to work full time in the Department of Industry to help educate the viewing public and to coordinate resellers and manufacturers to ensure widespread availability of teletext sets throughout the country. At the same time, Philips kept up the pressure on the Croyden factory to reduce costs of teletext sets and to improve the quality of reception.

Finally, in 1980, teletext took off, and U.K. sales reached half a million sets in 1982. In 1985, over three million teletext sets were in use in the United Kingdom, and the product spread abroad rapidly. Building on its early lead, Philips has established a dominant position in this market. Throughout the process, the U.K. subsidiary has played a lead role, and the Croyden plant has been formally recognized as the company's center of competence for developing and producing teletext TV sets.[18]

Contributors

Several companies we observed were trying to capture the benefits of certain local facilities or capabilities and apply them to the broader worldwide operations. This pattern was particularly characteristic of subsidiaries in which competence was high but the strategic importance of the market was limited. The Australian subsidiary of Ericsson provides a fine example of this contributor role.

A cornerstone of Ericsson's ascendancy in the telecommunications switching business has been the AXE digital switch, which the company introduced in 1982. By 1986, the system was sold in 60 countries and had become the anchor of Ericsson's ambitious strategy for winning share in the global telecommunications switching market.

Ericsson's Australian subsidiary made an important contribution to the development of the AXE system. Its engineers played a leading role in designing several key components, including the trunk distribution system, which expedited the planned conversion of the system from its initial analog design to the final digital form. More recently, the same group developed Ericsson's rural switch, which has been produced and sold as a global product.

The role of the Australian operation in developing and implementing such products is more significant than the relative size of the company and its local market might suggest. Its ability to contribute derives from a long history during which the subsidiary built up a strong technological capability. Two factors were particularly important: government pressure and strong managerial leadership.

Recognizing that Australia was one of the first countries to change from electromechanical to electronic central switching systems, the government insisted on a strong local technological capability as a precondition for market access. It forced Ericsson to cross-license its technology to two other local manufacturers, both subsidiaries of large worldwide companies, and demanded that the company maintain an Australian R&D team to service the licensing obligations and to promote local development. Gradually, these demands led to the creation of a large group of engineers with an intimate knowledge of the company's core technology.

Equally important was the influence of Ericsson's strong, independent, and entrepreneurial country manager, who saw local technological capability as essential for market success. He strengthened the R&D team, probably beyond the level required to meet immediate government demands, and often without full support from the headquarters.

As a result, Ericsson's technological capability in Australia was much more advanced than its R&D resources in other markets of similar size or strategic importance. The Australian subsidiary's ability to contribute to efforts such as the AXE development project illustrates the value of harnessing excess resources in a particular subsidiary to address the corporation's global tasks.

Without appropriate management, building excess resources in a noncritical environment can create problems. Lacking an external challenge, internal competencies tend to focus on increasing local autonomy and finding avenues for product or system differentiation that may be unnecessary for, or even detrimental to, the firm's global strategy. But if the company inhibits the development activities of these subsidiaries, the capabilities may be lost. If skilled, experienced personnel become frustrated, they may stop contributing or leave, perhaps even joining competitors. Many American companies have seen this happen in their Canadian subsidiaries, for example.

Companies escape from this dilemma by finding ways to redirect excess resources to global rather than local tasks. Ericsson did it by having half the R&D team in Australia formally attached to the headquarters. Worldwide development tasks were assigned to them, and they were given the information and resources they needed. Not only was the company able to capture and leverage the capabilities of this remote development group, it was also able to motivate and reward the Australian technicians, making them feel they were part of a truly worldwide operation.

Implementer

Some national organizations have just enough competence to maintain their local operations in a nonstrategic market. Corporate resource commitments reflect the market's limited potential. In most companies, the majority of national units play this role. It is characteristic of many subsidiaries in the developing countries of Latin America, Africa, and Asia as well as the national organizations in Canada and in the smaller European countries.

These national organizations cannot contribute much to the strategic knowledge of the firm. They do not have access to critical information; they do not control scarce resources. Fundamentally, they are implementers—deliverers of the company's value added. Their task is not unimportant, however. The implementers often maintain the commercial viability of the company and generate the resources that support strategic and innovative processes. For this reason, their efficiency is as important as the creativity of the strategic leaders or contributors. The implementers make it possible to capture economies of scale and scope that are critical to most global strategies.

In Chapter 5 we described how Procter & Gamble created intersubsidiary teams to develop various Euro Brands that could be marketed on a coordinated European basis. Key to the program's success was management's ability to convince previously independent subsidiaries to act as implementers during the product launch. By resisting the temptation to modify the formula, change the package, or adjust the advertising approach for the various Euro Brand products, subsidiaries in the implementer role made it possible to achieve the efficiencies and competitive advantage P&G had hoped for.

The Black Hole

There may be strategically important markets in which a worldwide company has minimal capabilities. This is true, for example, of Philips in Japan, of Ericsson in the United States, and of Matsushita in Europe. In each of these markets a strong local presence is essential for maintaining the global position of the firm.[19] Yet these competitors have only token positions in these markets.

The black hole is not an acceptable strategic position. The task for management is to find a way out of this thankless role. In essence, the national organization in a black hole situation should be playing the role of a strategic leader but lacks the competence to do so. Remedies will not come cheap. Developing a significant local presence in a large, sophisticated, and competitive national environment is extremely difficult, expensive, and time-consuming.

One common response to this challenge has been to create a small sensory capability to exploit the learning potential of the environment, even if its business potential is beyond reach. Thus, many American and European companies have established small organizations in Japan to monitor technologies, market trends, and competitors. The assumption is that such monitoring will allow the companies to analyze the global implications of local developments and at least prevent erosion of their positions in other markets.

In many cases, this strategy has proved disappointing, as the experience of Philips in Japan illustrates. Although it had previously set up two joint ventures with Matsushita, one for manufacturing electric lamps and the other for producing electronic components, Philips did not establish its own marketing organization in Japan until 1956. By the late 1960s, when Japan started emerging as a major force in the consumer electronics business, Philips wanted to develop a better understanding of the market but found it very difficult to penetrate the captive distribution channels controlled by the principal Japanese manufacturers. Since it seemed virtually impossible to build a viable business in Japan, a consensus emerged that what the company needed was a "window" to keep headquarters informed of local developments. To supplement the small marketing company, Philips set up a technology group to monitor Japanese technical developments.

But the "Japan window" never really achieved its objective. "Eyes and ears are not enough," a senior manager of Philips in Japan explained. "One must get inside the bloodstream of the business and gain access to distribution channels, component suppliers, and equipment manufacturers." Detecting a new development after it has occurred is not helpful, for there is no time to catch up. One needs to be aware of developments as they emerge, and for that one must be a player, not a spectator. By formally defining the role of the local unit as a "window," Philips kept it from ever developing a more important strategic role. In essence, it is condemned to permanent black hole status.[20]

At the other extreme, some companies have recognized the importance of escaping the black hole but underestimated the difficulty of doing so. Matsushita, for example, launched a frontal attack in Europe. Initially, it tried to enter the consumer electronics market with its full line of products, some through export, others through local production, hoping to capture a share in every segment, through all distribution channels. After ten years, the result was a 3 percent overall market share with a weak operation and no prospect of significant improvement.

The most promising approach to the black hole problem lies somewhere between these extremes. Both Philips and Matsushita have now modified their earlier strategies. The manager responsible for Matsushita's sales and marketing operations in Europe described his new approach as a "sniper strategy." Matsushita is now focusing on products in which competitors do not seem particularly interested. It has chosen a very small number of resellers in each market and is servicing them intensely. And Matsushita is trying to capitalize on any small competitive vulnerability—a competitor's stock-out or a gap in its line—to gain share. With 3 percent of the European market, Matsushita recognizes that it cannot behave as it does in Japan, where it is the market leader. Its priorities have shifted to a more careful development of local capabilities that will enable it to expand its toehold in the market to a foothold, and eventually to develop an organization capable of climbing out of the black hole.

Philips, similarly, is getting into the bloodstream of the Japanese market. The local organization now sees its task as selling, not sensing. But it is highly selective, focusing on areas of relative strength. It started with coffee makers and electric shavers, and supported these businesses with an integrated operation in Japan. The acquisition of Marantz, a leading Japanese hi-fi producer, has given Philips an opportunity to expand its strategic base as it attempts to move from a black hole toward a lead country role.[21]

Another approach is to develop strategic alliances. Such relationships have been historically difficult to manage, however.[22] Ericsson's joint venture with Honeywell in the United States and AT&T's alliance with Philips in Europe, are sometimes cited as examples of how an alliance can strengthen a company's position. In both cases, major telecommunications competitors hoped to exchange their technological capabilities for the local resources and competencies of a strong national firm. But both alliances subsequently experienced organizational and management conflicts stemming from divergent strategic objectives, suggesting that the strategic promise of such linkages is often much greater than the organizational compatibility of the partners.

Building the Differentiated Organization

Our framework suggests that the assignment of lead, contributor, and implementer roles will depend on the strategic importance of the unit's environment and its internal resources and capabilities. A third factor also needs to be considered, however: the organizational implications of the choice.

The potential organizational repercussions of role assignments are illustrated by the experience of companies that unquestioningly embraced the growth-share matrix popularized by the Boston Consulting Group in the 1970s. Many managers who found themselves in low-growth businesses classified as dogs or cash cows became defensive or demoralized. A similar effect is possible among managers in national organizations assigned an implementer role.[23] In the units destined to implement strategies developed elsewhere, skills may atrophy, entrepreneurship may die, and any innovative spark may sputter.

Accordingly, headquarters managers should allocate roles so as to raise the company's organizational effectiveness as well as its strategic efficiency. By finding opportunities to give lead or contributing roles to the smaller or less well-developed units, if only for a few strategically less important products, they can achieve two important organizational effects. First, they allow national organizations in major markets to focus on their leadership roles in the truly critical products. Second, they give a huge incentive and motivational boost to the smaller unit entrusted with an important role in the global strategy.

For example, although many other subsidiaries were closer to large markets or had better access to corporate know-how and expertise, Philips Taiwan was given the lead role for the company's small screen monitor business. The corporate vote of confidence was highly motivating and represented a major source of pride to that national unit. Incentives were especially strong because the project was critical to solving Taiwan's own problem of growing excess capacity for black and white TV picture tubes.

In allocating roles and responsibilities, management must distinguish clearly between the corporate headquarters of a worldwide company and the home country operations that also may be located at headquarters. Too many companies—particularly U.S.-based firms—tend to overlap or blur the roles. The home country operation should be treated no differently from the other national organizations—that is, it should be assigned the role it is best suited to play, not necessarily the leadership role it has probably traditionally enjoyed.

For many worldwide companies, particularly those based in countries such as the United States or Japan, the home country national organization will legitimately play a leading role, because it controls many key corporate assets and capabilities, and the home market is strategically vital. However, if the home market is not important to the global strategy (the Netherlands market in Philips's consumer electronics business is an example), then corporate management must be prepared to assign the domestic operation a contributor or even an implementer role.

Managing the Differentiated Roles

Having assigned roles and responsibilities to the national organizations, corporate management has to coordinate the complex, subtle system it has created. The nature of traditional organizations encouraged corporate management to apply the same methods of coordination and control throughout the company, using standard tools and techniques. Such an approach runs counter to the differentiated nature of the transnational, and corporate management must be prepared to develop a more flexible management process. This is the subject of Chapter 9.

In Chapter 7 we address the organizational capabilities that allow the transnational to respond to the third emerging strategic imperative—the ability to develop and diffuse innovations effectively worldwide. The value of differentiated subsidiary roles will become apparent.

7
FACILITATING LEARNING: MULTIPLE INNOVATION PROCESSES

Scholarly research has long identified innovation as an important reason for corporate internationalization. A firm invests abroad to derive further profit from innovations developed for the domestic market. Its market entrée in many countries is its ability to innovate (i.e., to develop new products and processes) and to create an organization through which it can appropriate the benefits of its innovations more advantageously than by selling or licensing its technology.[1]

In the current international environment, a company's ability to innovate is rapidly becoming *the* primary source of competitive success. Although worldwide companies once gained competitive advantage by exploiting global scale economies or arbitraging imperfections in the world's labor, materials, or capital markets, such advantages have eroded over time. In most industries today, worldwide companies no longer compete primarily with smaller national companies, but with a handful of other giants, comparable in size and geographic diversity. To survive, a company must have achieved global scale, international resource access, and worldwide market position; to emerge as a competitive leader, however, requires much more. The new winners are the companies that are sensitive to market or technological trends no matter where they occur, creatively responsive to worldwide opportunities and threats, and able to exploit their new ideas and products globally in a rapid and efficient manner. Companies that are insensitive, unresponsive, or slow are falling victim to the rising costs of R&D, the narrowing technology gap between countries and companies, and the shortening of product life cycles.

MANAGING INNOVATIONS IN WORLDWIDE COMPANIES

These new global competitive realities have forced companies to find new ways of creating innovations. Traditionally, there were two classic worldwide innovation processes. In the *central innovation process*, a new opportunity was sensed in the home country; the centralized resources of the parent company were used to create a new product or process; and it was exploited worldwide. Alternatively, in the *local innovation process*, national subsidiaries used their own resources and capabilities to create innovations that responded to the needs of the local environments. While most worldwide companies have tried to develop elements of both processes, one or the other usually becomes dominant in a particular organization. Quite naturally, the central process has been dominant in global companies with centralized hub structures, while local innovations have been common in multinational companies with their decentralized federation organizations.

These innovation processes also reflect the traditional mentalities of the two types of companies. The central process is usually associated with the global mentality, which sees the diversity of international environments as an inconvenience whose effects must be minimized. Thus, these organizations modify their central innovations only reluctantly, to meet specific needs. The local innovation process, on the other hand, reflects a multinational mentality, which sees conformity to local needs as the unavoidable price of admission to the market.[2]

Management attitudes have been changing in recent years. In documenting innovation cases in our nine core companies, we saw that successful firms are developing and managing different ways of creating new products, technologies, and even administrative systems. These *transnational innovation* processes fall into two broad categories, which we have labeled locally leveraged and globally linked. The first capitalizes on the resources and entrepreneurship of individual national subsidiaries but leverages them to create innovations for exploitation on a worldwide basis. The second links the resources and capabilities of diverse worldwide units in the company, at both headquarters and subsidiary level, to create and implement innovations on a joint basis. In this process, each unit contributes its unique resources to develop a corporatewide response to a worldwide opportunity.

While transnational innovations are becoming increasingly important, they are not substitutes for the traditional processes. In a competitive environment companies are recognizing the need to develop innovative products and processes in every possible way. The challenge is to develop an organization that can facilitate all processes simultaneously.

Central Innovations: Risk of Market Insensitivity

Central innovations are born of the fact that key capabilities of the worldwide company must remain at the headquarters, to both protect core competencies of the company and achieve economies of specialization and scale in R&D. NEC's development of the NEAC 61 digital switch is a good example of central innovations. The company's experience with its development helped it recognize the limitations of this process and adapt it in future product development for overseas markets.

The Japanese manager in charge of NEC's U.S. subsidiary sensed the possibility of a swing to digital technology as early as 1976, when TRW demonstrated a small digital switch to a group of enthusiastic customers. While he recognized the importance of this early warning signal and passed on the information to headquarters, corporate technical managers were wary about a supposed trend to digitalization that they saw nowhere else. They were skeptical about the claims of digital's technological superiority, and hesitant to begin development work on a new switch that would compete with NEC's existing electromechanical and electronic products.

When the U.S. managers were finally able to elicit sufficient support, the new NEAC 61 digital switch was developed almost entirely by headquarters personnel and the work was carried out fully within Japan. Even in deciding which features to design into the new product, the central engineering group tended to discount the requests of the subsidiary managers and relied instead on data gathered in its own staff's field trips to U.S. customers.

The need to centralize the development process was driven by three main forces. First, management wanted to maintain control over a technology that would be at the core of the company's long-term competitiveness. Second, the effort required close integration between hardware and software development, and subsequently between the development and manufacturing functions. Third, NEC knew it had to develop its new switch quickly to meet market demands; tenders were beginning to specify digital capabilities.

The major risks of the centralized development process are that the resulting innovations may be insensitive to market needs and may be difficult to implement if the subsidiaries resist a centrally developed product. For example, the NEAC 61 switch of NEC was generally acclaimed for the capabilities of its hardware but early sales fell below the company's expectations because the product did not meet some of the key requirements of the American operating companies.

Almost all the shortcomings of the switch could be ascribed to its designers' limited knowledge of the needs of American customers. For example, the software did not have appropriate facilities for allocating revenues among multiple operators that could be involved in routing a single long-distance call in the United States. The Japanese designers were used to a single government-owned company (NTT) handling all long-distance calls. Another limitation of the switch was the absence of what are called "revenue generating features." U.S. operating companies, particularly the small ones, depend on hardware suppliers to provide features in the switch that allow them to extend new and billable services to their customers. These features generate additional revenues for the operators and tend to have a significant influence on the acceptability of a switch in the U.S. market. Once again, the Japanese designers of the switch were handicapped because of their limited knowledge of the American customers, whose needs were very different from those of the Japanese operating company.

Local Innovations: Risk of Needless Differentiation

Local innovations are essential to meet the needs of the various national environments in which the worldwide company operates. As we have emphasized, the current fascination with globalization of markets downplays the continuing need for responsiveness to local differences.

For example, Unilever faces numerous pressures to develop globally standardized products. The cost and sophistication of R&D are increasing, economies of globally integrated operations are available, and competitive battles with major rivals like P&G are forcing global responses. However, Unilever's ability to respond in innovative ways to local opportunities has been a major corporate asset. For example, its advanced laundry detergents did not sell well in huge markets such as India, where much of the laundry was done in streams, so the local unit developed synthetic detergents in solid tablet form, enabling the company to capture much of the bar soap market. Similarly, in Turkey, where Unilever's margarine products did not sell well, the national company developed a product from local vegetable oils that competed with the traditional local clarified butter product, ghee.

Not all local-for-local innovations are as clearly justifiable, however. In Philips, for example, the British subsidiary spent substantial resources to create a new TV chassis especially suitable for the local market. The final product was almost indistinguishable from the standard European chassis that headquarters managers were trying to introduce, and the company had to operate five instead of four television set factories in Europe. While the managers in the national organization may have retained their identity and autonomy, the additional facility clearly compromised Philips's overall efficiency and competitiveness—a fact that was explicitly recognized by the closure of the facility in 1988.

Locally Leveraged Innovations: NIH Risk

Locally leveraged innovations permit management to use the most creative resources and developments of its subsidiaries worldwide, to benefit the whole company. In this way a company can often take the responses to market trends emerging in one location and use them to lead similar trends elsewhere. This kind of innovation requires management to develop and control the worldwide learning process, but it also allows the company to leverage its global innovative resources.

For example, Procter & Gamble created the fabric softener product category with a brand called Downy in the United States and Lenor in Europe. Unilever soon entered this fast-growing segment, but after years of effort its Comfort brand had done little to displace P&G's dominant position. Then, Unilever's German subsidiary developed a new brand with a product position and marketing strategy that proved enormously successful in gaining share rapidly. Management soon recognized that the reason for the success of Kuschelweich ("cuddles" in German) was the product's teddy bear symbol. Consumer research showed that the bear not only communicated the desired image of softness, but also evoked strong recognition and trusting associations among consumers. The German brand and the product market strategy were successfully transferred to other markets around the world, becoming Cajoline in France, Coccolino in Italy, Mimosin in Spain, and Huggy in Australia. So successful was the product and the cumulative learning that accompanied its worldwide transfer that when Unilever introduced it as Snuggle in the United States in the mid-1980s, the company tripled its market share in the softener category.

Yet local innovations are not always transferred so easily. Sometimes the new environment is not suited to a particular product or process; appropriate coordinating and transfer mechanisms may be lacking (a particular problem with technology transfer), and the Not-Invented-Here (NIH) syndrome may present problems.[3]

Despite the outstanding success of its fabric softener worldwide, Unilever management was unable to transfer a zero-phosphate detergent product developed by its German subsidiary to other European subsidiaries. Insisting that its market needs were different, the French subsidiary proceeded with its own zero-phosphate project. Product coordination managers at the central office believed that a NIH attitude was also an important factor in the French decision. This attitude particularly flourishes in an environment where national companies struggle to maintain their local R&D budgets against central pressures for more coordination.

Globally Linked Innovation: Coordination Cost

The globally linked innovation process is the one best suited to an environment in which the stimulus for an innovation is distant from the company's response capability, or several organizational units can contribute to developing the most innovative response to a sensed opportunity. By creating flexible linkages that allow the efforts of multiple units to be combined, a company can create synergies that significantly leverage its innovation process. Like locally leveraged innovations, the globally linked process captures the worldwide company's potential scope economies and harnesses the benefits of worldwide learning.

A good example of this mode of innovation was Procter & Gamble's development of its global liquid detergent. When Unilever's U.S. success with Wisk demonstrated the potential of the heavy-duty liquid detergent category, P&G and Colgate rushed to the market with competitive products (Era and Dynamo, respectively), but with limited success. All three companies tested their products in Europe, but because of different laundry practices and the superior performance of European powder detergents, which contained levels of enzymes, bleach, and phosphates not permitted in the United States, the new liquids failed every test.

P&G's European scientists were convinced they could enhance the performance of the liquid to match the local powders. After seven years' R&D they developed a bleach substitute, a fatty acid with water-softening capabilities equivalent to phosphate, and a means to give enzymes stability in liquid form. The new product beat the leading powder in blind tests, and the product was launched as Vizir, establishing the heavy-duty liquid segment in Europe.[4]

Meanwhile, researchers in the United States had been working on a new liquid to replace Era, which had not established a satisfactory share against Wisk. They worked on improving builders, the ingredients that prevent redisposition of dirt in the wash. During the same period, the company's International Technology Coordination group worked with P&G's subsidiary in Japan to develop a more robust surfactant (the ingredient that removes greasy stain), making the liquid more effective in the cold water washes that were common in Japan. Each unit had developed effective responses to its local needs, yet they were not sharing their breakthroughs.

When the company's head of R&D for Europe was promoted to the top corporate research job, one of his primary objectives was to develop more coordination and cooperation among the local development efforts. The world liquid detergent project became a test case. Plans to launch Omni, the new liquid the U.S. group had been working on, were shelved until the innovations from Europe and Japan could be incorporated in it. The Japanese and Europeans picked up on the new developments from the other laboratories. The result was the launch of Liquid Tide in the United States, a brand that was able to challenge market leader, Wisk, followed by the successful launch of Liquid Cheer in Japan and Liquid Ariel in Europe. All three products incorporated the best of the developments created in response to European, American, and Japanese needs.

But this process also has its limitations. It requires an expensive, potentially wasteful degree of internal coordination. The complex organizational links necessary to facilitate the process can create problems of ambiguity and excessive diffusion of authority. One company we studied estimated that a new system of periodic meetings— supposed to encourage integration of its European production plants— required company managers to spend 2,581 person-days in one year to attend the meetings.

Similarly, as we described in Chapter 2, ITT faced enormous problems in attempting to develop its System 12 digital telecommunications switch through a collaborative effort of its European subsidiaries. Coordinating the efforts of the units responsible for developing components of the switch proved to be extremely time-consuming and costly, and led to delays and budget overruns. Indeed, the inability to manage a globally linked innovation contributed to the failure that led to the company's exit from this core business.

The Management Challenge

Managers of worldwide companies must, at the same time, enhance the effectiveness of central innovations, improve the efficiency of local innovations, and create conditions that facilitate the newer forms of transnational innovations. To do so, companies need to overcome two related problems. First, they must avoid the particular pathologies of each innovation process. Second, to develop innovations simultaneously, they must overcome the contradictions among the organizational factors that facilitate the processes.

None of the companies in our sample had solved both problems fully. Some, however, had developed special competencies in managing one or another of the innovation processes and in overcoming the associated pathologies. A few companies had also made some progress in overcoming the inherent contradictions among the organizational processes. Differentiation of subsidiary roles and responsibilities appears to lie at the core of the solution. Instead of expecting each unit to contribute equally to all processes, these companies were creating an internally differentiated organization, so that each unit could participate in the innovation process to which it could make the greatest contribution.

MAKING CENTRAL INNOVATIONS EFFECTIVE: LESSONS FROM MATSUSHITA

The key strength on which Matsushita Electric Company has built the global leadership position of its well-known Panasonic and National brands is its ability to create central innovations and to exploit them quickly and efficiently throughout its worldwide operations. It also employs other modes of innovation, but, of all the companies we surveyed, Matsushita is the champion manager of central innovations. Three organizational mechanisms stood out as particularly important to its success: gaining the input of subsidiaries into the process, ensuring development efforts are linked to market needs, and managing responsibility transfers from development to manufacturing to marketing.

Gaining Subsidiary Input: Multiple Linkages

The two most important problems facing a company that innovates centrally are that those who develop the new product or process may not understand market needs, and that those who must implement the new product introduction are not committed to it. Matsushita managers are very conscious of the problems and spend a great deal of time building multiple linkages between headquarters and overseas subsidiaries, not only to help headquarters managers understand country-level needs and opportunities, but also to give subsidiary managers greater access to headquarters product development processes.

Matsushita recognizes the importance of market sensing as a stimulus to innovation. Rather than limit linkages between headquarters and subsidiaries or channel them through a single point, as many companies do for the sake of efficiency, Matsushita tries to preserve the perspectives, priorities, and even prejudices of its worldwide groups, and ensure that they are in touch with those in the headquarters who can represent and defend their views.

For example, multiple links connect different parts of the Matsushita organization in Japan with the video department of MECA, the U.S. subsidiary of the company. The senior vice president in charge of MECA's video department has his roots in Matsushita Electric Trading Company (METC), the organization responsible for Matsushita's overseas business. Although formally posted to the United States, he continues as a member of the senior management committee of METC and spends about a third of his time in Japan. This arrangement allows him to be a full member of the top management team of METC, which sets product strategy for the U.S. market, including priorities for new product development. As a senior executive in MECA, he ensures that the local operation implements the agreed-on video strategy effectively.

The general manager of the department is a company veteran who has spent 14 years in the video product division of the corporate headquarters of Matsushita Electric, the production and domestic marketing company in Japan. He maintains strong connections with the central product division and acts as its link to the local American market. The assistant manager in the department, who spent five years in the central factory in Japan, acts as its local representative and handles all day-to-day communication with factory personnel.

These links, deliberately created and maintained, reflect an awareness that the parent company is not a homogeneous entity, but a collective of constituencies and interests. The multiple linkages enhance the subsidiary's ability to influence key headquarters decisions relating to its market, particularly decisions about product specifications and design. At the same time, headquarters managers use the links to coordinate and control implementation of strategies and plans, including those for exploiting innovations.

Linking Development to Needs: Market Mechanisms

Matsushita has created an integrative process that exposes researchers and technologists to the pressures and constraints felt by front-line managers. A key element in this difficult organizational task is the company's willingness to employ internal "market mechanisms" for overseeing the activities of central researchers and development engineers.

Research projects undertaken by the central research laboratories (CRL) of Matsushita fall into two broad groups. The first consists of "company total projects," which develop technologies important for Matsushita's long-term strategic position and possibly applicable across many product divisions. Such projects are decided upon jointly by the research laboratories, the product divisions, and top management, and are funded directly by the corporate board. The second group consists of smaller projects relevant to particular product divisions. The budget for such activities, approximately half of the company's total research budget, is allocated to the product divisions. Each year the product divisions suggest a set of research projects that they would like to sponsor. At the same time, the various research laboratories hold annual exhibitions and meetings and write specific proposals to highlight research projects they would like to undertake. The engineering and development groups of the product divisions mediate the subsequent negotiation process through which the expertise and interests of the laboratories and the needs of the product divisions are finally matched. Specific projects are sponsored by the divisions and are allocated to the laboratories or research groups of their choice, along with requisite funds and other resources.

The system creates intense competition for projects (and the budgets that go with them) among the research groups, forcing researchers to maintain a close market orientation. At the same time, because the product divisions know they are paying for the product development effort, they are less inclined to make unreasonable or uneconomical demands on R&D.[5]

The market mechanism is also used to determine annual product styling and features. Each year the company holds merchandising meetings, which are in effect giant internal trade shows. Senior marketing managers from Matsushita's sales companies worldwide visit their supplying divisions and see the proposed product line for the new model year. Relying on their sense of their own markets, the managers pick and choose among proposed models, order modifications for their local markets, or simply refuse to take products they feel are unsuitable. Individual products or even entire lines might be redesigned as a result of input from the hundreds of managers at the merchandising meeting.

Managing Responsibility Transfer: Personnel Flows

In local innovations, it is relatively easy to transfer responsibility from research to manufacturing and finally to marketing, because of the smaller size and closer proximity of the units responsible for each activity. Problems arise when large central units take the lead role in the development of new products and processes. For example, Philips developed the V2000 video cassette recorder in its central research laboratory in Holland and faced enormous difficulties and delays while transferring the design to the production center in Belgium.

Matsushita has evolved some creative means for managing these transitions, relying heavily on the transfer of people. First, careers of research engineers are structured to ensure that most of them spend five to eight years in central R&D engaged in pure research, then another five years in the product divisions in applied research and development, and finally, in a direct operational function, usually production, where they take up line management positions for the rest of their working lives.[6] More important, each engineer usually makes the transition from one department to the next when the major project on which he has been working is transferred.

In many companies engineers move from research to development, but not at the same time as their projects. We saw no other examples of engineers routinely taking the next step, actually moving to the production function. This last step, however, is perhaps the most critical in integrating research and production: building a network that connects managers across functions and transferring common values that facilitate implementation of central innovations.

Another mechanism that integrates production and research at Matsushita works in the opposite direction. Wherever possible, the company identifies the manager who will head the production task for a product under development and makes him a full-time member of the research team early in the development process. This system not only injects direct production expertise into the development team, but facilitates transfer of the innovation once the design is complete.

Matsushita also uses this mechanism as a way of transferring product expertise from headquarters to its worldwide sales subsidiaries. A common practice among many worldwide companies, it carries additional significance in Matsushita because of the importance of internationalizing management as well as products.

MAKING LOCAL INNOVATIONS EFFICIENT: LESSONS FROM PHILIPS

If Matsushita is the champion manager of central innovation, Philips, its archrival in the consumer electronics business, is the master of local innovations. Of course, Philips has been extremely successful at central innovations too. Its central research laboratories have developed a long list of products and processes, from light bulbs to laser disk technology. Equally impressive, however, has been its ability to foster a process of innovation at the national organization level unmatched by any other company of comparable size, diversity, and maturity.

The first Philips color TV set was produced and sold in Canada, where the market had closely followed the U.S. lead in introducing color transmission. The K6 chassis used in those sets was designed in the central research laboratory in Holland, but the Canadian subsidiary played a major role in the development process and had an even greater input in designing the production system. Philips's first stereo color TV set was developed by the Australian subsidiary; teletext TV sets by its British subsidiary; "smart cards" by its French subsidiary; and a programmed word processing typewriter by North American Philips. The list of local innovations in Philips is endless.

Philips's ability to create such local innovations reflects both the company's administrative heritage and an explicit strategic choice to respond to local market needs. Over time, the company has accumulated substantial resources in its national organizations, which, in conjunction with decentralization of authority, has made dispersed entrepreneurship a key organizational asset. The most significant factors facilitating local innovations in Philips appear to have been the company's ability to empower local management in the different national organizations, to establish effective mechanisms for linking the local managers to corporate decision-making processes, and to force tight functional integration within each subsidiary.[7]

Empowering Local Management

Perhaps the most important factor supporting local innovations in Philips is the dispersal of its organizational assets and resources, and the decentralization of authority, which jointly empower local management to experiment and to seek novel solutions to local problems.

As we have described in Chapter 3, the decentralized organizational structure and dispersed resources in Philips are the outcomes of a historical process and have deep roots in the company's management philosophy. Since it was founded in 1891, Philips has recognized the need to expand its operations beyond its small domestic market, but the successive barriers—poor transport and communication linkages in the early decades of the century, protectionist pressures in the 1930s, and the disruption of World War II—encouraged the company to build national organizations with an unusual degree of autonomy and self-sufficiency. As manifest from our description in Chapter 6 of how the British subsidiary of the company created the teletext set, such dispersed managerial and technological resources coupled with local autonomy and decentralized control over the resources have enabled subsidiary managers to risk the trial and error involved in creating local innovations.

Linkages to Corporate Decision-Making Processes

While local resources and autonomy have made it feasible for subsidiary managers in Philips to pursue their own innovative ideas, linkages to corporate decision-making processes have given them the legitimacy that motivates such pursuit. In the following chapter we shall describe in greater detail why such legitimacy and access are necessary to build motivation, and how they can be developed within a worldwide organization. In Philips, a cadre of entrepreneurial expatriates has played a key role in developing and maintaining such linkages.

Expatriate positions, particularly in the larger subsidiaries, have been very attractive for Philips managers. Many of the national subsidiaries contribute much larger shares of the company's total revenues than the parent company (only 6 to 8 percent of total sales come from Holland). As a result, foreign operations have enjoyed higher organizational status than in most large worldwide companies. Furthermore, Philips's formal management development system has always required considerable international experience as a prerequisite for top corporate positions. Finally, the corporate headquarters are located in a small town in a rural setting. After living in London, New York, Sydney, or Paris, many managers find it hard to return to Eindhoven.

As a result the best and the brightest of Philips managers spend most of their careers in national operations, working for two to four years in a series of subsidiaries. In Matsushita or NEC, by contrast, an expatriate manager spends five to ten years in a particular national subsidiary and then returns to headquarters. This difference in the career systems has an important influence on managerial attitudes. In Philips, the expatriate managers develop close relations among themselves. They tend to identify strongly with the national organizations' point of view, and the shared identity creates a distinct subculture within the company. In companies such as Matsushita, on the other hand, there is very little interaction among the expatriate managers, and they tend to regard themselves as parent company executives temporarily on assignment in a foreign company.

Expatriate managers in Matsushita are far more likely to take a custodial approach that resists making local changes in standard products and policies, while expatriate managers in Philips are much more willing to advocate local views.[8] Their willingness to rock the boat and their openness to experimentation and change are the characteristics that fuel local innovations.

Because Philips has created an attractive environment in the national organizations, it has little difficulty in recruiting very capable local management. Whereas local managers in many Japanese companies often feel excluded from the decision-making process, local managers in Philips know their ideas are listened to and defended at headquarters.[9] This too creates a supportive environment for local innovations.

Integration of Technical and Marketing Functions within Each Subsidiary

Historically, Philips's national subsidiaries have not been headed by an individual CEO but by a committee made up of the heads of the technical, commercial, and finance functions. This three-headed management system had a long history in the company, stemming from the functional independence of the two Philips brothers, one an engineer and the other a salesman.

This management philosophy has recently been modified to a system that emphasizes individual authority and accountability, and almost all national organizations are now headed by a single general manager. But the long tradition of shared responsibilities and joint decision making has left the subsidiaries with many mechanisms for functional integration at multiple levels. These integrative mechanisms enhance the efficiency of local innovations in Philips, just as various means of cross-functional integration within the corporate headquarters facilitate central innovations in Matsushita.[10]

Most Philips subsidiaries employ integration mechanisms at three organizational levels. First, for each project, there is what Philips calls an article team consisting of relatively junior managers from the commercial and technical functions. It is the responsibility of this team to evolve product policies and to prepare annual sales plans and budgets. Subarticle teams may be formed to supervise day-to-day activities and to carry out special projects, such as preparing capital investment plans, if it seems major new investments are needed to manufacture and market a new product effectively.

At the product-group level cross-functional coordination is accomplished through the group management team. This team, including technical and commercial representatives, meets once a month to review results, suggest corrective actions, and resolve any interfunctional differences. Keeping control and conflict resolution at this low level facilitates sensitive and rapid responses to initiatives and ideas generated at the local level.

The highest-level coordination forum within the subsidiary is the senior management committee (SMC), consisting of the top commercial, technical, and financial managers in the subsidiary. Acting essentially as a local board, the SMC coordinates effort among the functional groups and ensures that the national operation retains primary responsibility for its own strategies and priorities. Again, local management has a forum where actions can be decided upon and issues resolved without escalation for approval or arbitration.

ENCOURAGING TRANSNATIONAL INNOVATIONS: LESSONS FROM ERICSSON, P&G, AND NEC

Innovations are created by applying resources to exploit an opportunity, or to overcome a threat. In worldwide companies, however, the opportunity (or threat) and the resources are often in different locations. Transnational innovation processes use linkages among dispersed units of the organization to leverage existing resources and capabilities, irrespective of location, to exploit any new opportunity that arises anywhere in the company.

Several of the companies we studied were developing such organizational capabilities. A few appeared to have become quite effective in managing the required linkages and processes. We identified three organizational characteristics that seemed most helpful in facilitating the new integrated innovation processes: an interdependence of resources and responsibilities among organizational units; strong cross-unit integrating devices; and a management attitude of strong corporate identification and well-developed worldwide perspectives.

Interdependence of Resources and Responsibilities

Perhaps the most important requirement for facilitating transnational innovations is that the organizational configuration be based on a principle of reciprocal dependence among units. Such an interdependence of resources and responsibilities breaks down the hierarchy between local and global interests by making the sharing of resources, ideas, and opportunities a self-enforcing norm.

In most companies, as we described in Chapter 5, relationships between the headquarters and the national subsidiaries are based on either dependence or independence. At Kao, for instance, these relationships have historically been based primarily on subsidiary dependence on the headquarters. Kao's national subsidiaries had neither the competence nor the legitimacy to initiate new programs or even to modify products or administrative systems developed by the parent company.

For example, believing that the traditional shampoo powder used in Thailand was a primitive product, the company launched one of its brands of liquid shampoo in that country. Four years after its introduction, the new brand had not met its market share goals. Although well suited to the sophisticated needs of the Japanese market, the product could not compete effectively with simpler but less expensive local products; it developed only a marginal 7 percent market share despite large marketing investments. Remedial measures were taken only after marketing experts from the headquarters along with executives from Dentsu, Kao's Japanese advertising agents, visited the subsidiary. The local manager acknowledged that "Japan's expertise, knowledge, and resources made it appropriate for them to make such decisions." In companies where subsidiaries had developed such highly dependent relationships with the headquarters, the central innovation process was often the exclusive source of new products and ideas. For example, we did not see a single case of any other innovation process in Kao.

In other companies, such as ITT, the subsidiaries enjoyed high levels of strategic and operational autonomy, though headquarters exercised administrative control through the budgeting and financial reporting systems. In these companies, local innovations dominated, and the independence of natural subsidiaries from headquarters control made collaborative efforts difficult.

Transnational innovation processes, in contrast, require joint involvement of a number of organizational units, including headquarters. Such joint efforts appeared to materialize and be effective only when the units were linked through relationships based on mutual interdependence, rather than on either one-way dependence or independence. Mutual interdependence is hard to build, but some companies, such as NEC, Procter & Gamble, and Ericsson, appeared to have developed such relationships, both between headquarters and the subsidiaries, and among the subsidiaries themselves. In essence, they made integration and collaboration self-enforcing by requiring each group to cooperate in order to achieve its own interests.

In Chapter 5, we described the emergence of Euro Teams in Procter

& Gamble. The company subsequently institutionalized the process as a fundamental product management tool for its European operations. It formed a number of Euro Brand Teams to develop product market strategies for various product lines. The subsidiary general manager nominally responsible for each team knew that he could expect more support from his team members if product managers from his subsidiary cooperated with other teams. The ability of the teams to foster cooperation through interdependence was dramatically demonstrated when the first Euro Brand Team developed a successful Europewide marketing launch for a new and revolutionary heavy-duty liquid detergent called Vizir, which paved the way for truly transnational innovations such as the world liquid detergent project described earlier in this chapter.

NEC, on the other hand, developed cooperation by building genuine specialization and complementarity of resources among different parts of the organization. As we described earlier, the company's first digital switch, the NEAC 61, failed in the market, despite the excellence of its hardware, because of software limitations. Learning from the experience, NEC subsequently built up significant software capabilities in the U.S. subsidiary, while hardware development remained centralized at the headquarters.

This approach has many advantages. It allowed NEC to tap into the rich pool of telecommunications software expertise available in the United States. It also led to the creation of explicit interdependencies between the central development groups in Japan and the U.S. subsidiary. As a result, the company's product development process moved from the classical central approach to a much closer approximation of the transnational model. The dependence of headquarters on the subsidiary for software design and support made the central hardware groups far more receptive to subsidiary ideas about hardware. The subsidiary, in turn, was sensitized to the need to make its software designs more robust and transferable.

The advantages of the new climate of cooperation showed up in the company's new digital adjunct switch, the NEAC 61E. Much greater involvement of the subsidiary in the development of the switch made it more responsive to market needs, and it has chalked up some significant successes in key world markets.

There are many other ways in which a company can build interdependencies among its units and create a self-reinforcing environment of cooperation. The internal market mechanism developed by Matsushita (described earlier in this chapter) is a distinctly different means of achieving the same objectives, and NEC uses a similar process for forging closer links between its R&D and operating departments. The appropriate tool will vary from company to company; what matters is that the company find some way to link and leverage its existing capabilities. In this process, building mutual interdependency is often a vital ingredient.

Interunit Integrating Devices

Central innovations require strong integrating mechanisms at headquarters, and local innovations are facilitated by coordinative capabilities within national units. Transnational innovation processes need a different kind of integration process—one that operates across units. Ericsson's experience provides some insight into how such a process can be achieved.

Unlike ITT, where the relationship among national companies was often competitive and headquarters-subsidiary interactions were often adversarial, Ericsson has been able to foster a more cooperative and collaborative organizational climate. Ericsson's success in interunit integration depends primarily on three factors: clearly defined and tightly controlled operating systems, a people-linking process employing such devices as temporary assignments and joint teams, and interunit forums, particularly subsidiary boards, where views can be exchanged and differences resolved.

Ericsson management believes that its most effective integrating device is strong central control over key elements of its strategic operation. Unlike ITT, Ericsson has not had sophisticated administrative systems (it introduced strategic plans only in 1983), but its operating systems have been carefully developed. For example, AXE's product specifications are tightly controlled, and the company's highly sophisticated CAD/CAM systems allow close central coordination of manufacturing. Management argues that these strong operating systems do not cause centralization of decision making, but encourage delegation, since the center can be confident that local decisions will be consistent with the overall interests.

Interunit cooperation also requires good interpersonal relations, which Ericsson has developed through a long-standing policy of transferring personnel back and forth between headquarters and subsidiaries.[11] Whereas NEC may transfer a new technology through a few key managers, Ericsson will send a team of 50 or 100 engineers and managers for a year or two; NEC's flow is primarily from headquarters to subsidiary, but Ericsson's is a balanced two-way flow, and while NEC's transfers are predominantly Japanese, Ericsson's multidirectional process involves all nationalities. The Australian technicians sent to Stockholm during the AXE development effort formed enduring relationships that helped in the joint development of a rural switch in Australia a decade later. Similarly, when an Italian team of forty spent eighteen months in Sweden learning about electronic switching, the groundwork was laid for greater decentralization of AXE software development and a delegated responsibility for developing transmission systems in the Italian company.

Any organization in which there are shared tasks and joint responsibilities requires additional decision-making and conflict-resolution forums. In Ericsson, differences between parent and subsidiary are often debated in the national unit's board meetings. Whereas many worldwide companies' local boards are pro forma bodies, designed solely to satisfy national legal requirements, Ericsson's local boards are legitimate forums for communicating objectives, resolving differences, and making decisions. At least one and often several senior corporate managers sit on each board, and subsidiary board meetings are an important means for coordinating activities and channeling local ideas and innovations across national lines.

National Competence, Worldwide Perspective

As ITT's development of its System 12 shows clearly, a company cannot create transnational innovations if its managers identify primarily with local parochial interests and objectives. Such innovation is equally difficult, NEC's experience shows, when management is unable to defend national perspectives and respond to local opportunities. One of Ericsson's most important organizational strengths is a management attitude that is both locally sensitive and globally conscious.

At the Stockholm headquarters, managers emphasize the importance of developing strong country organizations, not only to capture sales that require responsiveness to national needs, but also to tap into the resources that are available through worldwide operation. Ericsson is very conscious of the need to develop skills and capture ideas wherever they are. At the same time, local managers see themselves as part of the worldwide Ericsson group rather than as independent autonomous units. Constant transfers and frequent assignment on joint headquarters-subsidiary teams help broaden managers' perspectives from local to global, while the allocation of worldwide product responsibilities to national firms confirms their identity with the company's global operations.

MANAGING INNOVATIONS IN THE TRANSNATIONAL

As we noted earlier, the challenge of managing innovations in worldwide organizations is twofold: first, management must enhance the efficiency and effectiveness of each innovation process; second, it must create conditions that allow innovations to come about through all processes *simultaneously*. The second task often proves more difficult, because organizational attributes that facilitate one innovation process often impede the others.

The Organizational Dilemma

Quite different organizational attributes are required to facilitate local and central innovations. The former process requires that national subsidiaries have the necessary resources and the autonomy to deploy them. But independent and resource-rich subsidiaries tend to become victims of what Rosabeth Kanter calls the "entrepreneurial trap"—a mentality in which "the need to be the source, the originator leads people to push their own ideas single-mindedly."[12] As companies like Philips have found, this mentality impedes the subsidiary's ability and willingness to adopt central innovations. On the other hand, both creation and worldwide adoption of central innovations can be facilitated by centralizing resources and maintaining tight central control over the operations of national subsidiaries. Such an organizational arrangement, however, creates the reverse problem: perceived or actual scarcity of spare resources and local authority in the national subsidiaries lead to efficient adoption of central innovations, but constrain the company's ability to facilitate local innovations due to sheer incapability or lack of motivation on the part of local managers.

Overcoming the Dilemma Through Differentiation and Integration

The most transnational of the companies we studied had been relatively successful in overcoming this dilemma. They had recognized that national organizations are not all equally capable of handling each innovation process.

Innovation requires both external stimuli and internal response capabilities. Subsidiaries differ widely in both respects. These differences imply significant differences in the contributions that subsidiaries can potentially make to the innovation processes we have described. Thus, instead of choosing either to facilitate local innovation or to adopt central ideas in all subsidiaries (or worse, seeking to find the nonexistent grand compromise between the two), the successful companies allocate different innovative roles to various units of the company. In fact, this resolution of the organizational dilemma—facilitating all the innovation processes simultaneously—is one of the primary logics behind the differentiated network organization we described in Chapter 6.

Subsidiaries with the strategic leader role are the transnational company's innovative spark plugs. Many of the local innovations they create are subsequently diffused throughout the organization as new technologies, tastes, or business practices spread from their advanced markets to the rest of the world. The teletext TV innovated by the British subsidiary of Philips is a case in point.

The subsidiaries assigned an implementer role lie at the other end of the spectrum. Poor in environmental challenge and organizational capabilities, these units are not expected to create significant innovations from which the company as a whole can benefit, though they certainly should be able to represent the needs of their local market and make the necessary minor modifications to global products. Their major contribution is to adopt and implement central and global innovations efficiently.

Both contributor and black hole subsidiaries have some potential to advance the firm's global innovation processes, yet each suffers certain disabilities. The contributors have the resources but lack the exposure to stimulating environments; the black hole can be a vital sensor, but cannot itself respond because of limitations of resources and competencies.

Managing the Process

Clearly, it is far from easy to build and manage the diverse roles and simultaneous processes we have described. The company must develop an organization that prizes diverse perspectives and capabilities, and a management process in which diverse capabilities in widely dispersed locations can be flexibly linked and leveraged. In Section III, we will describe how such organizational capabilities and processes can be built and managed.

PART III
BUILDING AND MANAGING
THE TRANSNATIONAL

8
LEGITIMIZING DIVERSITY: BALANCING MULTIPLE PERSPECTIVES

In Part I, we described how companies developed strategic capabilities to respond to the dominant demands they faced at the time they internationalized their operations. Some became skilled at sensing and responding to national differences; others built cost advantages through global-scale operations; still others developed an ability to exploit the parent company's special knowledge and capabilities by diffusing and adapting them worldwide.

Managing each type of strategic capability required a distinct kind of organization, and most companies evolved characteristic management biases that reinforced their primary competitive strength. Multinational companies needed strong *geographic management* to sense and respond to opportunities country by country; global companies typically had organizations in which *business management* was dominant and pushed for manufacturing rationalization, product standardization, and low-cost global sourcing; and in international companies, *functional management* usually was the catalyst and prime mover for spreading knowledge and skills throughout the company.

Changing environmental forces and industry characteristics are now forcing companies to broaden their international strategic focus, to recognize that competitive viability now requires global efficiency, multinational flexibility, and worldwide learning—all at the same time. As ITT, Kao, and General Electric have found, an inability to break down unidimensional organization biases can limit the development of transnational strategic capabilities.

In this chapter we focus on the implementation tasks facing companies as they try to overcome the organizational biases of their administrative heritage. In the first section, we will describe the obstacles in converting a unidimensional organization into a truly multidimensional one, isolating the key tasks in the process. Then we will detail how managers might deal with the three major challenges in building the new management perspectives and capabilities: ensuring their legitimacy, facilitating their access, and expanding their influence. Finally, we will provide some guidance on how to manage the conflicts inherent in such multidimensional organizations, drawing lessons from the companies in our study that manage this task most successfully.

OFFSETTING ORGANIZATIONAL BIASES

In many companies the development of transnational strategic capabilities is impeded by the ingrained power of the organization's dominant management group. ITT's telecommunications business, for example, was unable to offset the organizational dominance of its geographic managers, who had been so successful in responding to host country political demands for half a century. Kao was equally unsuccessful in counterbalancing the power of the functional management groups that had been the source of the company's highly successful technological, manufacturing, and marketing innovations. These companies' experiences illustrate the strategic, organizational, and interpersonal characteristics that represent the three most important challenges in overcoming organizational biases.

Strategic Barriers

An attempt to change management perspectives and capabilities will probably be perceived as threatening the responsibilities of the core group on which the company's success has depended. These managers may regard any challenge to their decision-making power or dilution of their resource support as a direct assault on the firm's distinctive strategic capability.[1]

In the postwar era, Kao gave priority first to building its technology (largely through an intensive overseas licensing program), then to developing its marketing sophistication (often by imitating its greatly admired counterpart, P&G), and most recently to increasing its manufacturing efficiency. As Kao became one of Japan's most innovative developers and marketers of branded packaged products, the size, sophistication, and power of the corporate functional groups also grew.

Due to the company's success in developing new innovative products and selling them into a very competitive Japanese market, the technical and marketing functions dominated Kao's management, and almost all of the company's top officers came from one of these functions. The international group played a secondary role, and an overseas posting was not regarded as a prestige assignment.

P&G's entry into the Japanese market in 1972 reinforced Kao's commitment to developing innovative new products and marketing them aggressively, and entrenched the power of these functional groups in the corporation. It successfully defended its positions in detergent and personal care products and directly challenged P&G in new categories such as disposable diapers. By the mid-1980s, the company devoted almost 5 percent of its revenues to research and development—two to four times the level of most competitors—and more than 20 percent of its employees were engaged in R&D.

The managers responsible for the company's foreign subsidiaries increasingly depended on the headquarters functional divisions for product development, marketing assistance, and manufacturing support. The overseas group adopted the role of selling the products and implementing the strategy developed at the center.

By the early 1980s, Kao's top management recognized that the lack of strong geographically oriented management was limiting the company's potential outside Japan, and initiated a localization program to counterbalance its strong domestic market bias. In 1983, it opened regional headquarters in Singapore, New York, and Düsseldorf. Simultaneously, a corporate-level development program was initiated to upgrade the skills and organizational status of overseas personnel and to internationalize the perspectives of managers at headquarters.

But the changes had a limited impact. The functional groups saw the new international thrust as a response to the need for greater globalization of competitive strategies, product technologies, and even brands. They read the localization program as a signal for them to become more directly and intensively involved in overseas operations. As a result, the regional headquarters quickly adopted the role of communications channel and operations overseer while national subsidiary managers continued to deal directly with headquarters on strategy and for support. Even in the late 1980s, the geographic dimension of the company's organization was still dominated by the strong functional groups, and the rate of Kao's overseas expansion remained disappointing.

ITT's telecommunications business had similar problems. The ability of its national systems houses to integrate themselves into their host country environments was the key to ITT's success in supplying equipment to government-owned post and telegraph services. As a result, the company's geographic managers enjoyed remarkable independence, even within the tight systems introduced by CEO Harold Geneen.

Emerging trends in electronic switching technology and in the digitalization of signaling led the director of the relatively small technology group at the parent company headquarters to set up its Advanced Technical Center (ATC) in 1977 to begin work on a new generation of digital electronic switches. Within two years the project had made sufficient progress to attract the attention of several of ITT's systems houses in Europe. Because the company's technological capability had historically been concentrated in these national companies, a team of 200 European engineers came to headquarters to work on the project, subsequently known as System 12.

As interest in digital switching grew, the strong country-based managers began urging top management to "get the development out of the hands of theoretical corporate researchers and back to the practical engineers close to the market." The chief technical officer, however, argued that the project should remain a corporatewide effort to ensure that a standard ITT switch would be developed.

Top management tried to build corporatewide technological capability by establishing the International Telecommunications Center (ITC) in Belgium and giving it overall development responsibility for the System 12. Although ITC's role was defined as linking activities across systems houses and coordinating development between Europe and the United States (ATC in the United States was made responsible to ITC), it soon became clear that ITC did not have sufficient internal resources, and would have to rely heavily on the established R&D units in the national systems houses to do most of the actual development work.

Developing pressures in national telecommunications markets soon led to the reassertion of the country general managers' power and the failure of the company's attempt to develop a counterbalancing integrated technical group. First, the national units in Britain and Austria opted out of the System 12 project, citing the incompatible switching specifications of their host country telecommunications authorities. Then, in 1982, ITT's French company was nationalized by the new socialist government. The national units in Belgium and Germany, the most technologically capable of the remaining systems houses, began promising their local customers that their needs would become the company's technological priority. Supported by country managers in Italy and Spain, these two powerful national companies pressured top management to return responsibility for technological development to the country level before ITT compromised the strong political relationships on which its business had been built.

The showdown came at a meeting in 1982, when the heads of several major systems houses challenged the right of ITC's director to assign development responsibilities and control the specifications for System 12. The president of ITT Europe backed the national units, explaining it was vital that the company protect its strong host-country relationships. By allowing the systems houses to proceed with their individual digital switch development, he essentially gutted ITC's for-

nal power. The organization remained one in which geographic managers dominated the decision-making process.

As these examples show, it is not easy to break the biases in management perspectives and organizational capabilities that have built a
strategic legitimacy over many decades. Efforts to encourage a greater
diversity of management views and organizational capabilities can
create disruptive interpersonal tensions and interdepartmental turf
battles.

In dealing with this problem management has two key tasks to
which we will return later in this chapter. The first is to build an
internal understanding of the need to broaden the base of the company's competitive capability, so that it can be simultaneously globally
competitive, multinationally flexible, and able to capture the benefits of
worldwide learning.

Management's second task is to recognize that organization development need not be a zero-sum game. It is possible—indeed imperative—for a company to build new management perspectives and capabilities without compromising or undermining the individuals and
groups that embody the company's existing skill and knowledge base.

Organizational Barriers

The fact that the historically dominant management group—the functional units in Kao and geographic managers in ITT—have line responsibility also represents a formidable barrier to the development of
counterbalancing management perspectives and capabilities. Furthermore, an organization's formal systems are normally structured to meet
the needs of the line organization. This makes it difficult for newly
established management groups to gain access to information in a form
that allows them to make appropriate analyses, or to have significant
influence on the planning or central processes.[2]

At Kao, the influence of the central functional groups was greatly
strengthened in the late 1970s, when a medium-term planning system
was introduced. Overseas subsidiaries were required to prepare three-
year plans, to be reviewed with headquarters functional managers at an
annual planning conference in Japan. In the early 1980s, the planning
system was supplemented with a program to build a sophisticated on-
line information system designed to "centralize and quickly analyze all
the varied and complicated information emanating from all its activities." The new computerized reporting and control systems linked
managers at the corporate headquarters directly with the data systems
of the overseas units, further institutionalizing the central groups'
dominance.

When top management tried to reinforce the area dimension of its organizational capability by creating regional headquarters, the new management group found it was unable to interject itself into the strong strategic relationship that had developed between headquarters and subsidiary managers. As a result, the regional group settled into a more operational role. Even here, however, its effectiveness was limited by the corporate headquarters' access to on-line, real-time financial and operating data, consolidated by function or task rather than by geographic area. The availability of such data encouraged headquarters marketing, technical, and manufacturing managers to bypass the regional offices and communicate directly with subsidiaries when their reports identified an operating problem or issue of importance.

At ITT also there were organizational impediments to the establishment of an integrated worldwide technological capability. More than in any other company we studied, formal line authority and responsibility were sacrosanct at ITT. Almost certainly, the country managers' appeal for the return of product development responsibility succeeded because they emphasized the national units' final accountability for the success of System 12 in the local market.

According to one of the company's top technical managers, ITT's well-known systems were designed not to centralize information or decision making, but to make explicit the plans and objectives of line managers, to measure performance against those plans, and to hold the managers accountable. He described the failure of the International Technology Center to retain control of System 12 development in these terms:

> Although ITC was assigned the task of developing System 12, we never had unambiguous management support. The systems houses not only controlled most of the technical assets and resources, they also had the organizational advantage of being held accountable for operating results. This meant that whenever they escalated issues or conflicts for top management resolution, the outcome was a foregone conclusion. The national units were accountable, and that meant they had the final word.

Overcoming organizational barriers is every bit as difficult as counterbalancing the strategic biases. The management tasks center on challenging the formal structure and adapting the formal systems. To challenge the formal structure, management must reinforce the power and influence of the newly developed management group so it is less vulnerable to veto by formal line authority. To adapt the formal systems, management must ensure that emerging perspectives and capabilities not only gain access to the information and communication channels, but also have legitimacy in relevant decision-making forums. These, too, are issues we will develop in the later part of this chapter.

Cultural Barriers

The most enduring barriers to change in many of the companies we studied were cultural. At Kao, ITT, and other companies more successful in legitimizing greater organizational diversity, the entrenched position of the dominant management group was buttressed by norms or beliefs that had become institutionalized as organizational verities. In Procter & Gamble, the sanctity of exhaustive product and market testing before a new launch protected and reinforced the power and influence of the company's strong marketing managers; in Unilever, the deeply ingrained commitment to the maximum delegation of responsibility helped maintain the dominant role of geographic managers while product coordination groups were trying to establish themselves at the corporate level.[3]

Ingrained management mentalities and established informal relationships also became major impediments to the establishment of new organizational perspectives and capabilities in many companies. In particular, because top managers are often products of their company's administrative heritage, they also become its captive. In the face of changing environmental demands and new competitive realities, the bias in senior executives' experience can constrain an organization's ability to perceive its problems and to overcome the strategic misfit.

At Kao, the dominance of the technical and marketing groups was institutionalized in the company's published credo, which described technology as "the very spring of corporate life." The corporate philosophy committed the company "to strive for the development of the world's highest level, unique technologies"; and, viewing marketing as the vital function to bring its innovations to the consumer, Kao aimed at "the perfection of the marketing technology."

The dominance of the two functional groups was perpetuated by the success of individuals with such experience. Kao's president and several other top officers had advanced through the organization along the much-traveled product development route. This pattern clearly signaled the qualifications required to succeed and tended to reinforce the informal influence of employees from similar backgrounds. Relationships the senior managers developed as they worked together on projects often endured and influenced their decisions as they moved up the organization.

Overcoming these people- and culture-based barriers to management diversity and organizational multidimensionality involves several management tasks. The first and most time-consuming is to modify the norms that are blocking the development of different legitimate views. When P&G found that its exhaustive prelaunch market-by-market testing was preventing timely worldwide rollouts of new products, it emphasized a "time-to-market" approach. This new emphasis softened the ingrained marketing verity that demanded extensive product and market tests, thereby allowing competitors to leapfrog P&G with imitations of its own brands. Unilever has also backed off from the almost religious fervor with which it applied its delegation philosophy, and now tries to assign responsibility to national companies within more clearly defined broad global policies and strategies. Kao has held formal education sessions for its corporate management to explain the importance of developing international capabilities and break down the assumption that overseas operations were mere appendages to the domestic organization.

The attitude of the top management team is vital in bringing about such change. We saw individuals who were able to transform the company's administrative heritage from a liability into an asset. Their understanding of the firm's historical strengths and values gave them the credibility to propose change, and the sensitivity to implement it in a way that protected the company's heritage. But the leadership challenge is great. Strength and persistence are required to bring about the development of new organizational perspectives that threaten entrenched power groups and ingrained values. And in some situations, it may be necessary to underscore the company's commitment to change by bringing in new management, particularly at the top levels of the company.

BUILDING NEW MANAGEMENT PERSPECTIVES AND CAPABILITIES

There are risks in any attempt to impose a new structure on an existing organization. Structural change is a blunt instrument that can have devastating effects on established organizational processes and managers' motivations if used improperly.

The challenge in building organizational diversity is to protect the company's existing knowledge base and competencies while establishing new management perspectives and capabilities. Among the companies we studied, Procter & Gamble provides one of the best examples of how to manage such an organizational change process. P&G understood that the transition process had to be undertaken in a logical sequence gradually. The first step is to provide the emergent group with *legitimacy* within the organization; next, *access* to the company's information resources and communication channels; and finally *influence* in the organization's key decision-making processes.

P&G to the Mid-1970s: Unidimensional Biases

Until the 1950s, P&G's organization was a simple functional structure, dominated by marketing and geared to selling soaps and detergents in the U.S. market. Overseas operations were a small part of the total business, concentrated in Canada and England. Over the next few decades, however, a strategy of product and geographic diversification, coupled with an increasingly complex operating environment, forced the company to make some drastic organizational changes.

In 1955, P&G structured its domestic organization around businesses, forming three operating divisions—still dominated by marketing—to manage the detergent, personal products, and food products operations. As the company began expanding internationally, particularly in the late 1950s and early 1960s, it built its overseas organization around geographic markets and made the country subsidiary the dominant unit in its management structure.

The overseas expansion was built on three major corporate assets: superior technologies, an innovative product development capability, and a world-famous marketing expertise. But management soon learned that consumer tastes and habits varied widely from one country to another and that it was a mistake to impose on foreign operations products or strategies developed in the United States. Subsidiary general managers gradually established the freedom to develop, modify, and promote products to best suit local consumer needs.

Even though the managers had final responsibility for their operations, tight central administrative systems tracked performance against budget, and major investment decisions were carefully reviewed by top management. Even more powerful was the pervasive influence of P&G's culture. While product market strategies varied widely among countries, the company way of doing things did not. Around the world P&G subsidiaries looked and acted like miniatures of the parent company, with organizations built on the foundation of brand management, and policies and practices—like a commitment to extensive market research and endless product testing—that were straight from the U.S. experience. But within the framework of doing things "the Procter way," local general managers had great freedom and control over their national strategies.

While the functional organization of the parent company had an indirect influence on the geographically dominated overseas operations, there was no strong group that integrated product or business strategies across national boundaries. In Cincinnati headquarters the international division consisted of a president and his accounting and personnel managers; small staff groups at the regional office in Brussels served mainly to consolidate information and provide support services for the European subsidiaries. Until the mid-1970s, therefore, the country managers were clearly the dominant group in P&G's international operations.

All this began to change with the oil shocks of 1973 and 1979. Their double impact—on raw materials costs and on consumer spending—caused most companies in the consumer chemicals industry to make major adjustments to their strategic approach and organizational assumptions. By the late 1970s, P&G faced a saturated and increasingly competitive market abroad, particularly in Europe, which caused some worrisome profitability problems. Yet, like ITT and Kao, P&G found its attempts to address the problems were severely constrained by organizational biases.

With costs rising much faster than revenues, the company could no longer afford to let product development be driven by the local interests of each national subsidiary. The lack of coordination was obviously quite inefficient and led to a great deal of duplicated and overlapping effort. Furthermore, the autonomy of local subsidiaries left the corporation competitively vulnerable in some respects. Each subsidiary could decide which products should be introduced into its markets, when they should be launched, and how they should be marketed. This market-by-market approach allowed competitors to copy successful P&G product concepts and marketing programs, and beat the company to market with them in countries where the P&G subsidiary was slow to react. As growth slowed and competition escalated, the need for a more coordinated product strategy was becoming increasingly urgent.

Building Legitimacy

Given stiffening competition, a maturing market, rising costs, and declining profits, it was clear that the views of the geographic managers had to be supplemented by other managerial perspectives. In particular, the subsidiaries could no longer be allowed to stand in the way of a more integrated technology strategy, which promised both more new products and more efficient use of R&D resources. Nor could they be allowed to block the development of more effective means to coordinate product strategies across national boundaries. The question was how to strengthen the viability of the functional and product groups, without compromising the responsiveness and morale of the company's highly entrepreneurial and innovative national subsidiaries.

In P&G and in many of the other companies we studied, the first step in building the new management influence was to ensure its legitimacy and credibility. Although companies implemented this task through a wide variety of particular approaches, we identified two common broad characteristics that seemed vital to the task.

First, companies used the assignment of people to the emergent management group to develop face validity for its views and activities. Upgrading the legitimacy of the underrepresented group seemed to require bringing in new people, since the status and credibility of the managers already in the group were usually well established, and their relationships with managers in other parts of the organization were clearly defined. The most common practice was to transfer high-status managers from the dominant group to the new team, thereby upgrading the latter's perceived legitimacy and allowing it to tap into the contacts and relationships of the former.

The second common means of building early acceptance and legitimacy for the new group was to align its activities with the interests and needs of the dominant management group. This was typically a much more difficult challenge, since by definition the new group represented a management perspective that had not been supplied by the established dominant group. Nonetheless, some companies were able to position the new management group in a supportive rather than an adversarial role vis-à-vis the existing organizational interests. In this way P&G established the legitimacy and credibility of its technology function at the European headquarters (ETC).

The ETC group, which took a technology-driven approach to new product development, had long been regarded by the subsidiary managers as expensive overhead that they were required to fund. Although the European development facility represented about a quarter of the company's total R&D effort, by 1977 it had not generated a major new product innovation in over five years. As the economic crisis worsened, the company was urged to close the ETC lab, transfer basic research back to the United States, and enlarge the subsidiaries' role in development and application technologies. Instead, senior management strengthened the R&D function at ETC and gave it a clearer leadership role in the European product development effort.

Wahib Zaki was appointed head of R&D for Europe. His fifteen years at P&G, his rapid promotion through the R&D ranks, and his vice presidential status allowed him to move quickly at ETC. To build up the capabilities of the research group (and to improve its relationships with both the parent and the subsidiaries) Zaki persuaded several of the firm's best technical personnel, from both the United States and the subsidiaries, to transfer to ETC. He then organized the group along product lines, not only to give the staff a focus, but also to link it more closely to the market and the product-oriented subsidiary development units.

Zaki was now ready to begin his program of "Europeanization," a euphemism for rationalization of the product line and integration of development activities. He established Euro Teams (the precursors and models for the Euro Brand Teams we have discussed), technical groups that were asked to review all existing products and technologies in a particular product category, to determine how P&G's line might be improved, and savings achieved. A designated lead country tested the teams' ideas and reported back on field performance and consumer reaction.

Over the next few years, Zaki's group proved its value by delivering a string of developments that provided important product improvements and moved the company toward a more efficient and rational product line. When subsidiaries introduced the new formula developed for the company's leading European laundry detergent, Ariel, they were able to increase prices and still capture larger shares in every single market. Similar successes were reported by the Euro Teams working on Dash III detergent, Fairy dishwashing liquid, Lenor fabric softener, Camay toilet soap, and many other products. The credibility of the Europeanization program was established, and P&G now had a technical functional management capability that could counterbalance the company's dominant geographically oriented perspective.

Providing Access

The next stage is to make sure that managers with the new perspectives and capabilities can relate them appropriately to the company's objectives, interests, and priorities. Companies that managed this stage successfully ensured not only that the emergent group was plugged into the company's information system, but also that the system met their particular data needs. In addition, these companies created new channels and forums of communication to form linkages across management groups, and to encourage information sharing and joint decision making. P&G handled these tasks well when it established its European product management function.

Like the technology group, the product management function was intended to counterbalance the dominant influence of the geographically oriented managers. Because product management was not coordinated across countries, P&G had lost opportunities to competitors. In France, for example, Colgate launched a disposable diaper that preempted the traditional Pampers brand position, beating P&G to market even though Pampers had been launched ten years earlier in Germany.

P&G's initial attempt to build European product management capabilities involved the creation of a European Pampers czar who was responsible for coordinating disposable diaper strategy across subsidiaries. The experiment failed because the new position lacked legitimacy and credibility, and because the appointee had only limited access to the necessary market information.

Impressed by the success of the technical Euro Teams, P&G's European top management decided to adopt the concept in developing an integrated European business perspective. By co-opting subsidiary staff into the task and by aligning the new organization with their interests, it was able to build legitimacy and credibility for an integral approach to European business management. Product managers in designated lead countries could develop and propose coordinated product strategies across national subsidiaries in Europe. This re-alignment led to the birth of the Euro Brand idea: a team was created for each key brand. But these groups did not become effective until they gained access to the mainstream management processes.

The typical Euro Brand Team comprised brand and advertising managers from country subsidiaries, key functional managers from headquarters (marketing, manufacturing, development, logistics), and, as chairman, the general manager of the subsidiary that had been nominated lead country for the brand—typically the subsidiary that was most successful or most enthusiastic about the product. In this way P&G was able to leverage the best ideas and greatest energy beyond national boundaries and create a strong product champion with legitimacy among other subsidiaries.

As we illustrated in Chapter 5, Euro Brand Teams provided a forum in which managers could constructively discuss issues such as standard pack sizes, consistent brand positioning, and common advertising themes. They also attacked broader issues of competitive strategy such as the timing of product rollouts and the development of coordinated responses to competitive threats.

To ensure that a true integrated European business perspective could emerge, however, the company had to do more than create new and specialized information forums. It also had to modify its information and control systems, which had traditionally focused almost exclusively on the national subsidiary unit. Data now had to be consolidated so it could be analyzed by business Europewide. Then Euro Brand Teams, supported by specialists at the ETC headquarters, could analyze the cost savings that could be achieved by reducing product variations, consolidating manufacturing locations, or unifying packaging design. Furthermore, by showing competitive share data on a Europewide basis, the change in information systems made subsidiary managers aware that their competitors were increasingly pursuing integrated European strategies.

The liquid laundry detergent Vizir became the company's first Euro Brand. The German product group, which had lead responsibility in the Euro Brand Team, handled a coordinated product rollout. National views were still clearly heard, and certain subsidiaries were given special treatment. In the United Kingdom, for example, first priority was given to launching P&G's strong low-temperature laundry powder, Ariel. The important achievement was that the Europewide product perspective was incorporated into the decision process without invalidating the views of the country management.

Ensuring Influence

Perhaps the most critical management task is to ensure that the new management has the organizational clout to influence decisions. Legitimacy and access to management processes are not enough. To influence critical decisions, ideas must often be backed by more formal organizational power.

The companies we studied used a wide variety of means to ensure that the newly established groups had appropriate influence in the decision-making process. The two elements that seemed most important were an allocation of resources and a distribution of responsibilities that empowered the emerging group in its negotiations with more established management groups.

These elements can be seen in Procter & Gamble's experience as it transferred to the parent company the lessons it had learned in building its European organization. Top management had two clear priorities: to increase the influence and effectiveness of the technology and manufacturing groups, and to integrate the domestic and overseas parts of the business.

Impressed with Wahib Zaki's success at ETC, top management asked him to return to Cincinnati in 1981. Appointed a corporate senior vice president, Zaki set out to upgrade and integrate R&D on a companywide basis. In the United States he found that the R&D function had long been overshadowed by the marketing-dominated operating divisions, each of which controlled its own product development center. Corporate R&D was isolated from the market and out of the mainstream of the company's operations. Its primary task was developing new basic technologies and administering the corporate standards and policies for research.

Much as he had done in Europe, Zaki first focused on establishing his central R&D operations' credibility with the domestic operating divisions and the company's overseas units. He appointed four well-known and respected technical managers as his vice presidents and gave each of them responsibility for R&D in a business area that matched the operating divisions' interests and responsibilities—fabric and hard surface cleaners, paper products, food and beverage, and health and personal care. This organization allowed the central R&D groups to develop technologies directly linked to the business strategies of product and geographic line managers.

As the vice presidents and their organizations developed legitimacy and credibility within P&G, they became the focal points for the
company's worldwide technological information, and the integrators of
its product development strategy. As linchpins in the product development process, the R&D vice presidents played two vital brokerage roles
between the company's upstream scientific and technical resources
and the applied product development centers in the operating divisions, and between the domestic R&D capabilities and the worldwide
market trends and technological developments. As brokers, they made
important contributions to the business planning process of the domestic product and overseas geographic divisions.

The technological managers became a viable power group within
the P&G organization when Zaki convinced the CEO, John Smale, to
give them responsibility for leading the company's effort to revitalize
its product development efforts. Formerly, product or geographic line
personnel regarded the technological managers as support staff who
played an advisory role, but whose proposals they could dismiss. Now,
the technical managers were to be held jointly accountable for the
success of the company's products in the world marketplace, and this
responsibility represented a substantial source of power and influence
in the decision-making process.

Furthermore, as product innovations became a key weapon in the
global competitive battle of the 1980s, the assistance of the technological management group became more eagerly sought. In laundry detergents, there was an urgent need to respond to demands for higher
performance at lower temperatures, as well as a worldwide trend from
granules to liquids; in disposable diapers, a rapid sequence of changes
saw the introduction of shaped diapers, elasticized gatherings, refas-
tenable tapes, and thin profile products using super-absorbent poly-
mers; and even the mature toothpaste market was jolted by back-to-
back innovations such as gels, antiplaque formulas, and pump
dispensers. As controllers of the company's scarce technological resources, the R&D group found itself in a powerful and influential position.

In just a decade, Procter & Gamble has come a long way from its
historical position as a domestically oriented, marketing-dominated
company with a portfolio of overseas subsidiaries on the organizational
periphery. Although change has come slowly and with difficulty, the
company now has a much broader perspective on its changing environmental situation, and a much more robust response capability. Building on its existing strengths, P&G has created an organization that balances the influences of business, product, and area management.

MANAGING THE MANAGEMENT DIVERSITY: MAINTAINING A DYNAMIC BALANCE

Maintaining a balance among business, geographic, and functional management capabilities is a continuing challenge for the transnational company.

One company that has been able to maintain such a balance over a long period of time is Ericsson. Indeed, its ability to shift management responsibilities and organizational relationships continually in response to changes in its environment has helped Ericsson become a key player in the worldwide telecommunications switching business.[4]

Ericsson's organization has never allowed one organizational perspective to dominate and others to atrophy. Management has not hesitated to adapt its organizational processes and management structures to respond to environmental change. But rather than search for an idealized, static concept of organizational fit, Ericsson has pragmatically accepted that ambiguity, overlap, and change in management responsibilities are inevitable. The resulting organizational diversity and flux generates internal tensions and management conflicts, and Ericsson and other companies that have been successful in maintaining management diversity have found various means to resolve the differences that arise.

Building the Foundations: Ericsson's Historical Development

Like ITT, Ericsson built a substantial worldwide network of national operations in the 1920s to capitalize on the development of national telecommunications systems. Unlike ITT, however, Ericsson had a strong home market base and a parent company with the technological, manufacturing, and marketing capability to support its offshore companies as required.

During the 1930s, Ericsson's top management became concerned about the growing technological and marketing independence of its foreign manufacturing companies, each of which jealously guarded the geographic areas for which it had been granted a group sales monopoly. The independence of the foreign companies led to a divergence in technology, a duplication of effort, and a lack of competitiveness in sourcing. Gradually, Stockholm assumed responsibility for worldwide sales and distribution. In 1940, the incremental changes of the previous decade were consolidated in a new organization based on product divisions instead of the old functional departments. The intent was to achieve better control of technology and markets as well as a closer link between product development and customer requirements.

Ericsson's management then turned its attention to the business significance of the new electromechanical crossbar technology that was replacing the step-by-step Strowger switch developed in the 1920s. Although experimental research had been under way since the 1930s, it was only in the early 1950s that the new switching technology began to be used in large main exchanges. About this time, management became concerned that the product divisions should be focusing less on applications and more on the basic R&D necessary to capitalize on the new technology.

In 1952, the president issued a memo emphasizing the need for cross-divisional coordination and expanding the responsibilities of the functional staff groups. During the 1950s, functional management became as powerful as the product divisions. Thanks to a technological breakthrough made by the R&D department and drastic improvements in production costs and reliability, the company established a leadership position in the development of the crossbar switch that allowed it to enter new markets worldwide.

The 1960s brought new challenges and new organizational adaptation. Competitive bids for national telephone exchange contracts, and increasingly sophisticated and aggressive host government authorities forced Ericsson and other telecommunications companies to transfer their technology abroad and build manufacturing capacity in the countries buying the equipment. Since product design and manufacturing technology was well understood and fully documented, substantial development and production responsibilities could be delegated to the local subsidiary companies. The labor-intensive assembly process, which accounted for approximately half the cost of the crossbar equipment, could often be done much more efficiently in low-labor-cost countries. Extending the company's postwar shift from Europe to Latin America and the Pacific, Ericsson's operations in Mexico, Brazil, and Australia developed into major self-sufficient companies during this period.

In the mid-1970s, as the fully electronic generation of technology emerged, Ericsson management pulled research efforts and manufacturing responsibility back to Sweden. Where national capabilities, expertise or experience could be useful in the corporate effort to develop an electronic digital switch, the appropriate local managers were transferred temporarily to headquarters. Through the 1970s and early 1980s, responsibility for development and manufacturing of the company's AXE digital switch was clearly and deliberately concentrated in the parent company, which exported the product worldwide.

The transition to electronic switching affected capacity utilization in plants worldwide, as demand for the crossbar products declined. Even where the local companies had the volume and the skills to take over production or assembly of the AXE switch, the labor content of the electronic product was only a small fraction of the previous generation's. Like many other firms in the industry, Ericsson found itself in the politically delicate position of having to close down plants and lay off people in several of its overseas operations. Again, the company has been flexible in its organizational response. Since software represents a larger proportion of value added in an electronic switch than in older generations, and there is a shortage of software engineers in Sweden, Ericsson is shifting responsibility for peripheral development and software support to its more advanced overseas operations.

Managing Misfit and Ambiguity

Thus Ericsson's organizational development was entirely different from ITT's. Because of its emphasis on responding to the interests and demands of host-country governments, ITT made strong national systems houses its basic organizational building blocks. Ericsson, on the other hand, was more sensitive to changes in the international telecommunications businesses and in its operating environment, and constantly adapted its organization in response. In addition, Ericsson's top management was very conscious of the need to prevent a single management group from dominating the company's perspectives and capabilities. As the history of the company's development so clearly illustrates, when its overseas units became too independent, it increased headquarters' control; and when product divisions seemed too parochial or short term oriented, it built up the role of the functional groups. Rather than search for unidimensional strategy-structure fit, Ericsson management has historically focused on long-term environment-organization flexibility.

This gradual but continuous change in management roles and responsibilities, and the long-term evolutionary balancing of organizational power gave rise to internal tensions not felt in unidimensional organizations. While ITT's management processes were characterized by stability, clarity, and accountability, Ericsson's were marked by a degree of fluidity, ambiguity, and overlap. Where the ebb and flow of the company's history led to misfits in the distribution of assets or location of competencies—the development of a strong, independent R&D capability in the small Australian market is a good example—management felt no pressing need to eliminate them through restructuring. Indeed, the company seemed almost to encourage a degree of misfit, to create dynamic tension in the organization.[5]

In organizations that maintained this sort of multidimensional tension and balance, the resulting ambiguity and flux seemed to release managers from the constraints of organizations with tightly focused beliefs about "fit"; they were free to be more innovative and creative.[6] The tolerance of organizational overlap, and even misfit, seemed to encourage an entrepreneurial spirit in the units.

Creating Means to Resolve the Conflict

There are risks in putting such a managerial burr under the organizational saddle. Instead of encouraging innovative flexibility, ambiguous roles and overlapping responsibilities could lead to anarchy, yielding unproductive conflict rather than creative tension. Like several other companies we studied, Ericsson was aware of the potential problem and used several management processes to reconcile the diversity of perspectives and resolving the differences in interests.

One approach was to remove the issues most likely to arouse conflict from the organizational mainstream and resolve them in "off-line" forums: project teams, task forces, and committees, which isolate issues that are particularly conflict-prone so that they can be resolved in the least costly manner. By maintaining a large number of such decision forums—some permanent groups and some ad hoc committees to respond to a specific issue—Ericsson has developed the ability to isolate, yet legitimize, the intense and often disruptive debate necessary to resolve multidimensional issues.[7]

Ericsson also may ask one management group to arbitrate conflicts between others. Such conflict was often most acute between area and business managers. Ericsson's functional managers have traditionally served as the primary links between the central product divisions, which controlled most of the company's technology, and the national subsidiaries, which controlled market access. Their role is to transmit strategies and knowledge from corporate headquarters to the subsidiaries, and to act as the subsidiaries' representative at the headquarters. Corporate marketing and production managers travel constantly, and many of them sit on subsidiary boards—a position that facilitates their role as information links but allows them to monitor and intervene on issues on which the overseas subsidiaries and the central product divisions differed. Formal line authority rests with the product and area managers, but the functional group in its brokering role exerts considerable influence on the management process.[8]

LEGITIMIZING AND MANAGING DIVERSITY: A TOP MANAGEMENT RESPONSIBILITY

As companies like ITT and General Electric discovered, a failure to overcome unidimensional strategic biases can have dire consequences for a company. Yet entrenched management cliques and calcified decision-making processes can make it extremely difficult to implement change. In no company we studied was major change achieved without the substantial and enduring involvement of the firm's top management. Only top-level executives can provide legitimacy for a new management group; only with their support can the new managers gain access to the company's information sources and communication channels; and only top management can allocate the responsibilities and transfer the resources that give the emergent group real power and a continuing influence in decision-making processes.

The task for top managers is not just to authorize the establishment of a new department or to modify the company's formal systems. They must also use more subtle tools—upgrading personnel, broadening their responsibilities, building new channels for information flow, creating new and often temporary decision-making forums, and shifting the control of key resources.

In all the companies that established multiple management perspectives and capabilities, the transition was achieved over long periods of time. Procter & Gamble developed its functional and global business capabilities over a decade; it took Unilever almost twenty years to provide its product coordinators with legitimacy and power to offset that of the company's national managers; and Philips spent most of the 1970s and 1980s building the capability of its product divisions and giving them sufficient authority to counterbalance the strong national organizations.

By legitimizing the diversity of a truly multidimensional organization, management creates the core of an organization flexible enough to respond to environmental change and strong enough to compete on the basis of multiple strategic capabilities.[9] The next task is to build a coordinating process that allows the company to manage this diversity.

9
MANAGING COMPLEXITY: DEVELOPING FLEXIBLE COORDINATION

Apart from the complications associated with managing across geographic and cultural distance, the management process in traditional worldwide companies was comparatively straightforward. The type we have described as multinational organizations allowed their autonomous national units to respond to opportunities and threats in their local environment as they saw fit. As long as each unit could generate funds sufficient for its investment needs, produce products appropriate for its market, and amass the information and knowledge necessary to maintain its competitive position, there was little intervention from headquarters. In Chapter 3 we described the primary headquarters role in such companies as one of establishing administrative control of performance incentives, and managing the financial flows between the subsidiaries and the parent.

In global companies, management was relatively straightforward. Most foreign units were highly dependent on headquarters for funds, products, information, and expertise, and this dependency simplified the corporate coordination task. Headquarters provided strategic direction and operational support to overseas subsidiaries, and management at the center was responsible for deciding between competing subsidiary demands.

The transnational organization presents an entirely different management challenge. Its assets and resources are widely dispersed but mutually supportive to achieve global-scale efficiency; the roles and responsibilities of organizational units are differentiated but interdependent to maximize national flexibility; and its knowledge and initiatives are linked through a worldwide learning capability that assures the efficient development and diffusion of innovations. In such an organization, managers at the corporate and subsidiary levels will have sophisticated responsibilities, and the management processes linking the various organizational units will be complex.[1]

In this chapter we will describe the processes and mechanisms of coordination through which transnational managers can retain control of their complex organizations. More important, we draw on the lessons learned by our sample companies to specify how these tools should be applied. We begin with a description of the three major means of coordination, then show why most companies fully exploit only one or two of them. After highlighting the limitations of each tool, we explain why it is important for transnational companies to develop a full portfolio of coordinating mechanisms. In the final section, we describe how each means of coordination fits the major tasks of the transnational.

DEVELOPING THE MEANS OF COORDINATION: INFLUENCE OF ADMINISTRATIVE HERITAGE

The influence of a company's administrative heritage extends to the ways in which its international operations are coordinated. In our study we were struck by the similarity of basic processes among companies from similar backgrounds. Three distinctive coordinating mechanisms stood out in Japanese, American, and European companies, respectively.

Centralization: Dominant Process in Japanese Companies

Coordination in most Japanese companies was shaped by a consensus decision-making process that was culturally dependent and required intensive communication. The process was difficult to transfer abroad, since non-Japanese managers lacked both the language ability and the cultural background to participate in the subtle processes of *nemawashi* and *ringi*. Furthermore, Japanese companies typically expanded first into nearby, less developed Asian markets, where it was easy for managers in the parent company to manage the subsidiaries directly. For these reasons, most Japanese companies developed international coordination processes that relied on the direct actions and intervention of the headquarters management group. This simple and direct process we characterize as coordination through *centralization*.[2]

Centralization is relatively easy to establish and operate. By leveraging the organization and management resources already located at the corporate center, the process facilitates rapid decision making and minimizes the kind of headquarters-subsidiary arm wrestling that often occurs when authority is more widely dispersed.

At Kao, Matsushita, and NEC coordination by centralization was the management process of choice. Because centralization represented the best fit with the hub structure and the culturally driven organization process, specific tools and practices to implement the process were developed and institutionalized as "the company way." Even where environmental and strategic changes made the centralization process less appropriate than it had been, strong management traditions typically stretched traditional practices to meet the new demands.

For example, Matsushita concentrated assets and expertise at the corporate center, and even its largest and most sophisticated subsidiaries, such as the U.S. company, were more tightly linked to and more highly dependent on the center than subsidiaries in any of the European or American companies in our sample. Centralization of key international activities and decisions was all but inevitable despite Matsushita's philosophy of decentralization in its domestic operations. When environmental conditions forced an attempt to move more value-added tasks and more management responsibilities offshore, the effort was hampered by the subsidiaries' dependence on the center. Nonetheless, well into the 1980s, Matsushita still managed its increasingly complex coordination task primarily through a centralized process, although it was modified by the company's strong localization efforts.

As we described in Chapter 7, the Matsushita organization was structured to provide multiple linkages between the center and the overseas subsidiaries. As the offshore units grew in size and complexity, the company achieved close control and support primarily through its network of over 700 expatriate managers and technicians. Typically, the subsidiary general manager, the accounting manager, and the technical manager were all expatriates. These managers not only transmitted central decisions into the local contexts, they also forwarded (and interpreted) information about the local environment to headquarters, to make the company as responsive as possible to local market needs.

Thus, through the breadth and depth of these parent-subsidiary linkages, Matsushita maintained its strongly centralized coordination process despite the growing size and increasing complexity of its overseas business. Ironically, it was by sending more expatriates to its overseas companies that it was able to reinforce its central control. According to one manager in MECA, Matsushita's large North American subsidiary, the company had mastered the art of "decentralized centralization." As assets and responsibility passed to the subsidiaries, the company increased the number and strength of the linkages to ensure managers at the center were kept fully informed and completely involved in all key decisions.

Centralization is very costly to operate. As the overseas organization grows in size and complexity, managers at the center are swamped with requests for information, guidance, support, and decisions. To respond appropriately, they feel they need to reinforce their resources, capabilities, and knowledge base, thereby increasing the size and bureaucracy of the central decision-making unit. Eventually, the system reaches its limit, because of the overload of information or the inability of the central staff to respond to demands in a timely fashion.

The quality of decisions may suffer in an overloaded centralized process. The greater the diversity and complexity of the company's foreign operating environments, the more difficult it is for management at headquarters to be sensitive to local needs. Particularly during the 1980s, when host country pressures and demands intensified, corporate managers often had little knowledge or understanding of the changes.

Finally, because the centralization process both reflects and reinforces the dependency between overseas subsidiaries and the parent company, it can lead to strains and resentment within the organization. For example, as a subsidiary's operation matures and as local experience and ability are developed, country managers may find it demoralizing to have to refer to headquarters on issues they feel they understand best locally.[3]

NEC experienced all these problems as its overseas telecommunications operations expanded rapidly during the 1970s and 1980s. In the company's historical approach to coordinating its worldwide telecom switching business, most decisions and activities were managed by a central staff that had developed considerable expertise over the years. Such centralized coordination and control were highly effective as NEC moved into nearby markets in Thailand and Taiwan in the 1960s. And, despite some difficulties in managing the new wave of demands, the company continued to operate efficiently as it built an independent Brazilian switching company in the late 1960s, and even as it began to penetrate the more advanced U.S. market in the 1970s.

By the 1980s, however, the size and complexity of the overseas operations were straining the central coordination process even though huge staffs supported the offshore units. The Second Switching Division, the Switching Group unit responsible for sales and engineering for overseas markets, had grown to more than a thousand, and the Overseas Affiliates Support Office, responsible for assisting offshore production units, had a staff of several hundred.

To maintain the centralized coordination process, NEC corporate managers had to travel frequently to the overseas affiliates. An internal survey revealed that NEC managers logged 10,000 trips abroad in 1983 as part of the intensive commitment to centralization. Coordination by centralization was becoming extremely costly, not only in terms of travel cost but also in the strain it put on managers.

Furthermore, as the offshore telecommunications operations grew in size and capability, they began to resent their dependence on headquarters. Particularly in software, the headquarters group often found it difficult to make decisions appropriate to the diverse needs of its markets, as was the case during the development of the NEAC 61 switch, which we described in Chapter 7. By the beginning of the 1980s, NEC executives were concerned that costs of centralized coordination had begun to exceed the benefits; they began developing tools and approaches to reduce the load on the corporate staff.

Formalization: Preferred Coordinative Mechanism in American Companies

The administrative heritage of our American-based companies led them to rely on other coordinating tools and mechanisms. Most of these companies internationalized during a period in which divisionalization was the dominant organizational thrust in the United States. A new era of "professional management" had emerged in which greater delegation of responsibility was made possible by the development of sophisticated management systems that allowed corporate managers to control operations and hold other managers accountable for designated tasks. Thus, the coordination process in American-based companies was based largely on formal systems, policies, and standards. We refer to this process as coordination through *formalization*.[4]

Formalization represents one way to reduce the relatively high operating costs associated with centralization. Instead of shifting organizational power from subsidiaries to headquarters, formalization tends to decrease the power of both headquarters and subsidiary management. By subjecting decision making to an impersonal set of policies that assume a power independent of the interests and motives of either headquarters or subsidiary, formalization sweeps away many of the roles previously played by the two groups. The routinization of decision making delivers important operating efficiencies that are the hallmark of this means of coordination.

ITT built its coordination capability almost entirely on its formidable set of management systems. Although some outsiders saw the company's battery of detailed reports and the marathon review meetings as Harold Geneen's means of centralizing decisions, the architect of the system denied that was the case.

Geneen delegated substantial autonomy to ITT subsidiary companies, but held them accountable for bottom-line results. He insisted that his systems and processes were designed primarily as management training tools, whose main purpose was to lead managers to use their delegated authority responsibly. "To make careful and logical decisions on the basis of unshakable facts," as Geneen would say, "then force the logic out into the open."[5]

But the process has its costs. Most obvious is the high fixed cost of establishing the systems, policies, and rules so that they become effective and reliable surrogates for issue-by-issue decision making. More fundamental are the problems that arise when companies try to apply a routinized system to complex and changing tasks that require nonroutine decisions. Finally, in some companies the enforcement and control of the systems became so complex and time-consuming that even the potential low operating cost of formalization was lost.

For decades, Procter & Gamble operated under the philosophy established by Walter Lingle, the company's overseas vice president during its postwar expansion. In the mid-1950s, Lingle said, "The best way to succeed in other countries is to build in each one as exact a replica of the United States' Procter & Gamble organization as it is possible to build. We believe that exactly the same policies and procedures which have given our company success in the United States will be equally successful overseas."[6] While subsidiary managers were free to modify the company's products to respond to local preferences, they were required—by standard policies and even organization structures—to follow the well-developed "Procter way" of marketing. While the approach was very effective in transferring the company's legendary marketing skills abroad and in ensuring a consistent approach across markets, it led to problems that surfaced in the late 1970s and early 1980s.[7]

The most obvious was the cost of establishing an organization in each country that reflected the parent's marketing approach and administrative capabilities. In part because of Lingle's decision to create overseas subsidiaries as exact replicas of the parent organization, by the mid-1970s the overhead expense per unit in Europe was more than 50 percent higher than in the U.S. company. In addition, many of P&G's policies and practices were less appropriate in the overseas operations. Approaches that had been effective in the United States in the 1950s and 1960s were often impediments in dealing with the complex, rapidly changing European environment of the 1970s and 1980s. As we described earlier, P&G's exhaustive prelaunch product and marketing testing gave competitors so much advance warning and detailed knowledge that the company was continually pre-empted by rival companies rolling out imitative products. Furthermore, P&G's policy of sharing information only on a need-to-know basis—a by-product of the brand management system and the internal competition it fostered—impeded the vital task of transferring knowledge and experience among subsidiaries in closely related overseas markets. And the deeply ingrained procedure of committing new ideas and proposals to paper, then circulating them widely to refine and build support (P&G's famous one-page memos), delayed key decisions relating to overseas markets at a time when competitive pressures were demanding greater speed and flexibility.

In effect, the implementation of the policies and systems risked becoming an end in itself, and some managers expressed concern that operating policies were taking on the attributes of corporate dogma, and standard practices were being accepted as unquestionable verities. So much attention was paid to systems that managers were distracted from understanding and responding to consumer needs and competitive threats. In an internal environment driven by standardization and routinization, managers' willingness to be creative or innovative might be suppressed.

Socialization: Traditional Means of Coordination in European Companies

The European-based companies we studied had developed their own characteristic mode of coordination. Expanding abroad in an era of slow and expensive global communication, such organizations could not rely heavily on centrally directed coordination. Neither had they developed the systems expertise of their American counterparts. The European companies, many of them still strongly influenced by their founding families, often entrusted the management of subsidiaries to family members (or trusted retainers). The management process relied on these individuals' understanding of corporate objectives and on their close personal relationships. Thus, the dominant coordination process relied on the careful recruitment, development, and acculturation of key decision makers—an approach we will call coordination through *socialization*.[8]

Socialization is attractive because it overcomes centralization's problem of headquarters overload, and formalization's inflexibility. Unlike the other two means of coordination, it enhances the influence of headquarters and subsidiaries simultaneously, thereby facilitating the development and integration of resources and capabilities worldwide. Furthermore, because it relies on shared values and objectives, it represents a more robust and flexible means of coordination. Decisions reached by negotiations between knowledgeable groups with common objectives should be much better than those made by superior authority or by standard policy.

Since its earliest days of internationalization, Unilever management has relied on a select cadre of company expatriates to transfer knowledge and to develop operations abroad that were consistent with the parent company's values and objectives.[9] Today the company explicitly acknowledges that top management relies on three major means of coordination: its control over investments, the annual operating plan, and its manpower-planning process. "Of these," said former Unilever chairman H. F. van den Hoven, "our control over the development of people has been of greatest importance in managing the overseas operations."[10] One overseas committee director, who claimed he spent 75 percent of his time on personnel-related issues, stated the philosophy simply, "People are the glue that holds our worldwide operations together."

The company's recruitment, evaluation, training, and indoctrination processes, coupled with a lifetime employment policy, created an internal environment commonly described as a club. Members of the Unilever management club identified strongly with the company's values and objectives. Like any good club it had strong traditions, well-understood norms, and a distinctive style; many Unilever managers claimed they could easily identify another club member anywhere in the world.

There was no question that socialization represented "the company way" of dealing with complex coordination needs. Historically, other processes had been underdeveloped. The formal management systems were used primarily for fiscal reporting, and centralization was antithetical to everything the Unilever management philosophy stood for. (Even the terms "headquarters" and "subsidiary" were banned from the Unilever lexicon since they evoked an inappropriate sense of hierarchy. Instead the company preferred to talk about "the center" and "the national companies.") Yet this management philosophy also came under stress in the demanding international environment of the 1980s, and Unilever was obliged to strengthen some of the alternative means of coordination.

The major disadvantage of socialization is its cost. It is by far the most expensive means of coordination. Socialization takes the decision load off top management by institutionalizing its goals throughout the organization. However, ensuring that managers share objectives, priorities, and values, demands intensive indoctrination and training, requiring a substantial investment in such processes in a large organization. Furthermore, decision making is usually a slower, more ambiguous, and more complex management process than it is with either the centralization or formalization approach.

Unilever spends £100 million annually on management development and training, but that investment represents only the tip of the iceberg of socialization cost. The socialization process depends heavily on the transfer of managers, and Unilever has over 1,000 home-country or third-country nationals on assignment in other parts of its worldwide organization at any one time. Maintaining an expatriate manager costs two to ten times as much as hiring a local manager for the same position.

Still more costly in the long run, perhaps, was the complex decision-making process that Unilever's socialization fostered. One manager described it as "a coordinated disagreement system trying to arrive at consensus decisions." By the late 1970s, many recognized that the interminable negotiations over new product introductions, plant closures, or location of R&D responsibilities were costing Unilever dearly in terms of operating efficiency and competitive effectiveness. The company would have to broaden and reinforce its other coordinative mechanisms.

Limits to the "Company Way" of Coordinating

We have pointed out the dominant patterns of coordination found in particular companies and national groups, but we should emphasize that such distinctions and categorizations are of degree only. Indeed, all the companies we studied employed tools and practices that could be classified under each of the three coordination processes.

Even our classification of particular practices into centralization, formalization, and socialization categories is somewhat arbitrary. For example, Matsushita's practice of sending thoroughly indoctrinated company managers overseas and maintaining intensive communication links with them gives rise to a coordination process we have characterized as centralization ("decentralized centralization" we began to call it). But the intensive corporate training and the close personal contacts with headquarters managers indicate that the mechanism also has strong elements of socialization. In reality, the three general processes frequently intersect and overlap, and their collective influence can be seen in many of the more common means of coordination.

Nonetheless, there are clear company differences in the balance among the processes, and each organization's administrative heritage influenced its management's choice of approaches and tools. As a result, we noticed, companies typically stretched one coordinating process to the limit (e.g., Matsushita's use of centralization, ITT's refinement of its formalized systems and processes, and Unilever's development of the socialization process), while underutilizing other tools and mechanisms.

As they faced the new demands and changing environmental forces in the 1980s, many companies recognized for the first time that their coordinating capability was a scarce organizational resource that had to be deliberately developed and carefully allocated. Rather than adopt particular processes solely on the basis of tradition, managers had to understand a wide variety of approaches. Only then could they sensibly decide how to develop, link, and manage the new coordinating tools and processes they needed to supplement "the company way."

MANAGING THE COORDINATION PROCESS: ALLOCATING AND INTEGRATING MULTIPLE TOOLS

By the 1980s, many companies had reached a coordination crisis. New competitive pressures were requiring them to develop multiple strategic capabilities even as other environmental forces led them to reconfigure their historical organization structures. Familiar means of coordination characteristically proved inadequate to this new challenge.

By its very nature, the transnational organizational form toward which many companies have been moving requires both extensive and intensive coordination. To operate as an effective strategic whole, the transnational must be able to reconcile the diversity of perspectives and interests it deliberately fosters, integrate the widespread assets and resources it deliberately disperses, and coordinate the roles and responsibilities it deliberately differentiates.

How can managers approach this daunting coordination challenge? The experience of the companies in our study suggests the importance of overcoming the biases of administrative heritage by developing a full arsenal of coordinating processes, practices, and tools, and to use those mechanisms in the most effective and efficient manner.

Building Coordination Capability

The coordination crisis of the transnational has two sources. The first relates to the sheer volume and intensity of the task: the need to control the continuing diffusion of assets and resources and the increasing differentiation of organizational roles and responsibilities. The second source of the crisis is the need for a greater diversity of coordinating mechanisms: some integrating key international operations to achieve greater efficiency, others coordinating local units to maintain maximum flexibility, and still others linking worldwide sources of knowledge and expertise to build an organizational learning capability.

Increasingly, the coordination practices that had become "the company way" were not only overloaded, but also inappropriate for current needs. Managers clearly needed to build and apply the broad processes and specific mechanisms that had previously been underutilized. European companies began to see the power and simplicity of more centralized coordination of their far-flung empires; the Japanese increasingly adopted more formal systems and routine policies to supplement their traditional time-consuming, case-by-case negotiations; and American managers took new interest in shaping and managing the previously ignored informal processes and value systems in their firms.

In almost all the companies we studied, managers were actively trying to expand and strengthen their underutilized means of coordina-

ion. But, as with the reconfiguration of organizational structure and
the development of new management perspectives and capabilities (see
Chapters 5 and 8), the task could not be implemented quickly or easily.
Moreover, the installation of a new tool or mechanism did not automat-
cally guarantee the development of an effective new process.

For example, as early as 1972, with an eye to integrating activities
across national organizations, Philips tried to strengthen the coordination capability of its product divisions in Eindhoven. Product strategies
were deemed particularly important for worldwide coordination, and
the board of management issued a directive that clearly gave the product divisions responsibility to coordinate "worldwide article policy"
defined as product and market strategies and the implementation
plans to achieve them). When Cor van der Klugt became Philips's president in 1986, however, he found that the product divisions were still
struggling to establish their claim on the roles assigned to them four-
teen years earlier.

A senior staff manager observed, "There is a widely shared perception that the quality of managers in the NOs [national organizations] is
higher than at the PDs [product divisions]. What this means, of course,
is that NOs will not simply defer to the PDs. Product division management must win the right to direct strategy on a worldwide basis."

In other companies we saw much the same phenomenon. Soon
after becoming company president in 1977, Masaharu Matsushita, son
of the founder, made a major push to introduce new systems, particularly those that would foster more disciplined medium- and long-term
planning. Although the new systems had some impact on the organization, they were regarded by most international managers as operating in
parallel to, rather than being integrated into the mainstream management process.

Philips, Matsushita, and many other firms learned that new coordination processes, like new organizational capabilities or new management perspectives, require long-term consistent management attention
to their development and implementation. They cannot be created by
ingenious design or installed by management fiat. The newly defined
reporting relationship, the redesigned formal system, and the carefully
planned management development program can provide appropriate
frameworks for the development of centralization, formalization, and
socialization processes, but the management attitudes and organizational relationships required to make them effective are developed only
with substantial top management nurturing over an extended period of
time.

There is another important parallel between the development of
new processes of coordination and the implementation of structural
change or the legitimization of diverse management perspectives: the

key task is to protect the existing processes while building and overlay ing the new. The new tools and mechanisms must be introduced with subtlety and finesse, so that they do not short-circuit or undermine the established means of coordination, but also with strong support, so that they cannot be neutralized or co-opted by the existing systems.

Although Unilever's top managers recognized the need to improve the integration of strategy and operations in its independent national companies, they were concerned that any drastic change in management process might threaten the strong internalized values and powerful informal relationships that had historically linked organizational units. When they created groups at the corporate center with responsibility to improve the integration by product line across national units they deliberately did not designate them product divisions, or even product managers, preferring the vaguer title of "product coordinator." To ensure that they became part of the powerful informal processes managers of these product groups had to execute the coordination function with very little formal power for their first fifteen years. Instead they built their credibility and influence through the mechanisms that constituted Unilever's dominant socialization process of management Finally, when they were given formal line authority for businesses in Europe, they had a healthy respect for the informal relationships and values and were able to institute new tools of centralization and formalization without damaging the core socialization process.

On the other hand, Kao's attempts to broaden its means of international coordination were thwarted. Both a new sophisticated information and planning system and an integrative organizational development process were co-opted by the dominant management groups and used to reinforce the bias toward coordination by centralization. The functional managers used the new automated information system to obtain on-line, real-time data that allowed them to intervene more directly and more frequently into the overseas operations; they also gained control of the planning systems and made foreign subsidiaries bypass the regional offices and report directly to them. When top management implemented an organizational development program to make domestic managers aware of the importance of the international operations, it hoped to elevate the role and status of overseas managers and to give them more influence in the decision-making process. The functional managers at headquarters, however, read the program as a signal for them to become more involved internationally, and the dominance of the centralization process increased.

The companies that were most successful in enhancing their coordination capability built tools and mechanisms in two forms: self-regulating as well as managed. The interdependency among organizational units that was central to transnational operation made it possible to develop new coordination mechanisms requiring substantially less direct management. Matsushita's creative ways of linking its research and development efforts to market needs—the internal quasi-markets provided by product divisions "bidding" for research attention and the merchandise meetings that allowed sales units to negotiate with factories over product specifications—created a self-enforcing and self-sustaining means of coordination. Procter & Gamble's allocation of responsibility for its Euro Brand Teams created a similar self-regulating mechanism that encouraged intersubsidiary collaboration and coordination.

In these and similar examples, we saw companies allowing the invisible hand of internal markets to complement the visible hand of managed integration. Besides requiring less direct time and effort to manage, the coordination processes built on organizational interdependencies and internal market mechanisms often seemed to overcome the "stickiness" of managed organizational processes, and became more flexible and responsive to environmental changes. The risk was that if participants in the self-regulating systems were not thoroughly indoctrinated in broader organizational objectives, parochial attitudes or self-serving behavior could turn the process negotiations into horse trading, which produces acceptable compromises and trade-offs rather than shared commitments. But if management can protect the process against such risks, the "invisible hand" mechanisms can be powerful supplements to the managed tools we have described.

Allocating Coordinative Capability

Development of a diversified portfolio of coordination tools was only part of the challenge for managers of transnational companies. Equally important was the task of deciding which processes best fit which organizational needs. Given the scarcity of overall coordination capability and the wide differences in the establishment and operating costs of the tools, this decision was an extremely important one in most companies.[11]

In analyzing how managers might use various tools and processes most appropriately, we found it helpful to focus on two dimensions of the coordination task. The first involves the coordination of the flows between organizational units, while the second relates to the coordination of the units' strategic roles and responsibilities.

Three flows are the lifeblood of any organization, but are of particular importance in a transnational. The first is the flow of goods: the complex interconnections through which companies source their raw materials and other supplies, link flows of components and subassemblies, and distribute finished goods throughout an integrated network of specialized purchasing units, focused sourcing plants, broad-line assembly operations, and localized sales subsidiaries. The second is the flow of resources, which encompasses not only the allocation of capital and repatriation of dividends, but also the transfer of technology and the movement of personnel throughout the system. The third is the flow of information: raw data, analyzed information, and accumulated knowledge, which companies must diffuse throughout the worldwide network of national units.

It can be very difficult to coordinate the flows of goods in a complex integrated network of interdependent operations. But in most companies, this coordination process can be managed effectively at lower levels of the organization once clear procedures and strong systems are set up.[12] While the cost of establishing the coordination process may be high, in both financial and managerial terms, it should require limited resources to operate. The fact that such flows are reasonably constant or can be adequately forecast makes this a classic candidate for a formalized management process. Within its network of fifteen domestic plants, for example, Ericsson had learned to coordinate product and materials by standardizing as many procedures as possible and formalizing the logistics control, primarily through the use of telex reports. A senior manufacturing manager said this experience had helped the company understand how to operate highly interdependent yet widely separated worldwide facilities without developing burdensome coordination processes.

It is more difficult to coordinate flows of financial, human, and technological resources. Allocation of these scarce resources represents the major strategic choices the company makes, and so must be controlled at the corporate level. We have described the transnational as an organization of diverse needs and perspectives, many of which are conflicting and all of which are changing. In such an organization only managers with an overview of the total situation can make the critical decisions on the funding of projects, the sharing of scarce technological resources, and the allocation of organizational skills and capabilities. Managing the flows of resources is a classic case for coordination by centralization.

Centralization was the most consistently practiced form of coordination we observed. In every company, top management, including the board, explicitly reserved the right to decide on major capital requests and key personnel appointments. Less formally stated, but almost as universal, was its desire for direct control over licenses, joint venture agreements, or other arrangements involving the transfer or assignment of corporate patents and other core technological resources.

Perhaps the most difficult task is to coordinate the voluminous flow of strategic information and proprietary knowledge required to operate a transnational organization. The diversity and changeability of the flow make it impossible to coordinate through formalized systems or standardized policies; and the sheer volume and complexity of information would overload headquarters if coordination were centralized. The most effective way to ensure that worldwide organizational units are analyzing their diverse environments appropriately is to sensitize local managers to the broader corporate objectives and priorities, and to other units' needs and capabilities. That goal is best reached by transferring personnel with the relevant knowledge, or creating organizational forums that allow the free exchange of information and foster interunit learning. In short, the coordination of information flows is a classic candidate for the socialization process.[13]

Matsushita had been successful in developing this process to leverage the learning in its more advanced foreign units. By developing closer lateral relationships across subsidiaries, the company induced managers in these units to share their learning directly. So-called "block meetings" were held among subsidiaries in a region to compare performance and to highlight "best practices"; the company with the most advanced capability typically acted as host for the meeting. Besides engendering healthy interunit competition, the meetings allowed managers in companies with similar scale operations, similar operating problems, and at similar stages of production to develop relationships that became the source of regular information exchange and knowledge diffusion. Managers in video and home appliance divisions in Matsushita's Taiwanese company, for example, prided themselves on acting as "big brothers" to their counterparts in Malaysia and Indonesia.

Naturally, none of these broad characterizations of the fit between flows and processes is absolute, and companies employ a variety of coordinative mechanisms in managing all three flows. Goods flows may be centrally coordinated, for example, for products under allocation, when several plants are operating at less than capacity, or if cost structures or host government demands change; many routine information flows can be coordinated through formalization if appropriate MIS systems are installed.

Companies also differentiated their coordination processes to match the roles of individual units, which vary in the transnational company (see Chapter 6). For example, subsidiaries assigned an implementation role (those in nonstrategic environments, with limited capabilities), have little ability to contribute to corporate information flows and are normally out of the loop of the organization's resource flows. However, because implementer subsidiaries are usually highly dependent on other parts of the organization for the products they sell, they become focal points in the corporate processes involving goods coordination. Thus, given their organizational role, implementer subsidiaries tend to be managed by formalized systems, which allowed headquarters to coordinate their activities with the least expenditure of corporate management time.[14]

The situation was quite different in subsidiaries operating in a contributor role. Because of their substantial internal resources, such units were generally less reliant on other parts of the organization for products and materials. And the information from their local environments was rarely of major importance to other units of the corporation. But while their place in the goods and information flows was often limited, their role in the organization resource flows was important. Management had to ensure that the excess capabilities of these subsidiaries would not be focused on the noncritical local environments, but would be redirected to central or global tasks. To make these subsidiaries an integral part of the company's resource flow system, their activities were often placed under quite direct headquarters coordination.

In subsidiaries classified as black holes—those with limited internal capabilities located in strategically important environments—the key task was to ensure that the corporation had access to the critical information available in their environments. In companies trying to extricate the subsidiary from its black hole status, another vital task was to supply the additional resources needed to build local capabilities appropriate to the country's strategic importance. While the socialization process was most appropriate for information transfer, centralization was required to refocus corporate resources on the black hole subsidiaries. They were typically managed in a way that balanced central control with attempts to develop a sense of self-sufficiency and independence.

Finally, the subsidiaries that played a lead role were inevitably a prime source of the company's finished products and proprietary knowledge, and as such were deeply involved in the goods and information flows. They were most often managed through processes of socialization and formalization, with socialization predominating. Although socialization is the most expensive means of coordination, its high cost is justified by the substantial local resources under lead units' control and the complexity of the environment they had to manage. Socialization is the most appropriate way for corporate management to develop the entrepreneurial and innovative capabilities so critical to such units, since it gives local management both substantial autonomy and a framework that helps ensure that their actions fit overall corporate strategic objectives and priorities.

To test our broad observations of the nature of the differentiated coordination process, we conducted a more detailed analysis of the eadquarters-subsidiary relationship in three of our sample companies. 'his is presented in the Appendix, and the findings generally confirm ur hypothesis and support the broad conclusions presented here.[15]

Although a differentiated approach appears to be valuable, we are .ot suggesting that each organizational unit should be managed by a ingle coordination process. Indeed, our findings suggest the opposite: hat an effective organizational coordination process must be multi- .imensional and flexible. Moreover, since subsidiaries play a variety of oles by product or business, a subsidiary that is the leader for one roduct may play a contributor role for another, and an implementer ole for a third. The important finding is that companies can and should .ifferentiate the way they coordinate organizational units. Manage- 1ent should vary the mix of centralization of authority, formalization f systems, and socialization of managers according to the nature of the 1sk and the strategic role of the units being coordinated.

TRANSNATIONAL COORDINATION: FROM CONTROL TO CO-OPTION

'aced with an increasingly complex organizational coordination task, 1any companies have responded by simplifying the processes through vhich they manage the growing number and diversity of coordination 1sks. By relying on a limited set of tools and processes, organizations ould develop a "company way" of coordination that became familiar nd comfortable.

For many companies, however, the search for managerial simplic- ty was overtaken by the need for greater organizational sophistication nd flexibility. Managers began to recognize that the bias toward a ingle dominant coordination process was leading to inefficiencies: lecisions arbitrated at headquarters when central managers had little .nowledge to make the necessary judgments; routine issues resolved hrough expensive and time-consuming group negotiations. Similarly, he approach of managing all units by the same basic process led to the roblems associated with universal structures and responsibilities (the o-called UN model described in Chapter 6).

Eventually managers are forced to develop a broad array of coordi- 1ation mechanisms and apply them in a discriminating manner.[16] The ital ingredient in the resulting transnational management process is he ability of senior managers to use different tools and mechanisms, eparately and together, in a flexible way.

In developing a transnational organization, we have emphasized, he attention of top management must extend beyond the structure, ystems, and processes required to manage it. By recognizing that all

organizational processes are built on a foundation of individual under
standing and commitment, top management can develop a manageria
mentality throughout the company that co-opts individual employee
into sharing the corporate vision rather than subjugates them in a little
understood organizational system. It is to this vital element—buildin
and managing individual managers' commitment to the organization—
that we now turn our attention.

10
BUILDING COMMITMENT: CREATING A MATRIX IN MANAGERS' MINDS

The great strength of the transnational organization is its in-built flexibility. The integrated network of distributed assets and resources allows companies to capture the efficiency of specialization without suffering the exchange rate exposure, political risks, or diseconomies of centralization. The development of multidimensional management perspectives and capabilities permits them to sense potential opportunities and problems regardless of their source, and to respond to changes quickly and appropriately. And the differentiation of subsidiary units' roles allows them to link and leverage organizational resources and match them to environmental needs or opportunities.

But these characteristics of the transnational organization are also the source of its greatest problems. Such an organization must learn to cope with enormous forces of fragmentation and dissipation. Without a strong source of unification, such a company risks deteriorating into organizational anarchy—or worse, an international network of warring fiefdoms.[1]

Among the companies we studied, those that were best able to provide a sense of unity had moved beyond the initial steps of reconfiguring assets, redefining roles, and restructuring management systems. Top management was equally concerned with the perceptions and behaviors of *individual managers* within the organization, trying to ensure that they shared an understanding of the company's purpose and values, an identification with broader goals, and commitment to the overall corporate agenda.[2] Such a management mentality becomes the "global glue" that counterbalances the centrifugal forces of the transnational structure and processes.[3]

There is no easy way to build understanding, identification, and commitment at the level of the individual manager. But several characteristics were common to the companies that managed this task most successfully. Most fundamentally, they had developed a common understanding of a clear and consistent corporate vision.

It is often difficult for managers to interpret an abstract vision in day-to-day decisions, however, or to see the operational implications of generalized objectives. The key to converting the broad vision into action lies in the manager's understanding and acceptance of the logic and importance of the objectives and this is the second key task we will describe in this chapter. By helping individuals broaden their perspectives and relationships, companies can develop their personal identification with the total organization.

The third task is perhaps the most difficult, yet may be the most powerful in building individual commitment to corporate objectives. The most successful companies were those that had cemented individual understanding and identification through a process we describe as "co-option." Giving managers a direct role in the achievement of the broad vision can be a powerful tool in converting passive acceptance to active commitment.

BUILDING A SHARED VISION

The more complex and changeable the strategic task and the more dispersed and differentiated the organizational units, the more likely that individual managers are confused. In countless conversations with managers—particularly those in a company's overseas operations—we were struck by their apparently limited understanding of corporate strategies, priorities, or even broad direction. Yet in certain companies, managers seemed to have a much keener sense of corporate goals. These were the organizations that had created a clear sense of purpose and communicated it effectively to managers worldwide.

At its most effective, a carefully crafted and well-articulated corporate vision could become a beacon of strategic direction and (at the risk of mixing metaphors) an anchor of organizational stability; in other companies, it was nothing more than a catchy but ineffective public relations device. Three important characteristics marked the successful cases: a clarity that made the objectives both understandable and meaningful, a continuity in pursuing them, and a consistency in interpreting and applying them across all organizational units.[4]

Clarity of Purpose

Most managers in large worldwide companies specialize in one activity and focus on one aspect of the overall corporate task. A clearly articulated corporate vision provides these managers with a broader frame of reference, one that gives context and meaning to their particular roles and responsibilities. Objectives that are too vague, too complex, or too abstract, however, rarely become the touchstones that link individual managers' efforts to overall organizational priorities. Our observations suggest that the primary requirement for an effective shared corporate vision was that it be clearly articulated and communicated. Three complementary factors contributed to the clarity of companies' statements of purpose: simplicity, relevance, and reinforcement.

NEC's commitment to "computers and communications" was the best single example of a simple statement that focused managers' attention on the company's broad strategic thrust. The "C & C" philosophy—it was not seen as just a slogan—did much more than designate the company's business focus; it also defined the firm's distinctive source of competitive advantage, and thus its strategic and organizational imperatives. (Compared with NEC's C & C capability, AT&T's slow development of computers made it a c & C company, while IBM's capability was depicted as C & c.) By such symbolism, top management communicated a complex strategic and organizational concept in a very simple way. Managers worldwide understood that the integration of the two businesses and technologies represented an important strategic and organizational priority for NEC—and the source of competitive advantage over larger companies such as IBM and AT&T.

Relevance also contributed to the clarity of a corporate vision. Abstract goals are hard to communicate and harder to understand, but companies that linked their broad objectives to agendas that were relevant to managers achieved great clarity of meaning.

When Dr. Wisse Dekker assumed the leadership of Philips, he knew that the company needed a unifying purpose to motivate managers to coordinate their independent units more effectively. Together with his senior management team, he focused the organization's attention on the problem of achieving a viable competitive position against the Japanese. Indeed, the challenge was stated in terms as national as they were corporate—the United States had given up the battle to achieve global competitiveness in consumer electronics, and Philips was Europe's last defense against the insurgent Japanese. Management was then able to concentrate on a coordinated response to the challenge. A rationalization of plant operations, cost-cutting efforts, a quality improvement program, and a corporatewide campaign to achieve sales, income, and inventory targets were all driven by the shared concern to maintain competitiveness against the Japanese.

The third means of achieving clarity was top management's continual reinforcement, elaboration, and interpretation of the core vision, so that it never became obsolete or overgeneralized. The sample company that most effectively translated and updated its vision was Matsushita. Konosuke Matsushita's 250-year vision for his company (or even one of its 25-year phases) is far too broad to provide anything but the most general guidance to managers in their day-to-day operations. So too are the company's oft-cited "Seven Spirits"—service through industry, fairness, harmony and cooperation, and so forth. But top management has always been willing to translate its grand visions into specific objectives and immediate priorities. Each January the company's chief executive sets objectives for the organization, the central theme of which is typically embodied in an annual slogan. Even though the annual objectives further the broad long-term goals and values, they are stated in operational terms and guide managers in implementing the grand vision.

Continuity of Purpose

Even the most powerful unifying corporate vision can dissipate if it is not backed by a managerial commitment to consistent implementation. Despite the many international pressures and constraints, companies must remain committed to a core set of strategic goals and organizational values. Without such continuity, the unifying vision quickly vanishes.

In our study we saw several companies whose international expansion and development were undermined by a lack of continuity. Some were handicapped by major shifts of corporate leadership that resulted in an on again–off again commitment to the international operations; others were diverted by dramatic changes in international priorities (Brazil in the late 1970s, China in the early 1980s, and Russia in the late 1980s commanded international attention and interest); and still others were whipsawed when short-term profit pressures overtook longer-term strategic interests, particularly in countries with high economic and political volatility.

Nowhere was the impact of continuity (or lack of it) more clearly visible than in the Brazilian subsidiaries of our sample companies. The contrast between the experiences of the General Electric and Unilever subsidiaries there is instructive.

We described in Chapter 5 the evolution of GE's international strategic posture in consumer electronics under successive CEOs from Borsch to Welch. These strategic shifts, combined with fluctuations in local economic and political conditions, led to a gradual erosion of GE's competitive position in many countries, particularly in Brazil, which was once one of the company's international strongholds. Entering the Brazilian market in the 1930s, GE had developed a dominant position in consumer electronics and appliances in the postwar era. Indeed, GE was the first entrant in the Brazilian radio, TV, and audio businesses, and for several years the only significant foreign manufacturer of these products. In the early 1960s, GE's Brazilian subsidiary proposed becoming a low-cost source for GE's radios in the United States. The parent company responded that GE was de-emphasizing radios and (this was the era of the mini-GE) urged the subsidiary to focus instead on color TV, which was due to boom in the Brazilian market. GE Brazil complied. After the introduction of color TV in the mid-1960s, Japanese manufacturers streamed into Brazil, setting up plants in the low-labor-cost and tax-free northern region of Manaus. Despite its leadership position in Brazil, GE was not willing to develop the German PAL technology that had been adopted as the Brazilian transmission standard, or to relocate its plants to Manaus. By 1968, the company had decided to exit the TV business and focus on its attractive major appliances and housewares businesses.

GE had also been the first entrant in refrigeration and air conditioning in Brazil, importing products until the late 1950s, when local assembly was established. By the 1970s, with GE's Brazilian sales approaching $500 million, strong local competitors started taking share. Reviewing the detailed strategic plans that were now central to GE's decision-making process, corporate management became concerned about declining share, fluctuating demand, price controls, and aggressive competition in its Brazilian appliance business. Judging the product line and manufacturing efficiency to be vulnerable to global competition, they decided to withdraw from this business in 1981, and encouraged local management to concentrate on its strong position in the Brazilian housewares market.

In the Welch era, GE managers were forced to evaluate businesses on the basis of their global competitive position. In a last ditch effort to bring costs in line with those of Far Eastern competitors, the company launched its "World Iron Project," a bold experiment in competition in small appliances. Brazil and two other global-scale plants in low-labor-cost countries became the company's worldwide sources for irons. But in the Welch era, unless a business was number one or two in its industry worldwide, it was divested. A couple of years after the global iron project was initiated, corporate management sold its worldwide housewares business to Black and Decker.

Over a twenty-year period, the Brazilian company's dominant position in a broad line of consumer products had evaporated. The fundamental problem was that its managers had no idea, from one year to the next, what their role was in the overall corporate strategy. The lack of commitment and consistency led to the gradual weakening and eventual abandonment of GE's consumer businesses worldwide.

GE's approach to international strategy is very different from that of most other firms we studied. One of the best examples of a consistent approach to international operations was provided by Unilever, a company whose long history abroad has allowed it to develop a clear long-term view of how international operations should be managed. H. F. van den Hoven, then chairman of Unilever NV, summed up the company's philosophy in a 1983 speech to employees:

> If someone were to ask me to say in one word what aspect we devote most attention to in managing this company, my answer would be "continuity." Rather than short-lived successes we must set our sights on profitability over the long term. The interests of a very large number of people are directly or indirectly dependent on our company's continuity.

His successor, Floris Maljers, expressed it more colorfully in speaking of the company's enduring commitment to Brazil, despite volatile swings that had caused others to leave:

> In those parts of the world you take your management cues from the way they dance. The samba method of management requires you to take two steps forward, then one step back. Companies with a short-term perspective are unable to adopt this perspective. They will either not get on the dance floor because it looks too difficult or risky—as was the case with Procter & Gamble which has never entered Brazil, despite numerous opportunities—or they will choose to sit down when it comes to the part that involves one step back—as our other competitor Henkel recently did, selling its Brazilian business to us.

As a result of its long-term commitment, Unilever has built a profitable $300 million business in a rapidly growing economy, with a population of 130 million, and with no major global competitor fighting for a share.[5]

Consistency of Purpose

The third important task for top management in communicating strategic direction is to establish a consistency of purpose across organizational units—in other words, to ensure that the vision is shared by all. The cost of inconsistency can be horrendous. At a minimum, it can result in confusion and inefficiency; in the extreme, it can lead organization units to pursue agendas that are mutually debilitating.

Although most inconsistencies manifest themselves in the differences in objectives between headquarters managers and those in overseas subsidiaries, or between one subsidiary and another, their roots can often be traced to different views transmitted by executives in top management. If inconsistencies in the overall vision and direction are based on fundamental differences and disagreements among senior management, they will be very hard to eliminate.

Corning Glass Works found itself in this situation when a struggle developed between the company president, who was in charge of Corning's diverse domestic businesses, and the head of the international division, who reported separately to the vice chairman. Their different visions created a schism within the organization that made cooperation between domestic and overseas units or between individual managers difficult if not impossible. The situation was resolved only by having domestic and international operations report to a single top management position. Only then was one clear consistent objective given to all managers regardless of location.[6]

Even when top management is united in its commitment to a common objective, its views are not always reflected throughout the organization. As many companies learned at considerable expense, communicating a clear vision to a large diverse organization involves much more than developing a corporate slogan or addressing an annual management conference. In companies that had developed a truly shared vision of their overall strategy and priorities—companies like NEC, Procter & Gamble, and Ericsson—senior management used every available opportunity to communicate, confirm, and clarify the overall corporate vision and direction. It was prepared to devote considerable personal time and effort to ensure that managers in all parts of the organization were marching to the same drummer.

One company that for a while lost consistency of corporate purpose was Philips. For decades it had difficulty persuading its North American unit to play a supportive role in its worldwide strategies, as was most dramatically illustrated in the introduction of its ill-fated video cassette recording system, the V2000. Despite considerable pressure from the top management, North American Philips (NAP) refused to launch the system, arguing that Sony's Beta system and Matsushita's VHS format were already too well established and had cost, feature, and system support advantages Philips could not match. Relying on its managerial autonomy, its legally independent status as a trust, and its partial local shareholding, NAP management decided instead to source VHS format products from their Japanese competitors and market them under Philips's own U.S. brands. As a result, Philips was unable to build the efficiency and credibility it needed to challenge the Japanese dominance of the VCR business.

Formulating and communicating a vision—no matter how clear, durable, and consistent—is not enough. Central to the effectiveness of a shared vision is the ability of individual organization members to understand and accept the goals and objectives articulated. Often, this is not a problem of communication, but of receptivity.

DEVELOPING INDIVIDUAL UNDERSTANDING AND ACCEPTANCE

In organizations staffed by specialists who are physically and organizationally isolated from one another, managers tend to become narrow and parochial. Even when they intellectually understand the broad objectives and priorities implied by the corporate vision, their constrained organizational view and narrow experience base often make it difficult for them to internalize the more expansive perspective. Thus, if a shared vision is to harness managers' perceptions and actions to corporate goals, then individual perspectives and capabilities must be broadened.

An enduring barrier to the development of a transnational organization is the lack of individual understanding and acceptance that surrounds the international activities in most corporations. But companies can no longer delegate the complex issues relating to foreign markets, overseas sourcing, or global technologies to a specialized group of "internationalists." Managers at all levels and across all disciplines must make decisions with important worldwide implications. How should diverse national consumer needs or environmental conditions be taken into account in developing new products? What is the most strategically appropriate location for the next increment of plant capacity? What potential benefits accrue to raising finances in different countries?

Every company we studied had had major problems because of the limited perspectives of individual managers making such decisions. Because the person responsible for making the decision was uncomfortable with, or even unreasonably prejudiced against, a truly international point of view, products were developed for single-market needs rather than worldwide opportunities, capacity was added to existing plants rather than where it could capture greatest competitive advantage, and the company's traditional financial markets were tapped regardless of opportunities existing elsewhere. For several companies, the parochial behavior of a handful of managers in key positions was the major impediment to the development of transnational organizational capabilities.

The key to breaking down such attitudes and perceptions is a human resource function that aims to broaden perspectives, build experience, and develop relationships that result in management flexibility and close interunit linkages. Many companies we studied had consciously upgraded their personnel function from a low-level, isolated staff responsibility, focused on the administration of salary and benefit programs, to a central responsibility of all line managers supported by qualified specialists and sophisticated systems integrated into the mainstream decision-making process.

A central objective of the new human resource management program was to develop an organization in which the individual manager's perceptions, capabilities, and relationships would become the basic building block for an integrated, yet flexible worldwide organization. Three aspects of personnel policy—the recruiting and selection process, the training and development activities, and the career path management practices—were particularly important.

Recruiting and Selection

None of the companies we studied was satisfied with its ability to develop a pool of managers qualified to assume key roles in international operations. All the companies still had strong home country biases in their recruitment processes, and so the size, mix, and overall quality of the pool of available talent was unduly constrained.

For example, the managing director of Philips's Corporate Staff Bureau, the personnel function responsible for top management, said, "The Netherlands simply cannot continue to supply us with sufficient top-quality people who can become our next generation of senior managers. To get the best candidates we must draw from a worldwide pool." Ericsson was similarly hampered in its recruitment of engineers and technicians, particularly when it was developing the new AXE digital switch. Even after hiring almost two-thirds of the newly graduated Swedish engineers in electronics and data processing, the company still could not meet its demands.

Both companies solved this problem by breaking their historical linkage between specialization and centralization. Once Ericsson recognized it could delegate peripheral hardware development to leading subsidiary units and that new software could be written anywhere, as long as the effort was linked to the corporate system, the company began drawing on the larger pools of engineering talent in England, the United States, and other technologically advanced locations. Philips too broadened its recruitment policies, focusing on its entry program for young graduates. A new Star Track program was introduced to attract high-potential individuals from several European countries and give them the same overseas experience and same close top management attention historically reserved for newly recruited Dutch graduates.

Both companies hope to emulate the success of Unilever, which consciously initiated worldwide recruiting efforts in the 1930s. Having coupled its recruiting net to an intensive training and development program and a sophisticated worldwide expatriate transfer system, Unilever could boast that almost 400 of its 1,000 expatriates on assignment worldwide were from non-home countries. The corporate board of directors drew on Unilever executives from five countries.

A domestically oriented recruiting approach not only limited companies' ability to capitalize on a worldwide pool of management talent, but tended to bias their organizational processes. After decades of routinely appointing managers from its domestic operations to key positions in overseas subsidiaries, Procter & Gamble realized that this practice worked against sensitivity to the local culture. The lesson was firmly driven home after several painful product and marketing failures in Japan convinced management to make more extensive use of local nationals. P&G now relies much less on expatriate American managers to fill top international jobs. In addition to beefing up overseas subsidiaries' recruiting activity to meet local needs, the company has begun a major recruiting program at the corporate level aimed at internationalizing future senior corporate managers. Rather than focusing on good American candidates, P&G is working hard to attract foreign nationals attending leading American business schools, giving them exposure in the parent company, then transferring them to their home country to build their careers.

Many Japanese companies face a different problem in their management recruitment practices. Like their European and American counterparts, they have relied heavily on home country nationals to take the top jobs and the key linkage positions in overseas units, particularly in the early stage of a subsidiary's development. But local national managers feel isolated and excluded from the centralized decision that typifies such companies. Furthermore, the substantial language and cultural barriers that separate headquarters from most overseas units convince most non-Japanese that their career potential is limited to the national company and, even there, to positions not earmarked for expatriate Japanese. An American manager in Matsushita's U.S. subsidiary captured the frustration: "It is ironic that the very factors that have made this company's management of its production workers abroad so successful (participation in decision making, job security and advancement opportunities, and an egalitarian attitude) all seem to be missing from their treatment of management. I am becoming very doubtful that I can look forward to a satisfying career here." As a result of such attitudes, many Japanese companies have had difficulty recruiting and retaining the most talented individuals in their foreign operations. This problem in turn has often reinforced the decision to keep expatriate Japanese as the key decision makers.

To break out of this vicious cycle, several companies are conducting radical experiments in human resource management. Personnel is one of four key priorities in Matsushita's Localization Program, and the company is replacing expatriate Japanese with host country nationals wherever possible. Sony moved earlier to localize managers, but then had to deal with problems in headquarters-subsidiary communications. NEC has gone one step further and initiated a program in which top foreign-country executives are assigned to NEC headquarters. The objective is to build mutual understanding and positive relationships between headquarters and subsidiary managers, reducing the need to use Japanese expatriates in key linkage roles. Eventually, the hope is to open up key corporate positions to non-Japanese managers.

In many European and American companies too, nonparent-company managers felt excluded from positions of real power or influence. Companies as different as Philips and Procter & Gamble are both working to recruit more strong local nationals and open corporatewide opportunities for them.

But opening up the recruiting process is only a first step. Companies must also find ways to identify those individuals most likely to succeed in transnational organizational processes. Many managers have failed in their international postings, at a huge economic, organizational, and personal cost.[7]

One of the most effective ways to reduce the problem is to implement a more effective internal selection process—in effect, a second-level recruiting process—to identify the candidates best suited for these positions. Some of the companies we studied were still selecting managers for international service on the basis of success in domestic operations (or, in one company, on *poor* performance, since overseas markets were assumed to be "not as tough as the domestic environment"). A further problem was that overseas assignments often were not regarded as offering much prestige or potential. In Japanese companies, the expression "escaping overseas banishment" became part of the business jargon, and in one company in our study, an overseas posting was widely referred to as an "unlucky assignment." In American companies, managers seemed more concerned with the "re-entry problem"; many believed that a tour of duty abroad usually meant giving up one's position on the parent company's promotion escalator. These factors combined to create an environment in which many managers tried to withdraw themselves from the pool for international assignment.

Companies thus needed not only to enlarge the pool of internal candidates, but to develop criteria to select those with the greatest chance of success. NEC did particularly well in the first task. First, top management made it clear that international experience was an important, perhaps essential, qualification for promotion to senior levels. Then a new overseas personnel registration system was introduced to rate some 20,000 employees for their suitability for overseas assignment. Two superiors evaluated each person on both personal qualities and job skills. In essence, the company sent a signal to all key sales, engineering, and administrative managers that they were considered part of the worldwide pool of management talent. The top 25 percent of those in the system became the primary pool from which overseas candidates were drawn. The ratings, updated every three years, also became the basis for individual training and development to prepare candidates for such postings.

The companies in our study—Japanese, American, and European—all used much the same criteria to identify managers likely to succeed in a truly transnational organization. Dr. Wisse Dekker, chairman of Philips's board of management, described the desired qualities in a New Year's address (a vehicle often used at Philips to signal major strategic and organizational priorities):

> This brings me to the question of the optimum selection of our future managers. . . . We must look not only for professional skill and business acumen as our criteria, but also for the capacity to be able and willing to listen to others, openness, accessibility, and communication skills. Last, but not least, we must look for an understanding and knowledge of social developments. Managers no longer make the grade who treat society as something that bothers one, to be given a wide berth.

These themes were echoed in many of the companies we studied. Matsushita had reduced its experience in selecting expatriates to a simple acronym—SMILE—capturing five criteria remarkably similar to the characteristics detailed by Dekker: Specialty (the needed skill, capability, or knowledge), Management ability (particularly motivational ability), International (willingness to learn and ability to adapt), Language facility, and Endeavor (vitality, perseverance in the face of difficulty). At NEC, a systematic review process considered similar factors of personality (vitality, adaptability, tolerance, curiosity) and capability (management skills, job knowledge, language ability, negotiating skills, and problem-solving ability).

By developing such explicit criteria, companies found they could substantially improve the caliber of their overseas appointments. Moreover, by assigning more effective managers to the national subsidiaries, they raised the status and desirability of such assignments. By placing at the center of the international process managers who are more open to being transferred, better able to view issues from a broad perspective, and more willing to negotiate and collaborate on matters of shared interest, a company takes a large step toward creating a transnational organization.

Training and Development

Once it has identified managers more sensitive to international management realities, a company should develop their latent potential.

Many of the companies we studied found management training and development programs effective for this purpose. They used such programs to build cultural norms, shape organizational processes, and influence individual managerial behavior in a way that reinforced worldwide strategic and organizational objectives.[8]

Management typically had three aims in training and development efforts: to inculcate a common vision and shared values (called "cultural and spiritual training" in Matsushita, "organization cohesion" in Philips, and "indoctrination" in Unilever); to broaden management perspectives and capabilities ("widening career bases," as Dekker termed it); and to develop contacts and shape management relationships.[9]

No company we studied was more thorough in developing a common vision and shared values than Matsushita. During their first six months on the job, its white-collar employees are all exposed to intensive "cultural and spiritual training." They not only learn the company's credo and the seven spirits of Matsushita (which are repeated daily in morning assemblies held around the globe), they also study the fuller philosophy of Konosuke Matsushita. At the conclusion of the formal program, employees are grouped under a leader to continue discussions of how the philosophy translates into their daily responsibilities. Each unit's personnel department is responsible for ongoing "spiritual training" to ensure that corporate values are fully embedded in management behavior. In addition, video tapes on various aspects of Matsushita's philosophy and operations are translated into local languages and distributed worldwide.[10] As a result, corporate objectives and values are not meaningless concepts mindlessly checked off in rote repetition during morning assembly. Instead, they are thoroughly internalized beliefs that managers at all levels refer to daily, and that often become the basis for purely operational decisions.[11]

The use of training and development programs to broaden management perspectives has been particularly important at Philips. The company's long tradition of two-headed and sometimes three-headed management encouraged the development of technical, commercial, and administrative specialists who formed top-level committees to guide policy for the product division or national organization. As the company recognized the organizational complexity and operational awkwardness of such an approach, the training and development group was asked to "despecialize" the upcoming management group. The aim was to develop generalists who could take charge of an organizational unit in single-headed fashion, but who also had an understanding of and respect for all points of view. The traditional menu of specialist courses and functionally oriented programs was reinforced with more general management training, and the company has boosted its financial commitment to such programs severalfold.

Matsushita used training to develop a more international point of view in its management group. In the early 1970s, the company built an impressive Overseas Training Center (OTC) dedicated to this purpose. The most basic effort is to give a broad group of managers better access to the company's worldwide operations by improving their language skills. Over 5,000 students go through OTC's language courses each year; most learn English, but Spanish, Chinese, and other languages are also taught. During its first dozen years of operation, over 1,000 employees went through OTC's intensive training programs in preparation for overseas tours of duty. In the same period, over 3,000 foreign trainees came to the center for cultural and skills training. The underlying objective of all of the programs was to broaden the international perspectives of the students, making them more sensitive and responsive to other nationalities.

NEC's Institute of International Studies, founded in 1980, offered comparable programs and had similar objectives for internationalizing the company's management perspectives and capabilities. Indeed, NEC's personnel policy explicitly aimed to make the company "more flexible, more dynamic," and the company's training programs were supposed not only to transmit the new knowledge demanded by the dynamic business environment, but also to develop the broader management viewpoints needed for flexible decision making. It was this objective that led to the foundation of its Institute of International Studies.

In these and similar programs, management had an important additional objective that was well articulated by a senior personnel manager at Unilever.

> By bringing managers from different countries and businesses together at "Four Acres" [Unilever's International Management Training College] we build contacts and create bonds that we could never achieve by other means. The company spends as much on training as it does on R&D not only because of the direct effect it has on upgrading skills and knowledge, but also because such programs play a central role in indoctrinating managers into a Unilever fraternity or club where personal relationships and informal contacts are much more powerful than the formal systems and structures.

Career Path Management

Although recruitment and training were valuable, many companies recognized that the best way to develop a broad international perspective in their managers was through personal experience. By moving selected managers across functions, between businesses, and among geographic units, a company not only creates an organizational environment in which cross-fertilization of ideas can occur, but also develops individuals with the breadth of experiences and perspectives necessary to manage in a flexible manner.[12]

The foundation of such a process is an inventory and evaluation system that allows top management to identify and track the scarcest of all corporate resources, skilled management. Many of our sample companies had developed such systems on a worldwide basis, and began to regard personnel assignment as a management and organization development opportunity as well as a resource distribution task.

Introduced in 1973, Philips's career path management system was based on a reliable, current audit and appraisal of the company's worldwide management resources. To signal his commitment to the program, Dekker upgraded the Corporate Staff Bureau and had it report directly to him. "Those with responsibility for our management development system must have direct access to the most senior management of the company," he said. Together with the board, Dekker was personally involved in the selection, development, and career path decisions for almost 1,500 of the company's senior managers.

The objective of Philips's Corporate Staff Bureau was to focus the organization on the development of individuals. It viewed the task of filling vacant jobs as a means of building management capabilities and creating fulfilling careers. Central to this approach was the company's job rotation system, which was regarded as the centerpiece of the management of high-potential individuals, particularly during their first ten or twelve years.

To meet the company's stated need for more generalists and internationalists, management felt there was no substitute for diverse job experience in multiple functions and locations. High-potential employees were assigned internationally for at least three to five years. Gradually, Philips was breaking down the tight-knit group of expatriates, the "Dutch Mafia," who moved from one national organization to another over a good part of their career. The new system was aimed at internationalizing a broad group of managers, not just a select cadre.

Career path management practices at Unilever were in many ways similar to those at Philips, but the Unilever system had been in operation longer and its effects were already evident throughout the company. Unilever had a clear policy of rotating managers through various jobs, particularly in the early years of their careers, recognizing the importance of specialists' skills, but emphasizing too the need for generalists in top positions. An individual who showed high potential and continued good performance could expect to rotate through various functions, product groups, and geographic areas every two to three years.

As the company's strong commitment to localizing the recruitment and development of managers (the so-called "ization" process) began making overseas companies more self-sufficient, there was less need to send expatriates from the parent company to run operations around the world. But Unilever management knew that such transfers had been the glue that bound diverse operations together. Rather than halt the tradition of expatriation, they wanted to enrich it and manage it more effectively. They certainly did not want greater localization of national company management to result in greater isolation. For example, if Indian managers were to take responsibility for running Unilever's Indian company, then they would have to become more knowledgeable about corporate objectives and values.

In addition to the hundreds of overseas managers brought to its training programs in England (more than 300 a year by the 1980s), the company created short-term and long-term job assignments for international managers in the corporate offices. In 1986, there were more than eighty expatriates in the London headquarters and approximately fifty in Rotterdam, representing about 10 percent of the central staff. The company claimed this process brought diverse input to corporate thinking and helped guard against "ivory tower" decisions that were out of touch with marketplace realities. The central purpose, however, was to indoctrinate the managers in the ways of the company. Beyond learning about the company's products and strategies, they were to join the so-called Unilever Club. This unofficial cohort had a strong sense of identity with the company, conformed to tacit but well-understood norms, and shared a common bond that led to generally open and cooperative interpersonal dealings among club members.

Unilever makes two kinds of assignments in sending expatriates abroad. Some decisions attempt to meet the organizational need by transferring a manager who already has the required skills for the job; others try to meet the management development need by assigning an individual who would benefit from the job experience. The two types of assignments are carefully balanced, so that transfers are not driven primarily by the short-term needs of the overseas companies nor constrained by the administrative complications of managing expatriates on a worldwide basis. The company has abandoned its traditional practice of using a group of "circuit men" as the expatriate core. Today the management development value of such assignments is seen as too high to waste on "a group of old lags," as one manager called them.

Unilever expects that the great majority of its future top managers will have had substantial international experience. But since planning and managing career path development requires substantial effort, the company (like Philips) has developed a sophisticated international management identification and evaluation system that feeds its expatriation program. Unilever maintains four development lists that reflect both the level of the manager and his or her potential. The progress of managers on the most select A1 list is tracked by the company's Special Committee (the two company chairmen and the vice chairman) with the help of the corporate personnel division. Other groups in the company are responsible for following the B, C, and D lists of managers. Using these lists, Unilever managers appoint those two levels below them in the organization. Thus the chairman of Industries Gessy-Lever Limitada, Unilever's huge Brazilian organization, was appointed by the board's Special Committee; the heads of the detergent, edible fats, and personal products divisions in Brazil were named by the central Overseas Committee on the advice of the responsible director; and appointments to key functional posts within each division were made by the Brazilian country chairman. In this way, a much broader range of candidates could be considered for major job openings, no matter where they were located.

Using this system, Unilever maintains expatriates in about 5 percent of its worldwide management positions at any one time. In 1986, for example, 997 of the company's 18,583 managers were on expatriate assignment. Although Dutch and British managers are still the majority, approximately 250 of this group were from North America or other European countries, and an additional 87 were from 19 countries in Unilever's overseas group (Latin America, Australia, Africa, and Asia). Through this constant rotation of managers, Unilever developed an appreciation of global as well as local needs, and a network of contacts that facilitated informal information exchange and decision making.

CO-OPTING MANAGEMENT EFFORTS:
THE BINDING COMMITMENT

Gaining the active involvement and personal commitment of individual managers has proven next to impossible for many companies. Intellectually, most managers may understand the company's strategic vision and they may have had the training to develop a broad corporate frame of reference, but they are so consumed by their immediate operating responsibilities that they often think and act in a parochial manner when global issues impinge on their turf. In trying to create the involvement needed to develop binding personal commitment among managers, many companies pursued similar approaches. They reasoned that if managers were given direct responsibility for achieving part of the corporate vision and key roles in coordinating the new organization, they could be co-opted into the transnational agenda.

The means and level of involvement varied widely, but generally fell into two categories. Most widely used were structures for soliciting a broad range of input to key strategic decisions. By institutionalizing managers' participation in the deliberations leading to major choices, companies found they could greatly increase managers' personal commitment to the firm. In addition numerous approaches were used to give managers specific responsibility for the implementation of key parts of the transnational organization's core agenda. Procter & Gamble's Euro Brand Teams are a case in point. Particularly through the allocation of the strategic roles described in Chapter 6, companies co-opted individuals and even whole organization units into the corporate objectives and priorities.

The company that faced the most difficult challenge in co-opting management efforts was Philips. Historically, its cadre of expatriate Dutch managers had not been easily bound into the parent company's changing strategic needs or shifting organizational priorities. Although trained at corporate headquarters and rotated among posts, many of these managers tended to "go native." The culture of the company seemed to foster an attitude of strong independence and sometimes elitism in this group. Many of the expatriates believed that only they understood the real needs of their local markets and that executives at headquarters promoting new ideas and different priorities were "uninformed meddlers" and "unnecessary overhead."[13]

When Philips began increasing the strategic responsibilities and organizational control of the product divisions in the 1970s, management recognized the risk such changes involved. The Audio Division, which was then facing intense competitive pressure, was one of the earliest to take on the expanded central role. Knowing how important it was to retain the commitment of the national organizations, division management created numerous forums for developing a global strategy. The Audio Consultation Meeting brought together key division and national organization managers quarterly to discuss broad product policy issues and priorities; when product policies and market strategies were developed, they were presented at the annual Audio Product Meeting, where the input of national organization managers was elicited; and marketing and distribution strategies were developed and reviewed in collaboration with subsidiary managers at an Audio Policy Consultation Meeting.[14]

The Video Division made little serious effort to coordinate Philips's worldwide television strategies and operations until Japanese competition entered Europe in the late 1970s. Learning from the experiences of the Audio Division, management also structured numerous teams, committees, and task forces for developing the broad global business strategy and relating it to product line design and advertising policy. The top-level committees went through various formats and orientations before evolving into a top-level World Strategic Council and an operating-level World Policy Council involving key managers from the product division in Eindhoven and from the so-called strategic markets of the United Kingdom, Germany, France, United States, and Japan.

But although such meetings ensured that managers in the national organizations were included in decision making, they did not co-opt all players into major changes in direction. Some managers felt their views were not listened to. As one said, "The World Policy Council has a strong European bias. The members are unaware of and apparently unconcerned with a very different competitive battle we are waging in the United States." Others viewed the committees as merely another channel for informing the organization of strategies and policies developed by central management. A manufacturing manager in the huge consumer electronics operations in Croydon, England, implied as much:

> All of a sudden in 1983 we found ourselves having to follow directions from the center. Certainly the committees and councils kept us well informed, but there were just too many changes at once—new product designs, new processes, new equipment, new test gear. The feeling was that the pressure to move to standard European television chassis was leading to the production of overly expensive and inappropriate products.

Naming national companies as International Production Centers and giving them lead country status proved to be a much more effective way of co-opting subsidiary managers into the effort to integrate television strategy and operations on a worldwide basis. The Croydon manufacturing manager described the impact of his plant's becoming an IPC for television sets:

> It really forced us to build our relationships with Eindhoven [headquarters]. Where once we resented their visits, we started bringing people across; we started using the various meetings we were involved in as a way to represent our point of view; and we gradually began to understand the product division's systems and the reason for all the requests for information. We also started making more contacts with other plants in Europe and with 40 percent of our output being exported, for the first time we really felt that we were international managers.

Consumer electronics product division managers in Eindhoven had long regarded their colleagues in North American Philips (NAP) as the most isolated and independent in the company's worldwide operations. This, after all, was the group that had chosen to outsource VCRs manufactured by Japanese rivals rather than sell Philips's own V2000 system. In late 1985, however, when the NAP consumer electronics group was asked to coordinate development and manufacture of all Philips television sets using the NTSC transmission standard that dominated North American and Asian markets, relationships between Eindhoven and New York began to improve noticeably.

A senior manager in the North American consumer products business summed up the sentiment of American personnel:

> At last we are moving out of the dependency relationship with the center that was so frustrating to us. Rather than trying to sell NTSC versions of televisions developed for European tastes and adapted from the dominant European PAL technology, we can respond to our local market and competitive situation, and develop sets in collaboration with our labs in Japan and Taiwan with a more coordinated NTSC product line. We will be able to source from the United States, Mexico, Taiwan, or any other country using that standard. We are currently working with representatives from Eindhoven and the Far East to develop global NTSC facilities and a sourcing plan.

Two years later, after production of 13-inch NTSC standard sets had been moved from Taiwan to Mexico, the president of NAP's consumer electronics company was quoted in the press as saying, "It is the commonality of design that makes it possible for us to move production globally. We had splendid cooperation with Philips in Eindhoven." No NAP manager would have made such a statement even a few years earlier.

At the central product division, management was convinced that by using existing facilities, skills, and resources to meet worldwide needs, it was capturing substantial operating economies and also co-opting local managers into actively supporting its global mission. For this reason, Philips has not concentrated the high-status lead country roles in a few highly sophisticated units. Instead, it has assigned different responsibilities to different national organizations so that many of them have a high-status worldwide role for one or two products, even if these products represent only a minor part of their total portfolio. In so doing, the company not only frees up its major national organizations to concentrate their efforts and resources on the company's most important products, but motivates managers in the smaller or less sophisticated subsidiaries and gives them a sense of importance and belonging in the company's worldwide operations.

A MATRIX IN THE MINDS OF MANAGERS

There is a risk, as companies move toward an integrated network configuration, that managers will become so preoccupied with the necessary structural and systems changes that they will see the task as one of building a formal global matrix. Such structurally oriented approaches failed in the past because they did not recognize the importance of gaining the understanding and commitment of those who had to manage the new multidimensional and interdependent tasks.

The more successful companies in our study were those that extended their efforts beyond changing existing structures and systems. In these companies, we were struck by the substantial amount of top management time and attention focused on individual members of the organization. Examples include Unilever's worldwide recruiting efforts, its extensive use of training as a socialization process, and its well-planned career path management; Matsushita's continual efforts to instill common values and objectives in all corporate members; P&G's careful assignment of managers to teams and task forces to broaden their perspectives; and Philips's assignment of partial global roles to managers in its national organizations. These companies are trying to develop multidimensional perspectives and flexible approaches at the level of the individual manager.

One senior manager described the organizational task facing his company in a provocative way: "It is not so much to change the structure into a matrix as it is to create a matrix in the minds of our managers." The more that individuals can resolve complex and potentially contradictory issues, the less the organizational system has to cope with them. But for individuals to make such judgments and trade-offs in a way that fits overall corporate needs, they must have been selected for, developed by, and co-opted into the broader transnational organization.

11
THE TRANSNATIONAL SOLUTION

O nly the bravest—or most foolish—of futurists would try to forecast long-term trends in international business environments. Over extended periods of history, trade barriers have risen and fallen; currency values have fluctuated; successive waves of technological change have had dramatic effects; and consumer needs and preferences have ebbed and flowed. To the most experienced international managers, there is a great deal of truth in the old maxim, "nothing endures but change," to which they might be tempted to add, "and with every round of change the task becomes more complex."

The external forces for change and complexity are reinforced by equally important transformations occurring within many organizations. As we have seen, companies that once regarded their international units as entirely separate from the core domestic business now see the need to integrate their worldwide strategies and operations. Those that previously thought they could manage everything in much the same way globally now recognize the need to be sensitive to environmental diversity. In other words, companies are adopting more and more complex strategies to deal with ever-changing multidimensional demands in the international business environment.

To some extent, therefore, the task facing managers in worldwide companies is predictable. It will continue to be dynamic and to become more complex. But as we have stressed, these are the very organizational characteristics that have been historically the most difficult to manage. Our transnational model, unlike traditional organizational forms, is designed and developed specifically to respond to complexity and change.

In this final chapter, we will address three issues. First, we will consider how broadly the concepts and solutions we have proposed might be applied. Second, we will highlight the ways in which the transnational departs from traditional modes of organizing and managing worldwide operations. Finally, we will see if the transnational organization represents a generalized model for worldwide companies of the future, or are there legitimate alternative ways to organize and manage international operations?

THE TRANSNATIONAL ORGANIZATION: EXTENDING THE LESSONS

While the study and the findings it generated focused on the changing strategic and organizational demands being placed on worldwide companies, the more we talked to managers, the more we came to realize that our diagnosis and prescriptions had much broader applicability. What we were dealing with was the management of increasing complexity, diversity, and change, and this was the challenge facing all managers everywhere, regardless of how widely their operations were spread around the globe.

In particular, there are two broad trends that will make the "transnational solution" a relevant model for companies that are different from the large worldwide organizations we studied. The first is the continuing and accelerating changes in the international business environment, which are drawing more and more companies beyond their national borders. The second is the growing complexity of interorganizational relationships between companies and their stakeholders, which is challenging companies to find new and different ways to manage across once impermeable corporate boundaries.

New Challenges for Domestic Managers

By studying companies that conscientiously sought to internationalize their operations, we focused on a subset that was fully exposed to the forces of change that swept through the international economy in the 1970s and 1980s—oil shocks, trade agreements, floating currencies, global competitive gaming, national industrial policies, world debt crises, and so forth. In many ways, these companies absorbed the shock of the first wave of fundamental change in the world economy that has continued to reverberate through national economies, affecting all firms—large and small, local and global.

Those firms that did not seek the complexity, diversity, and change of the international environment are finding it thrust upon them through a variety of accelerating structural changes and environmental discontinuities. The historic United States-Canadian trade agreement, the 1992 initiative in the European Community, and the much-discussed extension of GATT agreements into the service sector represent some of the transformational changes that are forcing managers in even the most parochial companies to reexamine the way they think about and operate their businesses. They too are being confronted with strategic and organizational challenges once reserved for the largest and most sophisticated worldwide companies. Increasingly, the management of complexity, diversity, and change is the central issue facing all companies.[1]

New Demands on Focused Companies

The lessons learned by companies managing across national borders also have great relevance for companies facing another kind of organizational complexity—managing across corporate boundaries. As the pressures for global competitiveness, national responsiveness, and worldwide innovation increase, many companies recognize their inability to develop world-class competitive capabilities in all three areas, simultaneously. In a world undergoing technological revolution, companies that once defined themselves as being in the telephone business must now build strategies in telecommunications and information processing; banks must transform themselves into fully integrated financial services businesses; and computer companies must shift their focus from selling hardware to selling "solutions" that incorporate systems, software, and service.

The huge investment and diverse capabilities required to make this transformation have forced many companies to form strategic partnerships, coalitions, and alliances. This change too has forced managers to shift their thinking from the traditional task of controlling a hierarchy to managing a network.[2] Like the transnationals, such organizations are typified by units with multiple perspectives and capabilities, dispersed assets and resources, and differentiated roles and responsibilities. In many ways the task of managing across corporate boundaries has much in common with that of managing across national borders, and the findings we have presented—particularly those related to building and managing an integrated network—should have relevance for these firms.

MANAGEMENT IMPLICATIONS: TASKS, TOOLS, AND PROCESSES

The Task: Redefining the Objective

As we discussed in Chapter 2, many companies responded to the growing complexity of their environment by installing increasingly complex organizational forms. The assumption that management could best deal with conflicting demands by a formal structure led to the development of the global matrix—a structure that many felt fit the new environmental demands.[3]

The logic behind the adoption of the global matrix was compelling. Its dual reporting channels recognized the conflict between demands and provided a structural means for obtaining resolution; its multiple information channels allowed the organization to capture and analyze the external complexity; and its overlapping responsibilities were designed to provide in-built flexibility in the company's response to external changes.

But while the matrix structure appeared simple and rational, the organizational process it created in an international setting proved to be practically unmanageable. The dual reporting relationships led to confusion and conflict; the proliferation of formal channels created log jams in the information flow; and the overlapping responsibilities re sulted in turf battles and lack of accountability. Separated by distance language, time, and culture, managers could not clarify the confusion and resolve the conflicts the way they could in purely domestic or ganizations.

Gradually managers recognized that they may have been defining their objective in the wrong terms. By detaching themselves from the Stopford and Wells's stages model or from similar theories, many saw the task as more than simply seeking "structural fit." The real task was to build the organizational capability to deal with the emerging envi ronment, and no simple, static structural solution could create that capability. Attention shifted from the formal organization chart to the managerial decision-making process; the relevant unit of analysis changed from the company as a whole to the individual manager and his or her behavior.

The change in attitude was best captured by the international divi sion president at Corning Glass Works, one of the companies we studied in the pilot stage of our research. After almost a decade of pursuing the structure that would bring order out of the chaos that confronted its rapid overseas expansion, the company began to take a different approach:

> As we looked for the solution to the new challenges we faced, we kept returning to the structure. We looked at how other compa- nies had organized, we discussed the advantages of one form over another. But after a considerable amount of time, we came to realize that no structure could appropriately capture the complex- ity of Corning's international management task, with its multiple businesses in a diverse set of markets.
>
> The breakthrough came when we began to think in terms of pro- cess. How did information flow? Where and how should various decisions be made? What kind of roles and relationships were necessary business by business and issue by issue? It was when we began to look at these questions that we really began to make progress.

Many managers in large, sophisticated, and experienced world- wide companies, our study showed, have tried to reduce the complex- ity of the organizational challenge to simple choices to be resolved by a single tool—most often formal structure. Fortunately, many more have reached a conclusion like the managers at Corning. They understood that building the appropriate organizational capabilities required more than choosing among structural forms, and managing the worldwide company implied more than centralizing or decentralizing decision-making responsibility. The challenge was not to find the structure that provided the best fit, but to build and manage the appropriate decision process—one that could sense and respond to multiple changing environmental demands.

The Tools: A Biological Analogy

If the structural stages model is no longer rich enough to describe international organization development adequately, how can we conceptualize the building and management of the transnational? During our study we often found ourselves using a biological analogy to describe organizational characteristics.[4] Formal structure defines an organization's basic anatomy; systems and information flows shape its physiology; and culture and values represent its psychology. Change strategies that work through only one of these elements are less effective than those that address all three.

The definition of a worldwide company's formal organization structure is one of the most important decisions managers must make, since it defines formal decision-making channels and allocates responsibility and authority. Most managers in the companies we studied understood, however, this macrostructural tool has important limitations—it tends to define decision processes in unidimensional, symmetrical, and static terms. In a multidimensional, differentiated, and dynamic environment, managers soon found they had to compensate for the biases created by formal structure. This realization led them to some of the finer and subtler tools for shaping *organizational anatomy*.

To develop more transnational characteristics, managers were making greater use of mechanisms that might be called *microstructural* tools. Task forces, committees, and project teams became legitimate, and sometimes permanent parts of an organization's structure, allowing managers to fine-tune the decision-making channels and responsibility distributions defined by the basic macro structure. Because such off-line mechanisms can become an expensive and time-consuming way of managing, their use must be clearly focused and tightly controlled. Implemented effectively, however, these forums can be a good way to legitimize the nonline management perspectives and offset the mainstream allocation of responsibility and authority.

By shaping formal relationships among managers, macro- and microstructural tools also influence the way the organization's management processes operate. Yet, by adapting administrative systems, communication channels, and informal relationships, managers can exert an even more extensive control over the information flows that shape decisions in any large organization. Because the flow of information is the lifeblood of all management decisions, we see it as the *organizational physiology*.

Many researchers have shown the link between the complexity and uncertainty of tasks and the need for information. Operating an interdependent system in a changeable and often contradictory environment, managers in transnational organizations must gather, exchange, and process large volumes of information.[5] Furthermore, because decision making is no longer concentrated at corporate headquarters (as it is in a centralized hub structure) or at the local subsidiary (as it is in a decentralized federation configuration), the transnational's physiology must be able to carry a great deal of complex information to diverse locations in its integrated network of operations.

As we have seen, formal systems alone cannot support such huge information-processing needs. Indeed, many companies found they were being strangled by the increasingly demanding requirements of information, planning, and control systems. New channels and forums for information processing and exchange had to be created, most often by managing informal systems.

Managers have long recognized that a great deal of information exchange and decision making—perhaps the majority—is carried out through informal channels and relationships.[6] Yet, particularly in worldwide companies, this part of the management process has often been dismissed as either unimportant ("nothing more than gossip and rumor") or unmanageable ("you risk creating disruptive cliques or unholy alliances"). In organizations where information needs are intense and existing systems overloaded, such biases need to be re-examined. In many of our companies we saw managers trying to exert some control and influence over informal systems. Paradoxically, many found informal processes relatively easy to influence in companies with worldwide operations. Because of the widespread distribution of organizational units and the relative infrequency of direct contacts among those in disparate units, top management had a better opportunity to shape relationships among managers simply by being able to influence the nature and frequency of contacts. Most recognized that it was legitimate and often important for them to do so.

Major advances in international telecommunications and transportation, particularly in the 1970s, made it feasible to replace many formal systems and reports with more direct personal communications. Faster, more convenient, and lower-cost international air travel enabled managers at all levels to make trips abroad on brief, well-defined missions, rather than rely on data extracted from the formal reporting system. For the first time, many worldwide companies began to regard personal contacts, not formal systems, as their primary means of communication. The impact of this new approach on understanding among organizational units was profound.

By influencing the frequency and agenda of international management trips, participation in key meetings, or the nominees for important committee assignments, top management realized it could harness the potential of the personal information exchange network. A good example was Corning Glass Works' "analog management" system. Rather than create yet another set of formal systems and procedures to reconcile inconsistencies in information and to resolve conflicts in the recommendations that reached top management, the company simply legitimized an informal communication channel. "Functional analogs"—managers responsible for various functional tasks—were charged with the task of coordinating their activities and sharing their knowledge across national boundaries. If a dispute arose between a business manager and his geographic counterpart regarding the need for additional plant capacity, for example, or between two country managers about which country should add the capacity, the manufacturing managers in each location and the manufacturing staff managers at headquarters—all of them functional analogs for manufacturing—would try to negotiate a solution informally.[7]

We found companies using a variety of tools—formal and informal, macro and micro—to develop the physiology of the transnational organization. While the formal tools generally reinforced the broad mainstream of communication that paralleled the formal structure, the informal systems and processes created a network of tributaries, feeder streams, linking canals, and temporary channels for information that shaped the decision-making process and influenced its outcome in more subtle and flexible ways.

Most companies also have a powerful *organizational psychology*—a set of explicit or implicit shared values and beliefs—that can be developed and managed just as effectively as the organizational anatomy and physiology.[8] For companies operating in an international environment, this is a particularly important organizational attribute, for several reasons. When employees come from a variety of national backgrounds, management cannot assume that all will share common values and relate to common norms. Furthermore, when managers are separated by distance and time barriers, shared management understanding is often a much more powerful coordinating tool than either structure or systems. Yet managers attempting to guide organizational change tend to reach for the more familiar tools of structural reorganization and system redesign.

Our review of transnational organizations highlighted three techniques that seem particularly important in shaping an organization's psychology. The first is a clear, shared understanding of the company's mission and objectives. Matsushita's 250-year vision of its role in a world society, NEC's commitment to Computers and Communications (C&C), and Komatsu's objective to surround Caterpillar ("Maru C") all represent variants of this approach applied at different strategic and operational levels.

The second tool is the visible behavior and public actions of senior management. Particularly in a transnational organization, where other signals may be diluted or distorted by the sheer volume of information sent to foreign outposts, top management's actions have a powerful influence on the company's culture. When Sony's founder and chief executive, Akio Morita, relocated to New York to build the company's U.S. operations, he sent the most convincing possible message about Sony's commitment to its overseas businesses.

The third and most commonly used set of tools for modifying organizational psychology are those of the company's personnel policies. To develop a multidimensional and flexible organization process, human resource systems must encourage the appropriate kinds of people and behaviors. In earlier chapters we have shown how Unilever used its personnel policies not only to develop human resources, but also to shape the organization's decision processes and to influence corporate values. Its selection policies emphasized the need for team players rather than soloists; its management development process moved high-potential managers across product lines, between countries, and from national companies to corporate headquarters, thereby broadening their perspectives while developing their skills and knowledge; its education and training programs reinforced corporate values and provided numerous opportunities to foster informal personal contacts across organizational lines; and its performance evaluation process considered not only measurable output, but also cooperation with colleagues and adherence to organizational values.

To modify an organization's culture, values, or beliefs is a slow process. Yet progress in this area is particularly important in the development of a transnational, since changes in the organizational anatomy and physiology without complementary modifications to its psychology can lead to mechanical responses without understanding or commitment.[9]

The Process: Two Contrasting Models

Many managers have assumed that the organization change process was driven and dominated by changes in the formal structure. This belief was particularly strong in American-based companies, whose heritage favored the formalization of management processes.

Figure 11.1

Model I: The Traditional Change Process

Change in Formal Structure and Responsibilities
(Anatomy)

Change in Interpersonal Relationships and Processes
(Physiology)

Change in Individual Attitudes and Mentalities
(Psychology)

Among worldwide companies, we have seen many examples of structurally driven organization change processes, from Corning's serial attempts at reorganization to GE's shift from worldwide mini-GEs to the direct-connect concept. One of the most dramatic examples was Westinghouse's reorganization of its operations. Dissatisfied with the worldwide product organization it had installed eight years earlier, in 1979 top management assigned a team of executives to study the company's international organization problems for ninety days. Its proposal that Westinghouse adopt a global matrix was accepted, and the team was then given three months to "install the new structure."

The example is far from unusual—literally hundreds of other companies have done the same thing. The managers involved seemed to assume that changes in formal roles and reporting relationships would force changes in the organizational linkages and decision processes, which in turn would reshape the way individual managers think and act. This model of the process of organizational change is illustrated in Figure 11.1.

It is tempting to view the task of managing change as one of sketching alternative chart structures by moving boxes and redrawing lines. Too often, managers lose sight of the real organization behind those structural representations. The boxes they casually shift around represent people with abilities, motivations, and interests, not just formal positions with specified roles. The lines they redraw are not just formal reporting channels, but interpersonal relationships that may have taken years to develop. As a result, forcing changes in organizational process and management mentality by altering the formal structure can have a high cost. The new relationships defined in the reorganized structure will often take months to establish at the most basic level, and a year or more to become truly effective. Developing new individual attitudes and behaviors will take even longer, since many employees will be frustrated, alienated, or simply unequal to the new job requirements.

We noticed a somewhat different attitude toward the organizational change process in most European and Japanese companies. As we have described, top management in both Philips and Unilever consciously used personnel assignments as an important mechanism of organizational change. Building on the "old boy network" that dominated their earlier management processes, both companies used assignments and transfers to forge interpersonal links, build organizational cohesion, and develop policy consistency. Such mechanisms were at least as important as structural change for developing their desired international processes.

In Japanese companies, we were always conscious of the emphasis placed on socializing the individual into the organization, and shaping his or her attitudes to conform with overall corporate values. Organizational change often seemed to be driven more by intensive education programs than by reconfigurations of structure or systems.

Although the specific change process and sequence varied from one company to the next, the overall pattern that emerged was in marked contrast to the process driven by structural realignment. Indeed, the sequence often seemed to be the reverse. The first objective for many of the European and Japanese companies seeking major change was often to influence the understanding and perceptions of individuals, particularly those in key positions. Then followed a series of changes aimed at modifying the communication flows and decision-making processes. Only in a final stage were the changes consolidated and confirmed by structural realignment. This process is represented by the model in Figure 11.2.

Of course, these two models of organizational change in worldwide companies are both oversimplifications of the process and overgeneralizations of national differences. All change processes inevitably involve substantial overlap and interaction in the alterations in organi-

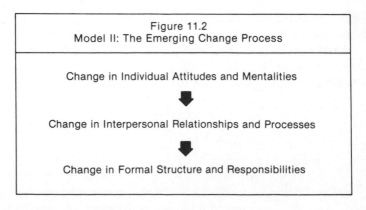

Figure 11.2
Model II: The Emerging Change Process

Change in Individual Attitudes and Mentalities

Change in Interpersonal Relationships and Processes

Change in Formal Structure and Responsibilities

zational anatomy, physiology, and psychology; the two sequences merely reflect differences in the relative emphasis on each set of tools during the process. Furthermore, while the two models reflect historical national biases, those differences seem to be eroding. American, European, and Japanese companies appear to be learning from one another with the Americans recognizing the power of socialization processes and the others developing greater structural and systems sophistication.

While the emerging change process is much less organizationally traumatic and therefore less likely to result in major problems or even outright rejection, it will sometimes be appropriate to employ the traditional approach, relying first on changes in formal structure.[10] Particularly in times of organizational crisis—chronic poor performance, a badly misaligned structure, or major structural change in the environment, for example—it may be necessary to achieve rapid and sweeping restructuring. For most organizations, however, dramatic structural change is also highly traumatic and can distract managers from their external tasks as they focus on the internal realignment. Fortunately most change processes can be managed in a more evolutionary manner. When a company focuses first on modification of individual perspectives and interpersonal relationships before tackling the formal redistribution of responsibilities and power, the process seems to have a greater chance of success.

THE TRANSNATIONAL ORGANIZATION: WHAT IT IS AND ISN'T

What really distinguishes the transnational from its predecessors, the international, multinational, and global organizations? Our emphasis on multidimensional management perspectives and flexible processes of coordination and control may suggest that the transnational is simply an updated form of the old worldwide matrix. Such a conclusion, however, misses the central point of our argument. By reducing the transnational's carefully developed and subtly balanced organizational capability to this level, one risks returning to the simplistic structural terms that constrained earlier thinking.

More than a Matrix

Just as the term *global strategy* has been reduced in many minds to a formulaic approach of standardizing products, rationalizing operations, and centralizing decision making, the concept of a *global matrix* has become too contaminated to be helpful in describing our proposals. We certainly are *not* proposing a rigid structurally dominated solution that imposes multiple formal reporting relationships and communications on a company's worldwide management processes. As we have seen, the apparent logic and simplicity of the global matrix design led to enormous organizational complexity, due to generalized joint responsibilities and formalized multidirectional communication.

The transnational organization is built up in a much more gradual and differentiated way. Ironically, its design complexity and subtlety facilitate greater clarity and simplicity in the management processes it defines. Rather than assign joint responsibility for everything, as the classic matrix structure suggests, top management in the transnational retains the clarity of line authority, but pays a great deal of attention to the allocation of responsibilities. In such organizations, it is important that country subsidiary managers, product division managers, and corporate staff managers all have the legitimacy, influence, and resource access to represent their viewpoints; at the same time the company must guard against extensive overlap in responsibilities, which might leave managers bogged down in internal negotiations and conflict resolution.

Transnational managers know it makes little sense to base organizational decisions on gross generalizations. Indeed, many problems of the past were due to oversimplified notions of global versus multinational businesses requiring centralized or decentralized organizations. The challenge is not to categorize industries or even strategic postures, but to decide task by task and even decision by decision where issues should be managed.

Some decisions will tend to be made on a global basis, often at the corporate center (most often research priorities and financing decisions, for example); others will be the appropriate responsibility of local management (typically sales and service tasks and labor relations, for instance). But for some issues, multiple perspectives are important and shared responsibility is necessary. Product policy decisions, for example, often involve negotiation between global product division managers pushing for greater standardization to achieve scale economies, and local subsidiary managers advocating modifications to fit the product to their local market needs.

As we have seen, transnational companies often isolate such joint decisions from the mainstream of decision making, handling them in specially constructed decision environments. Procter & Gamble's Euro Brand Teams allowed subsidiary and product managers to negotiate coordinated marketing strategies for brands being launched Europewide; Philips's consumer electronics division created a World Policy Committee and a World Strategy Council to provide a forum in which business and functional managers from headquarters could resolve strategic and operating differences with managers from key national organizations; and NEC linked its worldwide operation units to the central R&D lab with a network of integrative devices including an annual strategic conference, quarterly theme meetings, and several product development committees.

In effect, these companies are creating a series of mini-matrix organizations to encourage shared decision making and coordinated joint action. But because these off-line decision forums have all the potential problems of the global matrix, they should be used only for those few issues for which responsibility cannot be clearly allocated. The experience of our companies indicates that top management has to be closely involved in structuring and monitoring the operation of the teams to ensure that they do not degenerate into bureaucratic roadblocks or arenas for power sharing and horse trading.

The transnational appears to be a complex organization, with roles and responsibilities differentiated by business, by function, and even by task. But at least they are clearly defined, not subject to the constant overlapping and shared responsibility that create so much tension and confusion in the global matrix. Coordination and control in the transnational organization are accomplished as much through the socialization of its members as through formal systems. This approach greatly simplifies the decision-making process, takes a huge burden off top management, and unclogs the company's overloaded communication channels, all important benefits.

A Universal Solution?

Is the transnational organizational form appropriate for all companies with worldwide operations? In a sense, the question is misleading, since the transnational is less a structural classification than a broad organizational concept or philosophy, manifested in organizational capability and management mentality.

Thus companies as diverse as NEC and Procter & Gamble, Ericsson and Philips, or Matsushita and Unilever developed the organizational capabilities and characteristics that we call transnational. Because of major differences in industry environments and administrative heritages, they faced quite different strategic tasks and organizational challenges. Nonetheless, these and many other companies shared a new set of beliefs about how to manage organizations whose operations transcended national boundaries. Management not only recognized the importance of the complex and changeable external forces affecting operations, but tried to reflect those characteristics internally through the development of an organization with multidimensional perspectives, dispersed and differentiated organizational capabilities, and a flexible management process able to coordinate the conflicting, yet interdependent, interests.

Clearly there are vast differences between the international organizational challenge confronting management at NEC, and the tasks facing Unilever. The pressures for global-scale efficiency, responsiveness to national political demands, and continuous and costly technological innovation are much greater in telecommunications than in the consumer products industry. Furthermore, NEC's problems of reconfiguring its centralized Japanese management structure to accommodate the shift of manufacturing and development activities offshore is undoubtedly more difficult than Unilever's task of increasing the coordination of its decentralized units.

Nevertheless, in our view both companies are becoming transnationals. Both are consciously trying to develop the strategic capabilities of global competitiveness, multinational responsiveness, and worldwide learning. To do so, both are building organizations in which multidimensional management perspectives and capabilities are kept legitimate and viable, dispersed assets and resources are developed in a differentiated and interdependent network, and the whole system is integrated with a flexible coordinating process.

But the cost of developing such organization characteristics is high, and the complex processes that are created demand managers with superior administrative and interpersonal skills, particularly at the top levels of the organization. Some companies are simply unwilling or unable to develop such sophisticated capabilities, and choose to retain one of the more traditional global, international, or multinational organizational forms. While these simpler approaches may compromise the company's ability to respond to the environment, that strategic disadvantage is at least partially offset by the administrative advantage of a simpler decision-making process and lower overhead.

How, then, does a company decide if it should develop a transnational organization? Three important areas of management responsibility should be reviewed in making this complex decision. The first task is to review the nature and strength of the forces shaping the industry structure and competitive environment in which the company is operating. This is a task of analysis and prediction, not classification and projection. It involves developing an in-depth understanding of emerging industry trends and changing competitive characteristics, not a quick categorization of the business as "global" or "local."

Such an analysis will shed light on the need to develop the capabilities of the transnational organization. Unilever management, for example, recognized the opportunity to build competitive advantage in the branded packaged goods business by supplementing the company's well-developed ability to sense and respond to local markets with new strategic capabilities. The gradual trends toward converging tastes and lowered barriers between markets, particularly in Europe, made it possible for Unilever to develop and diffuse innovations in a more coordinated fashion and to capture more of the scale economies accruing to integrated operations. But these industry forces were mild compared with those of the telecommunications industry. NEC was virtually compelled to change its approach to the international telecommunications market. For it, internationalization was much more than a nice incremental market opportunity. Widespread deregulation of telecommunications services around the globe, coupled with the industry-wide transformation from electromechanical and analog devices to electronic digital switches, created discontinuities in market, technological, and economic forces. In the major competitive shakeout that was expected, the only survivors would be companies that could provide innovative and cost competitive products tailored to different national markets and backed by intensive local service. Such competitors have little choice—their industry demands transnational capabilities.

The decision to build a transnational organization depends not only on environmental considerations, but also on the company's ability to create and manage such an organization. Thus, management's next step is to evaluate the company's administrative heritage. Such an evaluation will suggest whether the company can develop the response capability to fit the emerging external demands, or, more ambitiously, to shape and influence the forces of change.

The second option is the only one available to a company whose industry is becoming transnational (i.e., global competitiveness, multinational responsiveness, and worldwide learning capabilities are increasing), but whose administrative heritage makes it difficult to adjust appropriately. Companies in such a situation may still be able to build viable worldwide positions either by offsetting the transnational competitors' advantages, or by approximating them through other means. The former approach is the one favored by "national champion" companies that rely on the support of their home country government. By financing capital investments, subsidizing exports, and funding R&D, these governments give their national champions the opportunity to compete with transnational companies.[11]

Alternatively, a company can try to approximate the strategic capabilities of its transnational competitors by linking up with firms with complementary skills or strategic positions. The current attention to international alliances reflects the fact that many companies find it difficult to meet increasingly complex strategic demands on their own. By forming alliances with Philips in Europe and GoldStar in the Far East, AT&T is trying to build sensitivity and responsiveness to worldwide markets quickly, and reinforcing cost competitiveness by adding offshore manufacturing capability.[12]

The history of global strategic alliances, however, is not an altogether happy one. The interests of partners tend to diverge over time, and capabilities that once were well balanced and complementary can quickly become one-sided and threatening. It is not easy to coordinate and control multidimensional perspectives and dispersed assets within a single organization; it is immensely difficult to do so across corporate boundaries.[13] However, changing industry forces may leave firms like AT&T no alternative.

After analyzing the external need for change and assessing the internal capacity to manage it, top management has one more major task: assessing implementation of the change.[14] Building a complex structure and flexible process is difficult enough, but, as we have continually emphasized, the development of a transnational organization requires more than multidimensional capabilities and interdependent assets. It is crucial to change the mentality of members of the organization. Diverse roles and dispersed operations must be held together by a management mindset that understands the need for multiple strategic capabilities, views problems and opportunities from both local and global perspectives, and is willing to interact with others openly and flexibly. The task is not to build a sophisticated matrix structure, but to create a "matrix in the minds of managers."

Developing appropriate organizational capabilities has always been vital to companies' success, indeed to their very survival. In the view of the eminent business historian Alfred Chandler, a company leader's "most important entrepreneurial act" is the creation of an effective administrative organization. Today the leaders of most companies recognize the strategic challenge they face in the global environment. What they lack is the organizational capability to implement increasingly complex and changeable strategies.

In the future, a company's ability to develop a transnational organizational capability will be the key factor that separates the winners from the mere survivors in the international competitive environment.

APPENDIX
RESEARCH METHODOLOGY

A s we indicated in the preface, the concepts and conclusions pre- sented in this book represent the culmination of lines of inquiry that began over ten years ago. Bartlett's dissertation, completed in 1979, highlighted some of the limitations of seeking structural fit as a solution to the strategic challenges of managing across borders and sensitized us to the important role of evolving management processes for building requisite organizational capability in large worldwide companies.[1] This research builds on that foundation.

DEFINING THE PROBLEM: CASE RESEARCH IN TWENTY COMPANIES

The issues we address in this book were further defined and formulated between 1979 and 1984 while developing a course on management of multinational enterprise for MBA students at Harvard Business School. Our discussions with a wide range of managers in over twenty large European, American, and Japanese companies convinced us that while many researchers were writing about the changing strategic impera- tives in the new international environment, they were, to a large extent, preaching to the converted. By the mid-1980s, most managers in worldwide companies recognized *what* they had to do; their real chal- lenge was *how* to develop the organizational capability to survive and prosper in the changing world environment.

Although there were times when we were surprised at an individ- ual manager's apparent lack of understanding of the nature and impli- cations of the trends that were reshaping the competitive dynamics of his or her business, such occurrences were very rare. In our study of ATI, the disguised name of a major American telecommunications company, for example, we found that managers were acutely aware of the way in which globalizing forces were restructuring their industry;[2] their counterparts in EMI, the U.K. company that developed the first brain scanner, were very conscious they had to be responsive to local differences in health care delivery systems and to the political pres- sures as it expanded abroad;[3] and in our study of Merloni, the Italian appliance company, executives explicitly recognized the need for the company to use its expansion into Northern Europe as a way to stimulate new, more innovative products.[4]

Yet, despite their recognition of the environmental changes, each company (and many others we studied) stumbled as it attempted to implement its international strategic intentions. ATI was unable to develop its Mexican subsidiary as a viable global source; EMI failed to respond to the market and political changes in the U.S. scanner market; and Merloni's intention to use its European companies as sources for needed product innovations was stillborn. The problem that these and other companies faced was not one of being insensitive to environmental changes or even of developing inappropriate strategic responses. They fell short by not building the *organizational capability* that allowed them to implement their strategic intentions.

Intrigued by this observation, we continued to research the ways in which companies adapted to the new organizational challenges. In studying companies in many diverse industries, we quickly recognized that the forces of change in the international environment were affecting businesses very differently. In the European operations of American Standard, the plumbing and heating company, we saw how understanding and responding to national markets were vital to the success of the business;[5] in Molex, the electrical connector company, the need to standardize product designs and capture scale efficiencies dominated the strategic task;[6] but in Kentucky Fried Chicken's international franchising efforts, we observed that the ability to organize to transfer knowledge and expertise to operations worldwide was the secret of the company's rapid international expansion.[7]

We were also struck by the wide differences in strategic and organizational response by companies from Europe, the United States, and Japan even where they were in the same business and faced the same forces for change. The importance of the company's history and management's cultural background in shaping the organizational response to the new challenges became increasingly clear. The differences were particularly evident in some of the comparison research where, for example, we were able to contrast the way in which Dominion Engineering Works' management system, as part of Canadian General Electric, constrained the company's response to important international changes in the paper machinery business in a way that the family-owned European company Voith was not.[8] Similarly, both the power and the limitations of Caterpillar's strong management structure and institutionalized strategic beliefs became more clearly defined as seen in contrast to the more organic, flexible, and opportunistic management process of its Japanese rival, Komatsu.[9]

But perhaps the most important piece of field research in this phase of the project, was the work done at Corning Glass Works.[10] It

Figure A.1

The Research Process

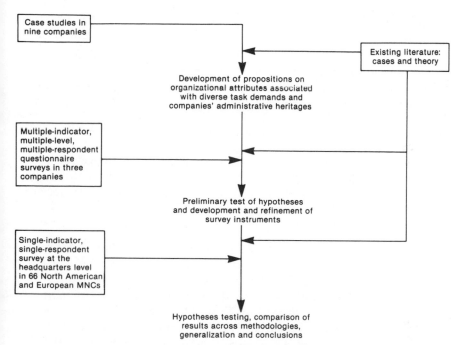

was here that we first defined differences in the strategic task facing
diverse businesses; and began to grapple with the organizational implications of managing complexity, diversity, and rapid change in organizations where managers were separated by distance, language, time,
and culture. It was here where we began to develop some initial hy-
potheses about the nature of what we later called the transnational
organization.

THE STUDY: A THREE-PHASE RESEARCH PROCESS

While these case studies provided the background and defined our
research questions, the structured research that led to this book was
carried out between 1984 and 1986 and consisted of three different
phases (see Figure A.1). In the first and core phase, we interviewed 236
managers in both the corporate headquarters and in a number of different national subsidiaries of nine large worldwide companies. Data collected from these companies provided the opportunity for in-depth
analysis of how managers in different contexts were coping with the
new challenges.

While the detailed case research in the nine core companies provided contextual grounding and clinical richness to our observations and analysis, we felt it necessary to test some of the ideas more rigorously in order to develop the reliability and generality of our conclusions. The second and third phases of the study were aimed at carrying out such tests. In essence, we adopted a different methodology for each of the three phases to achieve the benefits of triangulation—covering a spectrum from relatively "fine grained" to relatively "coarse grained" approaches within the same project.[11]

Phase I: In-Depth Studies in Nine Companies

The twenty companies studied during the problem definition phase had alerted us to the significant variations in the strategic challenges faced by different businesses. To capture the implications of these differences, we selected companies in three industries likely to be affected in very different ways by the international environmental forces:

- The branded packaged products industry (packaged food, personal care products, detergents, and so forth) is a business that has traditionally been regarded as highly nationally differentiated. Consumer tastes and habits vary by country, as do the structure of the distribution channels and nature of the advertising media. Few benefits accrued to those seeking global-scale economies in soup canning or detergent packaging, and the ability to innovate on a worldwide basis has been constrained by historical differences across markets. Those skilled in the downstream end of the value-added chain (in distribution and sales, for example) historically have enjoyed a substantial competitive advantage.
- In contrast, the radio, television, and hi-fi businesses were transformed by the electronics revolution that required investment in product and process development that was difficult to recoup over short product life cycles in single markets. The advent of printed circuit boards and integrated circuits also triggered opportunities to develop mass-production techniques that yielded substantial scale economies. Sony's ability to flood world markets in the early 1960s with a standard design, inexpensive transistor radio (a feat it repeated two decades later with the Walkman) demonstrated the low need for national product differentiation in consumer electronics.
- The telecommunications switching industry traditionally required a more multidimensional strategic capability. The high R&D cost involved in developing successive generations of central switching systems, and the significant scale economies in

producing key components demanded global integration and coordination. Yet, because national telephone authorities are normally controlled by the host government, suppliers must also develop nationally tailored systems and local manufacturing and development capabilities. Traditionally, successful competitors in this industry developed innovations in the advanced markets—typically their home countries—and transferred them around the world.

Recognizing that, within any industry, companies can and do respond in different ways to the diverse pressures, we chose to focus on three companies in each industry. To capture the differences in strategic position and organizational approach reflected in companies from different national backgrounds, we chose the leading multinational company based in the United States, Japan, and Europe in each of the three businesses. In branded packaged goods we concentrated on the soap, detergent, and household products business in which Procter & Gamble is the leading U.S. company, Unilever, the major European representative, and Kao, the dominant Japanese competitor. In consumer electronics, the companies selected were General Electric, Philips, and Matsushita; and in telecommunications switching the sample was ITT, Ericsson, and NEC.

Figure A.2 is a schematic representation of our sample in terms of the strategic characteristics of the industries and the competitive approaches of the companies. For each box in the figure, the vertical axis represents the strength of the globalizing forces in the industry or the extent of global integration in the strategic posture of the company, and the horizontal axis represents the need for national responsiveness in the business or the extent of country-by-country differentiation in the company's overall strategic posture. This way of viewing both industry demands and company strategy was our starting point (and one from which we departed substantially in the course of the study) and was based on the integration-responsiveness framework originally proposed by Prahalad and subsequently developed and used by other researchers in the field of international management.[12]

We interviewed 236 managers in the nine companies, both at their corporate headquarters and in a number of national subsidiaries, such as those in Japan, Singapore, Taiwan, Australia, the United Kingdom, Germany, Holland, Belgium, France, the United States, and Brazil. At the subsidiaries, the respondents invariably included the local general manager and the heads of the major functional areas—marketing, production, finance, planning, and engineering. For greater depth and to cover perspectives from different hierarchical levels, we interviewed managers in middle and relatively junior positions within each func-

Figure A.2
Phase I: The Sample of Nine Companies

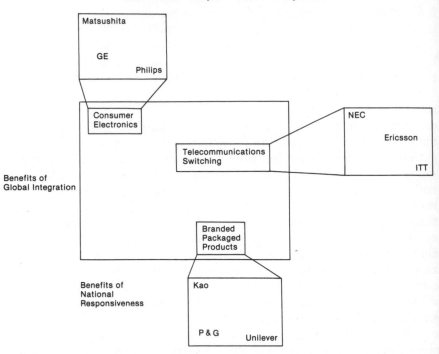

tion. At the headquarters, the respondents included the divisional president and all his direct reports. In addition, in each company a minimum of six and a maximum of 35 other corporate managers were interviewed to cover specific product, functional, or area issues.

All the interviews were conducted from January 1984 to May 1986. Most of the interviews were relatively unstructured and were not taped. They usually lasted for about an hour and a half, though some managers were interviewed on multiple occasions for total periods in excess of ten hours. Professor Hideki Yoshihara of Kobe University also participated in many of the interviews in Japan.

Besides the interviews, we also collected large volumes of documents from the companies about their historic strategic plans and organizational arrangements. These surveys and archival data provide the main database for the analysis, arguments, and illustrations in this book.

Phase II: Questionnaire Surveys in Three Companies

In the second phase of the research project, we conducted a multiple-indicator, multirespondent mailed questionnaire survey of headquarters and subsidiary managers in the consumer electronics business of Philips and Matsushita Electric, and the public switching business of NEC. This was a purely convenience sample, because these three companies were the only ones that agreed to host the survey.

The objectives of the surveys were to formalize some of the ideas that emerged from our analysis of the interview data, to carry out some preliminary tests on some of those ideas, and to develop suitable instruments for conducting a large sample survey to test those ideas more rigorously in the third phase of the study. Only some of our concepts and proposals were amenable to such testing and the instruments were focused on those issues, the most important of which pertained to managing innovations (covered in Chapter 7).

The case studies suggested that innovations could come about in worldwide companies through three different organizational processes. We have described them as local, central, and transnational innovations. These processes imply different tasks for a company's national subsidiaries. For the local process, the subsidiary's task is to develop and adopt new products and processes locally, using its own technical and managerial resources to respond to local circumstances: a task we call "creation" of innovations. For the global process, the subsidiary's main task is "adoption": to implement innovations created by the parent company, or a central R&D facility. For the transnational process, subsidiaries may be required to create, adopt, and "diffuse" innovations to other units: the third task lying at the core of what we describe as locally leveraged innovations. The main objective of the questionnaire survey was to explore how organizational attributes, such as the level of local resources, subsidiary autonomy, extent of shared goals and values, and the density of intrasubsidiary, headquarters-subsidiary, and intersubsidiary communication affected the subsidiary's ability to carry out innovation tasks.

Samples and Data Collection.   Ten wholly owned subsidiaries each of Philips and Matsushita and five of NEC (which had relatively fewer wholly owned national operations) were surveyed. The subsidiaries were selected in consultation with corporate managers of the companies and represented a wide variety in terms of size, local activities, and characteristics of host country environments. In each subsidiary, questionnaires were mailed to all departmental managers.

Our data analysis procedure required aggregation of the responses of all managers from a particular subsidiary to arrive at subsidiary-level scores for each variable. However, for such aggregation to be valid, it was necessary to have usable responses from *each and every* departmental manager of the subsidiary. For example, subsidiary-level scores for the number of innovations created locally could not be computed unless we knew the number of innovations created by each department. Similarly, our earlier case research made it quite clear that within a subsidiary, the relationships with the headquarters could be different for different functions, and unless responses from all functional managers were included, subsidiary-level measures for such variables as autonomy or communication would not be comparable. Therefore, in the analysis we included only those subsidiaries from which we received responses from every departmental manager. Eight subsidiaries of Matsushita (56 respondents), seven of Philips (52 respondents), and all five of NEC (33 respondents) met this condition and provided the data for our analysis.[13]

For such variables as creation, adoption, and diffusion of innovations, comparable data could be obtained from these subsidiary-level respondents. However, since subsidiary managers' responses to other variables such as slack resources, local autonomy, or normative integration were often subjective, these measures required a reliability and comparability check. This was done by obtaining comparative estimates of the variables from some corporate-level respondents. The procedure and results of these reliability tests are presented later in this Appendix.

Variables and Measures. All respondents were asked to *enumerate* and *describe* the innovations that were created, adopted, and diffused by their departments within the preceding twelve months.[14] The final measure for each indicator was based on evaluation of the descriptions; we excluded some cases included by the respondents since they did not qualify as innovations (e.g., "instituted a system for recording employee attendance"). In some instances, we sought additional information from the respondents and from the subsidiary general managers to decide if the cases should be included in the final count. Subsidiary-level scores for each variable were arrived at by simply adding the total number of innovations created, adopted, and diffused by the different departments of the subsidiary.

Each respondent was requested to report the frequency of his or her communication with managers of other departments in the same subsidiary and with managers in the headquarters and other subsidiaries of the company. The instrument developed by Professor Tom Allen of MIT was used and data were collected in five categories that varied from daily communication to communication less than once a year.[15] However, only daily, weekly, and monthly communication was scored as 3, 2, and 1, respectively, and communication with lower frequencies was ignored. Based on this scoring system, "internal," "headquarters," and "other subsidiary" communication densities were computed for each respondent as the average frequency of his or her communication. For each variable, the density scores of all the managers in the subsidiary were then aggregated to arrive at a subsidiary-level measure.

To avoid normative bias and as an alternative to purely perceptual and subjective measures, we adopted three indicators of normative integration that both received theory[16] and our own case studies suggested were valid.[17] Given the well-documented role of executive transfers as a key mechanism for promoting shared goals and values in MNCs,[18] our first indicator was the amount of time the subsidiary manager had actually worked in the corporate headquarters. Managers who had worked at least one year at the headquarters were assigned a score of one; all others were assigned a score of zero. The second indicator, justified primarily on the basis of our own case research, was having a mentor at the headquarters. If the manager reported having a mentor, he or she was given a score of one; if not, a zero. The third indicator was based on the number of trips the manager made to the headquarters:[19] managers who visited the headquarters at least once a year received a score of one; others, a score of zero. The three scores were aggregated to yield a single composite measure of the level of normative integration for each respondent; the scores of all respondents from the subsidiary were further aggregated to provide a subsidiary-level measure for the variable.

The level of local autonomy was measured by estimating, on a scale of 1 (low) to 5 (high), the relative influence of the subsidiary on six types of decisions: (1) introduction of a new product; (2) minor but significant modification of an existing product; (3) modification of a production process; (4) restructuring of the subsidiary organization which involved creation or abolition of departments; (5) recruitment and promotion to positions just below that of the subsidiary general manager; and (6) career development plans for departmental managers.[20] The average scores of all these decisions for all the respondents from the subsidiary were aggregated to yield a subsidiary-level measure for local autonomy.[21]

Finally, the level of slack resources was estimated by requesting the respondents to describe on a scale of 1 (significant disruption of activities) to 5 (no perceptible effect), the consequence of a 10 percent reduction in the operating budgets of their departments. The respondents were similarly aggregated for all respondents from a subsidiary to compute a subsidiary-level measure for slack.

Reliability Test through Corporate-Level Respondents.   In each company we identified two senior managers at the headquarters who had direct line responsibilities for all subsidiaries of the company that were included in the survey, or were otherwise knowledgeable about the operations of those subsidiaries. These managers were requested to rate, on a scale of 1 (low) to 5 (high), each subsidiary on the following attributes: slack resources, local autonomy, and normative integration. As we have indicated, these direct and single-indicator measures were obtained to test the reliability of the indirect and multiple-indicator measures of these variables that were obtained from the subsidiaries. A comparison of the responses obtained from the headquarters and the subsidiary-level respondents revealed the following:

1. To all three companies, inter-rater convergence was high for the two headquarters' respondents. For each variable, the ranks of the different subsidiaries were assessed similarly by both as shown in the rank correlations in Table A.1.
2. For each of the three variables that were estimated by the head-quarter-level respondents, Table A.1 also shows the correlations among the ranks of subsidiaries obtained by aggregation of responses from the subsidiary and the headquarters' managers. As can be observed readily, in each company inter-rater convergence was high among headquarters and subsidiary-level respondents.

Given such convergence, only the responses from subsidiary managers were used for further analysis.

Findings. The findings from this phase of the project have been reported in detail in academic journals and are briefly summarized below.[22]

For each company, we computed the ranks of each subsidiary for all the measured variables. Subsidiary ranks for creation, adoption, and diffusion of innovations were then compared with the ranks for the different organizational attributes. Results of these comparisons are shown in the Spearman's rank correlations in Table A.2. We adopted the rank correlation approach to avoid excessive influence of outliers. The findings, however, remained unaltered, even if the absolute measures are considered and Pearson's correlation coefficients are employed.

Given the small number of subsidiaries in each company, the statistical significance or otherwise of these rank correlation coefficients should not be overemphasized. Furthermore, the same constraint of sample size prevented analysis of partial correlations and the zero-order correlations could be influenced significantly by interaction effects. However, we have indicated in the table the significance levels (one-tailed test) for each of the correlation coefficients based on Olds' (1938) method for estimating the significance of rank correlations for small samples when variables are not assumed to be distributed normally. Comparison of these correlation coefficients with the propositions led to the following conclusions.

Table A.1
Spearman's Rank Correlations for Assessing Inter-Rater Convergence on Selected Variables

	HQ-HQ Raters			HQ-Subsidiary Raters		
	Matsushita	Philips	NEC	Matsushita	Philips	NEC
Slack resources	0.79	0.84	0.76	0.84	0.53	0.77
Local autonomy	0.71	0.69	0.86	0.95	0.70	0.75
Normative integration	0.62	0.59	0.43	0.60	0.75	0.70

Table A.2
Spearman's Rank Correlations between Creation, Adoption, and Diffusion of Innovations and the Different Organizational Attributes

Organizational Attributes	Matsushita			Philips			NEC		
	Creation	Adoption	Diffusion	Creation	Adoption	Diffusion	Creation	Adoption	Diffusion
Slack resources	0.66	0.71*	0.85***	0.96***	0.73**	0.78**	0.89*	0.58	0.66
Local autonomy	0.52	0.17	−0.22	0.89***	0.83***	0.65	0.48	0.63	0.71
Normative integration	0.67*	0.71*	0.67*	0.86***	0.79***	0.91***	0.89*	0.94*	0.86
Intrasubsidiary communication	0.76*	0.86***	0.70*	0.85**	0.55	0.81**	0.90*	0.71	0.77
HQ-subsidiary communication	0.61	0.83***	0.69*	0.68	0.79**	0.87**	0.71	0.90*	0.93*
Intersubsidiary communication	0.56	0.80**	0.91***	0.61	0.81**	0.86**	0.43	0.69	1.00*

Note: Significance of α for one-tailed test indicated by * ($\alpha < 0.05$), ** ($\alpha < 0.025$), and *** ($\alpha < 0.01$), based on Table 11 in Olds (1938).

First, some of our conclusions based on the case studies of the project were supported by the data. This was particularly true with regard to the effects of normative integration and communication on creation, adoption, and diffusion of innovations by MNC subsidiaries. In all three companies, normative integration was positively and significantly correlated with creation and adoption of innovations. Similarly, the relationships between intra- and interunit communication and creation, adoption, and diffusion of innovations were all significant and in the right direction.

Second, some of our propositions were not confirmed. The hypothesized effects on local autonomy, in particular, found no support in any of the companies. There was no evidence that local autonomy facilitated creation and diffusion of innovations, or that it impeded adoption.

Third, results on the effects of local slack resources were mixed. There was some evidence that slack facilitated creation and diffusion (correlations significant in two out of three companies), but its proposed effect on adoption was rejected. Contrary to our contextual observations, the association between slack and adoption was not negative in any of the three companies.

Categories of Subsidiaries. In both Matsushita and Philips, some subsidiaries were found to only create innovations but not adopt or diffuse any (group 1), others created and adopted innovations but did not diffuse (group 2), and only a few subsidiaries simultaneously engaged in creation, adoption, and diffusion as we have defined them (group 3). In NEC (perhaps because of the smaller number of subsidiaries that were considered) we observed only the second two groups: subsidiaries that created and adopted innovations but did not diffuse, and subsidiaries that did all three. Furthermore, in all three companies, subsidiaries that engaged in all the activities (group 3) were also the ones that recorded the highest scores in all three tasks.

Table A.3 shows the number of innovations created, adopted, and diffused by the eight subsidiaries of Matsushita, as well as their scores for the different organizational attributes. E and F are group 1 subsidiaries; G and H belong to group 2; and subsidiaries A, B, C, and D belong to group 3.

The different organizational attributes of Matsushita subsidiaries belonging to the different groups are compared in Table A.4. The table shows, for each group, the mean levels of local slack resources, local autonomy, normative integration, and the densities of intrasubsidiary, headquarters-subsidiary, and intersubsidiary communication. Results of one-way ANOVA tests revealed significant (F-statistic significant at the 0.01 level) differences among subsidiaries in the three groups for all organizational attributes except intersubsidiary communication.

Table A.3
Creation, Adoption, and Diffusion of Innovations by Matsushita Subsidiaries

| | Number of Innovations | | | Slack Resources (Scale 1–5) | Local Autonomy (Scale 1–5) | Normative Integration (Scale 1–3) | Communication Density (Scale 1–3) | | |
| | Created | Adopted | Diffused | | | | Intra-subsidiary | HQ-subsidiary | Inter-subsidiary |
Subsidiary									
A	20	3	1	3.9	3.4	3.1	1.9	1.4	0.0
B	16	8	4	4.3	3.2	2.6	1.6	1.4	0.1
C	17	6	9	5.0	3.5	1.9	1.9	1.5	0.3
D	22	12	7	4.1	4.2	1.7	2.2	1.8	0.4
E	14	0	0	2.2	4.5	0.7	0.8	0.1	0.0
F	11	0	0	3.4	3.7	0.6	1.1	0.7	0.0
G	8	2	0	3.2	3.0	1.1	1.3	1.6	0.1
H	7	4	0	2.8	2.9	0.8	1.4	1.5	0.0

Table A.4
Organizational Attributes of Matsushita Subsidiaries Belonging to the Three Groups

| | Mean Values | | | F-Statistic | Scheffe's Test (pairs that are not significantly different) |
	Group 1	Group 2	Group 3		
Slack resources	2.8	3.0	4.3	8.3*	(1,2)
Local autonomy	4.1	2.9	3.6	14.9*	None
Normative integration	0.6	1.0	2.1	17.6*	None
Intrasubsidiary communication	1.0	1.3	1.9	11.6*	None
HQ-subsidiary communication	0.4	1.5	1.5	8.4*	(2,3)
Intersubsidiary communication	0.0	0.0	0.2	1.9	All

Further investigation of the pair-wise differences among the three groups (Scheffe's test) showed the following:

1. Subsidiaries in group 1 had significantly higher levels of local autonomy and significantly lower levels of slack resources, normative integration, intrasubsidiary communication, and headquarters-subsidiary communication compared to subsidiaries in the other two groups.
2. Subsidiaries in group 2 had significantly lower levels of local autonomy compared to subsidiaries in the other two categories.
3. Subsidiaries in group 3 had significantly higher levels of local resources, normative integration, and intrasubsidiary communication compared to subsidiaries in the other two groups.

Exactly identical patterns were observed in Philips: two subsidiaries could be categorized in groups 1 and 2; and three in group 3. Group 1 subsidiaries had the highest levels of local autonomy, but the lowest levels of normative integration and intrasubsidiary as well as headquarters-subsidiary communication. Group 2 had the lowest levels of local autonomy. Group 3 subsidiaries had the highest levels of normative integration, as well as the most dense communication, both within the subsidiary and also with the headquarters. In the case of NEC, three subsidiaries belonged to group 2 and two to group 3. Here again, the key differentiating factors were the higher levels of normative integration, local autonomy, and internal and headquarters communication in the group 3 subsidiaries.

In a normative sense, group 3 subsidiaries had the most desirable innovation characteristics: not only did they engage in all three tasks of creating, adopting, and diffusing innovations, but also recorded the highest scores in each task. In all three companies, these subsidiaries were differentiated from the others by higher scores on normative integration and higher densities of intra- and interunit communication.

Phase III: Large Sample Survey of U.S. and European MNCs

In the third phase, our objective was to test statistically some of our ideas through a large sample survey. First, we wanted to pursue the issue of innovation-organization association with greater rigor and generality. Second, we wanted to check and see if companies actually differentiated the roles and management processes for different subsidiaries (as we described in Chapters 6 and 9, based on our clinical observations in the nine core companies). Full details of the survey methodology and key findings have been reported elsewhere and are briefly summarized below.[23]

Sample and Data Collection.   We mailed a questionnaire to the chairman or CEO of the 438 North American and European MNCs listed in Stopford's *World Dictionary of Multinational Enterprises.*[24] We did not receive any response from 215 companies; another 50 declined participation on different grounds; 31 questionnaires were returned because of wrong mailing addresses; and completed questionnaires were received from the remaining 76 companies. Of these, 66 were complete in all respects and were used for the statistical analysis reported below. In 50 of the 66 companies, the respondent was the corporate vice president responsible for all international operations or someone with even greater responsibility such as the CEO or the chairman.

While the response rate was modest, the respondents were distributed across geographical boundaries and industries in a manner quite similar to that of the relevant population and no discernible pattern could be found among the nonrespondents.[25]

Thirty-six of the 66 companies were headquartered in North America and the remaining were headquartered in Europe. Four had annual sales below $1 billion and 11 had annual sales above $10 billion; the remaining were within this range. Collectively, the 66 companies reported data on 618 national subsidiaries—five companies had less than five subsidiaries, 44 had between five and 15 subsidiaries, and 12 had more than 15 subsidiaries. A wide range of industries was represented by the companies including aerospace (2 companies), building products (3), chemicals (7), food and drink (7), electrical and electronic (3), health care (3), industrial equipment (9), metals (11), motor vehicles (3), office equipment (2), and others (3).

Variables and Measures.   The questionnaire was the same one we used for the corporate level in the second phase with only the addition of a few new variables. It required the CEO of the company or another manager who was responsible for overall assessment of the company's international operations to rate, on a scale of 1 (low) to 5 (high), each of the company's foreign subsidiaries on its ability to create and adopt innovations, and its overall performance relative to corporate expectations. Besides these performance indicators, two other sets of variables were measured. The first pertained to the subsidiary's environmental context: the intensity of competition, the extent of regulation, and the level of technological dynamism. The second pertained to the subsidiary's organizational context: the level of local resources and slack, the extent of centralization formalization and normative integration (socialization) in the headquarters' relations with the subsidiary, and the intensity of the communication between the two. Our objective was primarily to measure differences among the subsidiaries within the companies. We used measures which were related not to an absolute anchor but to the average level of the particular variable for the company.

It is important to emphasize that all measures represented perceptions of a senior manager in the headquarters for all the subsidiaries of the company. The issue of objective versus perceptual measures has been the topic of an on-going debate in the literature[26] and perceptual measures from a single key informant could clearly suffer from some deficiencies. Our justification for using this measurement system was based on two grounds. First, the close correspondence in the findings from the single-indicator perceptual measures obtained from corporate-level respondents and the multiple-indicator objective and perceptual measures obtained from subsidiary managers in the second phase of the study provided some support of the reliability and validity of the first measurement system. Second, collecting objective-level measures for the relatively large number of variables for a large enough number of subsidiaries for meaningful statistical analysis presented enormous and, for us, insurmountable practical problems. However, because of this measurement system, we could not measure three variables of interest: the subsidiary's ability to diffuse innovations, the density of its internal communication, and the densities of its communication with other subsidiaries. We felt that headquarters managers had little basis to make reliable estimates for these variables.[27]

Innovation-Organization Association

Table A-5 shows the correlations between the subsidiary scores on creation and adoption of innovations and their scores on local resources, local autonomy (obverse of centralization), normative integration (socialization), and headquarters-subsidiary communication. Only

Table A.5
Zero-Order Correlation Matrix

	Creation of Innovations	Adoption of Innovations	Local Resources	Local Autonomy	Shared Goals
Local resources	0.63	*			
Local autonomy	0.54	*	0.51		
Normative integration	0.37	0.15	0.45	0.20	
Headquarters-subsidiary communication	0.23	0.21	0.39	*	0.32

Note: All correlations significant at 0.001 level except those marked *.

correlations that were significant at the 0.001 level have been included and significant intercorrelations (at the same 0.001 level) among all the variables are presented in the table.

The high intercorrelations among the variables restrict the inferences that can be drawn from these zero-order correlation coefficients. However, it was manifest that creation of innovation by the subsidiary was very highly correlated with both local resources and local autonomy, while adoption was not significantly correlated with either of the two variables. Normative integration and headquarters-subsidiary communication, on the other hand, had significant positive correlations with both creation and adoption of innovations.

To develop a better understanding of these innovation-organization associations, we made a second analysis to look for differences between high- and low-performing subsidiaries on both creation and adoption of innovations. The creation and adoption scores were first normalized for all subsidiaries of the same company and these scores (z-scores) were divided into categories of high ($z > 1$), medium ($1 > z > -1$), and low ($z < -1$).

Table A.6 shows the means values of the different organizational attributes for subsidiaries scoring high, medium, and low on creation of innovation. The "F" probabilities indicate whether the differences among the categories are statistically significant. The Scheffe's test results indicate whether the differences between the high- and low-scoring group are statistically significant. This analysis reinforced the findings from the correlation analysis: subsidiaries with higher scores on creation of innovations had significantly higher levels of local resources, local autonomy, normative integration, and communication with the headquarters compared to other subsidiaries of the company.

Table A.7 shows the results of the same analysis for subsidiaries scoring high, medium, and low on adoption of innovations. As was suggested by the correlation analysis, local resources and autonomy did not discriminate among the different categories of subsidiaries, while normative integration and headquarters-subsidiary communication did.

Finally, to analyze the joint affects of the different organizational attributes on a subsidiary's ability to create and adopt innovations, a step-wise regression analysis was made. The results of the analysis are shown in Table A.8 (the right-hand side variables are listed in the order in which they entered the equation). Given the high correlations among the influencing variables, the beta coefficients could not be interpreted unambiguously. We present the results, however, only to highlight that the four variables (local resources, local autonomy, normative integration, and headquarters communication) collectively explained 52 percent of the total variance in the subsidiary scores on creation of innova-

Table A.6
Distinguishing Attributes of Subsidiaries' Ability to Create Innovations

Subsidiary Attributes (Measured on Scale) 1 (Low) to 5 (High)	Creation of Innovations by the Subsidiary			"F" Statistic	"F" Probability	Is High-Low Pair Distinguished at the 0.05 Level? (Scheffe's Test)
	High	Medium	Low			
Local resources	4.3	3.2	1.9	97.5	0.0000	Yes
Local autonomy	3.0	2.2	1.2	75.0	0.0000	Yes
Normative integration	4.2	3.5	2.9	28.9	0.0000	Yes
Intensity of headquarters-subsidiary communication	3.5	3.2	2.7	19.6	0.0001	Yes

Table A.7
Distinguishing Attributes of Subsidiaries' Ability to Adopt Innovations

Subsidiary Attributes (Measured on Scale) 1 (Low) to 5 (High)	Adoption of Innovations by the Subsidiary			"F" Statistic	"F" Probability	Is High-Low Pair Distinguished at the 0.05 Level? (Scheffe's Test)
	High	Medium	Low			
Local resources	3.3	3.1	3.0	1.3	0.2713	No
Local autonomy	2.2	2.1	2.3	3.2	0.0428	No
Normative integration	3.7	3.5	3.2	6.5	0.0016	Yes
Intensity of headquarters-subsidiary communication	3.5	3.2	3.0	11.6	0.0001	Yes

Table A.8
Regression Results

Dependent Variable	Influencing Variables				"F" Stat Significance	Adj. R²
	Local Resources	Local Autonomy	Normative Integration	Headquarters-Subsidiary Communication		
Creation of innovations by the subsidiary	0.43 (11.69)	0.30 (9.06)	0.12 (3.70)	0.10 (2.41)	187.7 (0.000)	0.52
Adoption of innovations by the subsidiary	—	—	0.21 (5.76)	0.19 (4.62)	20.22 (0.000)	0.09

Note: The values in the table are the beta coefficients under which the t-statistics are shown in parens. Coefficients not significant at 0.05 level are not shown.

tion. Variance in adoption scores, on the other hand, could not be explained to a significant extent by the variables, although both normative integration and headquarters-subsidiary communication appeared to have statistically significant impacts.

Types of Subsidiary Contexts. In Chapter 6 we argued that subsidiary contexts should be differentiated into four categories based on the joint conditions of (1) relatively low- or high-resource levels; and (2) the associated low- or high-environmental complexity. While we had direct indicators for the level of local resources available to each subsidiary in our database, we constructed a measure for environmental complexity by aggregating the measures for competitive intensity and technological dynamism (Cornbach's α was 0.67). We then clustered all the subsidiaries on these two variables to determine if there was a natural empirical pattern that coincided with our proposed scheme. We used McQueen's K-means clustering method and the existence of the clusters and the number of clusters were determined by using Calinski and Harabasz's C-Ratio, as recommended by Milligan and Cooper who found this to be the best stopping rule among thirty examined.[28] As we varied the number of clusters in the solution from 2 to 8, the C-Ratio varied as 600, 473, 656, 571, 610, 560, and 544, respectively. The maximum at the four-cluster solution indicated the existence of four different categories of subsidiaries.[29] The robustness of the membership in the various clusters was checked by comparing the K-means four-cluster solution with the solution from Ward's method. Ninety-one percent of the cases were classified into the same cluster by both methods. A graphic representation of the four clusters and the cluster centroids is presented in Figure A.3.

Given two input variables, a four-cluster solution was not surprising. However, as evident from Figure A.3, the four clusters represented combinations of local resource and environmental conditions that were very consistent with the conceptual framework we presented in Chapter 6.

Differentiation in Management Process. To test if companies differentiated their management processes for subsidiaries belonging to the different categories, the top performing subsidiaries (z-score > 1.0) were selected to determine the ideal combination of centralization, formalization, and socialization for each contextual situation. The mean scores of each structural variable for these subsidiaries in the different clusters were considered as empirically derived representations of the ideal structural combination for the four categories of subsidiary context. These ideal types were tested using one-way ANOVA and MANOVA to determine if the patterns actually differed across the

Figure A.3

Empirically Derived Clusters of Subsidiaries Based on Contextual Conditions

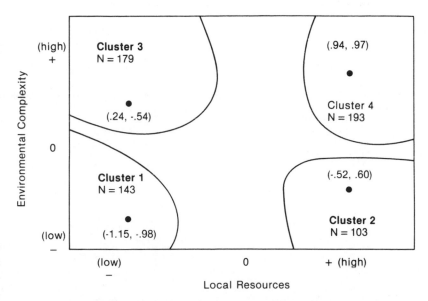

Note: (x,y) represents the standardized value of the local organizational resources 'x' and the environmental complexity 'y' at each of the cluster centroids shown.

clusters. The results are shown in Table A.9. The significant F-statistic (p < .01) for every structural variable showed that these ideal types were very different. An overall MANOVA using all three structural variables was also significant (F = 32.9; p < .001). Furthermore, while there were some deviations between these empirically derived ideal management processes for the different categories of subsidiaries and those we proposed in Chapter 9, there was a good match that supported our conclusions and prescriptions.

However, there was one discrepancy that is worth noting. The results indicated that, contrary to our expectation, in situations of high-local resources, subsidiaries that confronted more complex environments were governed by greater formalization than those in less complex environments. This finding contradicted our view that formal systems inhibit adaptation and responsiveness, which is so crucial in situations involving environmental complexity. While this finding needs to be explored further, a possible explanation may be found in the work of Burgelman of Stanford University, who contends that even autonomous behavior or innovation must take place within a structured context if it is to be effective.[30] Perhaps this was the reason why

Table A.9
Differences in the Mean Values of Top Performing Subsidiaries
across Clusters**

Structural Variables	1 N = 30	2 N = 16	3 N = 15	4 N = 49	Scheffe's Test	F
Centralization	.40	−.46	.12	−.56	(3,2) (3,4)	10.8*
Formalization	−.52	.2	−.20	.44	(3,4)	13.2*
Socialization	−.17	0.8	.32	.84	(3,4)	12.0*

*F-values in ANOVA (p < .001).
**Top performing subsidiaries are those with z-scores > 1.0.
Note: Scheffe's test is a pair-wise comparison of differences in group means (Scheffe, 1953). The pairs listed in the column are those groups for which the means are significantly different (p < .01).

these subsidiaries were managed with the greatest degree of formalization.

Having found broad support for the structural profiles that we proposed, we calculated deviations from these ideal profiles for the remaining subsidiaries, using a Euclidean weighted distance metric. The resultant distance calculations were between the structure of a focal subsidiary and its respective ideal type, according to the focal unit's contingency category. The distance measure was calculated as follows:

$$Dist = \sqrt{\Sigma[Bs(Xis - Xjs)]^2}$$

where Xis was the score of the ideal unit on sth structural dimension, Xjs was the score of the jth focal unit on the sth dimension, and Bs was a weight given by the standardized beta or contribution of the sth dimension in a multiple regression with performance and the dependent variable and all the structural dimensions as the dependent variables.

The calculated distance measure was correlated with the performance of the subsidiary. A negative correlation would demonstrate the validity of our normative proposals in Chapter 9, since the greater the distance from the respective ideal type, the lower the expected performance. The results of this analysis are shown in Table A.10. There

Table A.10
Correlations of Distance Measures with Subsidiary Performance
(Excluding High-Performing Units)

Distance	Performance	N	P-Value
All subsidiaries	−.14	508	.001
Cluster 1	−.08	113	.201
Cluster 2	−.11	87	.160
Cluster 3	−.18	164	.012
Cluster 4	−.17	144	.022

Table A.11
Associations between Innovation Tasks and Organizational Attributes: Comparison of Findings from the Different Methodologies

	Case Research in 9 Companies (Phase I)	Multiple-Indicator, Multiple-Level, Multiple-Respondent Survey in 3 Companies (Phase II)	Single-Indicator, Single-Respondent, Headquarters-Level Survey in 66 Companies (Phase III)
Association between creation of innovations by the subsidiary and:			
—local resources	+	+	+
—local autonomy	+	0	+
—normative integration	+	+	+
—headquarters-subsidiary communication	0	+	+
—intrasubsidiary communication	+	+	Not measured
—intersubsidiary communication	0	0	Not measured
Association between adoption of innovation by the subsidiary and:			
—local resources	−	+	0
—local autonomy	−	0	0
—normative integration	+	+	+
—headquarters-subsidiary communication	+	+	+
—intrasubsidiary communication	0	+	Not measured
—intersubsidiary communication	+	+	Not measured
Association between diffusion of innovations by the subsidiary and:			
—local resources	+	+	Not measured
—local autonomy	+	0	Not measured
—normative integration	+	+	Not measured
—headquarters-subsidiary communication	+	+	Not measured
—intrasubsidiary communication	0	+	Not measured
—intersubsidiary communication	+	+	Not measured

Note: Symbols in the table indicate positive (+), negative (−), or insignificant (0) associations.

Table A.12
Associations between Subsidiary Context and Management Process: Comparison of Findings from Different Methodologies

Subsidiary Context	Case Research in 9 Companies (Phase I)	Multiple-Indicator, Multiple-Level, Multiple-Respondent Survey in 3 Companies (Phase II)	Single-Indicator, Single-Respondent, Headquarters-Level Survey in 66 Companies (Phase III)
High-environmental complexity and high level of local resources (leader)	Coordination based on a mix of socialization and formalization	Coordination based on a mix of high socialization and moderate centralization and formalization	Coordination based on a mix of high socialization and moderate formalization
High-environmental complexity and low level of local resources (black hole)	Coordination based on a mix of centralization and socialization	[Not covered in the sample]	Coordination based on a mix of moderate centralization and socialization
Low-environmental complexity and high level of local resources (contributor)	Coordination based primarily on centralization	Coordination based on a mix of high centralization and moderate socialization	Coordination based on a mix of high centralization and moderate formalization
Low-environmental complexity and low level of local resources (implementer)	Coordination based primarily on formalization	Coordination based primarily on formalization	Coordination based on high formalization and moderate centralization

was a significant negative correlation between subsidiary performance and the distance measure of the deviation of the structure of the head-quarters-subsidiary relation from its ideal type (r = -0.14; p < .001). The same table also shows the component correlations between distance and performance within each contextual category.

Triangulation

Our objective in adopting the relatively complex and multiphase research approach was to compare the findings across the different methodologies and achieve some benefits of triangulation. Each of the methodologies we adopted suffered from many limitations, some of which were inherent in the methodology itself, and others were imposed by flawed application due to the practical problems we faced in its implementation in the specific context of our study.

Tables A.11 and A.12 summarize the findings across the three phases for the two issues—associations between achievement of innovation tasks and the organizational attributes of subsidiaries, and the differentiation of subsidiary contexts and the headquarters-subsidiary relations for the different contexts. As is manifest, the findings broadly converge, but there are significant differences across the different methodologies.[31]

In separate papers written for academic audiences we have explored these differences and their implications.[32] In deriving our recommendations, we have been governed not by the findings from a particular methodology, but from our overall learning from the entire research process. Our conclusions, therefore, are informed by each finding but represent the beliefs that we came to at the end of the study rather than the specific observations or statistical associations that were revealed in a particular part of it.

NOTES

CHAPTER 1

1. The implications of these major changes in the international economic environment have drawn attention from several quarters. One major focus is on changes in the relative competitiveness and comparative advantage of nation states. The dominant concerns are the decline of U.S. domination, the stagnation and restructuring of Europe, and the rise of Japan and the East Asian NICs. See Scott and Lodge (1986) for a key contribution and edited volume of papers on some of the major empirical trends and theoretical issues and Krugman's (1986) review of the book as exemplar of the neoclassical economist's position. A second focus is on how the forces of change have led to the restructuring of the dominant patterns of industrial organization, particularly the decline of institutions associated with the mass production system and the emergence of more flexible forms of industrial organization (Piore and Sabel, 1984; Powell, 1987). A third focus, and the one that is central to this book, is on the changing dynamics of competition among firms. See Porter (1986) for an important contribution and key collection of papers on this theme.

2. See Levitt (1983). Also see Porter (1986, 1987) for a comprehensive discussion of the forces driving the need for global integration and coordination in several industries during this period.

3. For instance, Owen (1976) conducted a study that showed that most firms in Europe had manufacturing operations that were well below the optimal scale afforded by the advances in production technology and the integration of markets such as EEC.

4. The economic benefits of international rationalization and coordination of production, particularly via scale and factor cost efficiencies, have been analyzed by Scherer et al. (1975) and Flaherty (1986). A classic case study of how manufacturing rationalization can also lead to the adoption of newer scale enhancing technology is Pool's (1976) description of how SKF, the Swedish ball-bearing manufacturer, integrated its batch operations and supplanted it with a continuous manufacturing technology. Doz (1978), on the other hand, draws attention to the enormous difficulties in implementing such a strategy.

5. While the difficulties of globalizing downstream activities such as marketing are aptly captured in Buzzell's classic rhetorical essay—"Can You Standardize Multinational Marketing?"—several opportunities and examples for global standardization in marketing and advertising are discussed by Killough (1978), Keegan (1980), and Takeuchi and Porter (1986).

6. These are perhaps the most prominent cases that support Levitt's provocative thesis of the globalization of markets.

7. The dynamics of the global strategic game are discussed at some length by Kiechel (1981), Hout, Porter, and Rudden (1982), Kogut (1985a,b), and Hamel and Prahalad (1985). This metaphor emphasizes the calculated sequence of strategic moves and countermoves such as entry deterring investments, cross-national price differentiation, and so forth that competitors can employ in global competition. The theoretical underpinnings of these insights may be found in the formal models of strategic oligopolistic interaction in contemporary industrial economics. See Porter (1981) for a review of these developments and their implications for strategic management.

8. The strategy of using financial resources generated in one part of the world to fight

competitive battles in another is called cross-subsidization and lies at the core of Hamel and Prahalad's (1985) conception of a global strategy. Also see Watson (1982).

9. See Levitt (1983).

10. Porter (1986, 1987) explicitly contrasts these countervailing forces of national responsiveness with his own discussion of the forces of globalization. A more detailed analysis of the tensions may be found in Prahalad (1976), Doz (1976), and Doz, Bartlett, and Prahalad (1981).

11. Piore (1987) contends that the result of the trend toward systems and modularization of components is a hybrid form of production between mass production and flexible specialization that may be termed "flexible mass production."

12. Traditionally, scale has been seen as an unmixed blessing—something that always helps and never hurts. Recently, however, many researchers have argued otherwise (e.g., Evans, 1982). It has been suggested that scale efficiencies are obtained through increased specialization and through creation of dedicated assets and systems. The same processes cause inflexibilities and limit the firm's ability to cope with change. As environmental turbulence has increased so has the need for strategic and operational flexibility (Mascarenhas, 1984). The extreme of this argument has led to predictions of a re-emergence of the craft form of production to replace the scale-dominated assembly form (Piore and Sabel, 1984). A more typical argument has been the need to balance scale and flexibility, through the use of modern technologies such as CAD/CAM and flexible manufacturing systems (Gold, 1982).

13. The strategic interaction between governments and MNCs in the context of global competition has been the focus of significant research by Doz (1976, 1979).

14. Indeed, there was a "storm over the multinational" (Vernon, 1977). For "sovereignty at bay" see Vernon (1971).

15. See Poynter (1985) for a discussion of various forms of government intervention and multinational response.

16. The importance of innovation for competitiveness in the global economy has by now almost become passé (e.g., Kanter, 1983; Teece, 1987). Surprisingly, comparatively little attention has been given to how MNCs should be organized to realize their enormous potential for worldwide innovation. Some exceptions are the work of Terpstra (1977), Ronstadt (1977), Behrman and Fischer (1980), Ghoshal (1986) and Ronstadt and Kramer (1982).

17. The trend for cooperation among firms that may be direct competitors—so-called strategic alliances—has been the subject of considerable attention. For cooperation in the context of global R&D see Fusfeld and Haklisch (1985); Perlmutter and Heenan (1986), and for a more general review see Horwitch (forthcoming).

18. See Ronstadt and Kramer (1982) and Harrigan (1984).

19. For a contribution and excellent collection of essays on technology standards and global competition see Gabel (1987).

20. The shortening of product-life cycles and the enormous advantage of first-movers in terms of jumping from one generation of technology to another have been stressed by Foster (1985).

21. The product-cycle theory, first formalized by Vernon (1966) suggests that multinational companies typically develop new products in their home countries, utilizing local resources and technologies to respond to local market needs, and then diffuse the innovations around the world step-by-step, first to countries that are close to the stage of development achieved by the home country (such as Europe, for U.S.-based MNCs), and then to lesser developed nations.

CHAPTER 2

1. *Newsweek*, April 14, 1986.

2. For a more detailed discussion of these and other aspects of national differences in the market for soaps and detergents, see Bartlett, "Procter & Gamble Europe: Vizir Launch," Harvard Business School case #9-384-139.

3. Emergence of the giant chains has led to a significant increase in concentration in disintegration channels, resulting in a shift of power away from manufacturers to distributors. For example, in 1970, 2,000 largest resellers accounted for about 50

percent of the consumer electronics market in the United Kingdom. Twenty-six resellers accounted for the same market share in the United Kingdom in 1984. This concentration also existed in other markets including Japan (away from company-owned stores to mass merchandisers), Germany, France, the United States, and most other large, advanced markets.

4. Another factor that facilitated globalization of this industry was the progressive decline in the need and importance of local service capabilities. Adoption of new components (transistors, ICs, PCBs) and new manufacturing processes (automated insertion, computerized on-line testing) increased product reliability, and reduced need for service. Moreover, the development of replaceable service boards practically eliminated the need for skilled service technicians. Need for local service acts as a powerful entry barrier for global firms, and progressive lowering and final elimination of this barrier has been almost as important for globalization of this business as some of the other factors we have described.

5. The term *global* applied to industries, companies, and strategies has been subject to widely differing definition and usage (see Ghoshal, 1986 for a discussion and illustration of these differences). We use the term *global industry* or *global strategy* in its purest sense: for example *global strategy* here is one that defines product design, location and scale of manufacturing facilities, choice of technology, sourcing patterns, and competitive strategy on the assumption of a unified and homogeneous world market. It is the classic approach of exporting standardized products from a centralized and global-scale plant to be marketed worldwide according to a centrally devised and controlled plan that Porter (1980) called the *pure global strategy* and Prahalad and Doz (1987) call the strategy of *global integration.*

6. This corresponds to what Porter (1986) describes as a multidomestic strategy, and Prahalad and Doz (1987) call a strategy of local responsiveness.

7. For a detailed discussion on the need for local responsiveness because of the role of the national PTTs, see Doz's (1986) discussion on the telecommunications switching industry. The tendency of these PTTs to restrict their patronage primarily to "local" companies is manifest from the high concentration and remarkable stability of market shares in each national market. In the United States, AT&T had a virtual monopoly in providing telecommunications services and converted it into a near monopoly in the equipment market by sourcing 70 percent of its hardware requirements from Western Electric, its wholly owned subsidiary. In Japan, the Nippon Telegraph and Telephone Public Corporation (NTT) sourced its needs from the "Denden" family of NEC, Fujitsu, Oki Electric, and Hitachi. In the United Kingdom, the British post office placed orders with a "telephone ring" of local manufacturers. The result was a remarkable stability of the market shares of GEC, Plessey, and STC. Similar direct or indirect "quote" systems for placement of orders by PTTs had been in operation in France, Germany, Belgium, Holland, and Italy, and in all these countries four-party concentrations varied between 65 and 95 percent, and these market concentrations have been remarkably stable over two decades.

8. The notion of "fit" between industry requirements, a firm's strategy, and its organization has played an extremely important role in recent management literature. Economists have argued that differences in the performance of companies can be explained by looking at such fit between industry structure and the company's strategy: Labeled the Structure-Conduct-Performance paradigm, this concept has, in fact been central to the development of the new substream of economic theory that has come to be called industrial economics (see Caves, 1980 for a review). The same concept of fit, both between industry characteristics and the company's strategy (Venkatraman, 1987) and between the company's strategy and its organization (Chandler, 1962) has also been used extensively by organization theory, business policy, and strategy scholars to explain why some companies do better than others. Much empirical evidence has been gathered by academic researchers to support this concept, and Hrebeniak et al. (1988) provide an exhaustive review of such evidence.

9. See Stopford and Wells (1972).

10. The matrix organization was proposed by Davis and Lawrence (1977) as a solution to the problem of balancing functional and project inputs in organizations that face multiple contingencies—for example, aerospace firms. In the contemporary interna-

tional context, this basic form has been elaborated upon as the organizational solution to the challenges of global integration and national responsiveness confronted by MNCs (Prahalad and Doz, 1987).

11. Walter Wriston, then chairman of Citibank, even wrote the foreword to the Davis and Lawrence book, *Matrix*.

CHAPTER 3

1. This argument, developed inductively from the experiences of the nine companies we studied, finds some strong support in a well-established thesis in organizational theory. Stinchcombe (1965) was the first to try and explain why many organizations retain their structural characteristics long after their founding. He documented that there are waves of organizational building during certain periods in history and that organizations change only very slowly after the founding period. Thus organizations are "imprinted" with indelible characteristics of the founding period and those formed in one period are likely to differ from those formed in another. The explanation for this pattern is that organizational inventions made at a particular point in history depend on the social technology available at that time. Because those organizations that are successful function effectively with the practices of their particular period, the practices become institutionalized and the basic structure of the organization tends to remain relatively stable. Our study reiterates this valuable insight. As we discuss later, European MNCs such as Philips owe their multidomestic character to the social conditions in Europe at the time of their founding. At that point, European nations were great mercantilist powers and the mercantile trading companies were organized on a country-by-country basis and were the natural models for these firms. Moreover, colonial experience provided a supply of expatriate managers who were comfortable operating in foreign environments.

2. Many organizational theorists have addressed the issues of organizational inertia and the influence of what we have termed *administrative heritage* on an organization's ability to adapt and change. Readers interested in exploring these theoretical implications are referred to the population ecology program of research spawned by Hannan and Freeman (1977, 1984). According to them, organizational inertia often stems from administrative heritage. Once standard operating procedures and distribution of tasks and authority have been agreed upon, they are very difficult to change. Normative agreements constrain adaptation in at least two ways. First, they provide a justification and an organizing principle for those elements that wish to resist reorganization (i.e., they can resist in terms of a shared principle). Second, normative agreements preclude the serious consideration of many alternate responses. This view emphasizes the dysfunctions of administrative heritage. But, administrative heritage is also the source of distinctive competencies (Selznick, 1957) and represents an "invisible" asset (Itami, 1987) that a corporation can use as a source of competitive advantage. Powell (1987) presents an interesting contrast of the uses and liabilities of organizational memory.

3. Our description of Unilever's historical evolution draws on a number of published sources besides our own discussions with managers of the company. For more detailed accounts of Unilever's evolution, see Wilson (1970), Knox (1976), Fieldhouse (1978), and Reader (1980).

4. For a detailed account of P&G's evolution see Schisgall (1981).

5. The impact of founders on the character of their organizations and its pattern of institutionalization has been stressed by Selznick (1959). Empirical support for this view has been provided by Kimberly (1980) in his discussion of the evolution of a medical college, when the founders' personal values and management style shaped the organization's evolution in a distinct manner.

6. See Schisgall (1981), p. 182.

7. The contrast between the social environment at the time of founding of Unilever and P&G and the subsequent very different structural evolution of these companies' international operations drives home the point made by Stinchcombe (see Note 1). As we will show later, the evolution of the Japanese MNCs agrees with this important theoretical insight.

8. The role of leaders in shaping the strategies, organizations, and cultures of leaders was central to the study of organizations into the 1960s. Authors such as Barnard (1939) and Selznick (1957) highlighted the powerful impact of leadership on behaviors of companies and Andrews (1967) placed it at the core of a company's strategic capability. The interest in leadership was pushed to the background in the 1960s and 1970s for reasons that are explored in Horwitch (forthcoming). There is now a renewed interest in the study of leadership, and some excellent contributions made by scholars such as Bennis and Nanus (1985), Schein (1985), and Kotter (1988), among others.

9. Matsushita is exemplar of Meyer and Rowan's (1977) discussion of how an organization's charter and the normative agreements arrived at early in an organization's history shape its evolution.

10. Stories—sometimes called myths—develop around important events and the actions of great leaders in an organization's past. These stories gradually define the historical identity of an organization. As this occurs, the "administrative organization," in Selznick's terms, is converted from an expendable instrument for the accomplishment of externally imposed goals into an "institution" (Selznick, 1957). A system with a life of its own, it acquires a self—a distinctive identity. A classic illustration is Clark's study of Antioch, Reed, and Swarthmore—the "distinctive colleges." In this context, he talks about the importance of "sagas"—collective understanding of a unique accomplishment based on historical exploits. Believers in the "saga" give loyalty to the organization and take pride and identity from it (1972:198). The saga, embellished through retelling and recruiting, links the organization's present with its past. The saga around the life and philosophy of Konosuke Matsushita is perhaps the strongest source of institutionalization of Matsushita's organizational systems and the ways in which they were influenced by Konosuke Matsushita. See Ghoshal and Bartlett, "Matsushita Electric Industries LTD" (MEI), Harvard Business School case #9-388-144.

11. The influence of national cultures on corporations has been the subject of much research. The empirical results do show consistent differences and general patterns across different MNCs. (See for example, Negandhi and Baliga, 1981.) The research is, however, less satisfying in terms of offering an explanation. One strand is social/psychological in orientation and stresses the different value structures and need orientations of the society (e.g., Hofstede, 1983; Laurant, 1986). The other strand examines the social institutions and structures of the society such as class structure, education levels, labor market characteristics, and so forth, and treats those as primary explanatory variables (e.g., Dore, 1973; Rohlen, 1974). The problems with these explanations have been raised recently by the empirical evidence presented by U.S. plants of Japanese MNCs such as Honda. Its U.S. plant, which employs primarily U.S. nationals, exhibits a surprisingly Japanese character. This has led some researchers to suggest that cultural explanations perhaps obscure the importance of organizational processes and structures which may historically have had a cultural basis but are not necessarily tied to it (e.g., Shimada and MacDuffie, 1987).

12. See Chandler (1986).

13. "Managerial Capitalism" is dramatically captured by the title of Chandler's (1977) superb history of the development of the M-form corporation, The Visible Hand.

14. See Servan-Schreiber (1968).

15. For a fascinating biography of Geneen and his impact on ITT, see Schoenberg (1985).

16. See for example, Abegglen (1958) and Yoshino (1968) for details of the social organization of Japanese firms, and Rohlen (1974) and Westney (1987) for aspects of the interaction between Japanese firms and their broader social environment.

17. These practices are discussed at some length in Rohlen (1974).

18. Readers interested in a more detailed historical analysis of the evolution of multinational companies are referred to the classic work of Chandler (1962, 1977, 1986). In Scale and Scope (forthcoming), he provides detailed evidence to suggest that the potential to realize scale and scope (the ability to amortize capital investments across multiple product lines) economies was the rationale for the growth of the MNC.

19. Both Franko (1976) and Dyas and Thanheiser (1976) provide illustrations and evi-

dence of why and how the differentiated and protectionist environment of these periods fitted the capabilities and orientations of European multinationals and led to their rapid successful expansion abroad.

20. See Buckley and Casson (1985:200).

21. Wilkins (1977) provides the most detailed analysis of the international expansion of American companies during this period.

22. See also Servan-Schreiber (1968). This author, both reflecting and shaping a view that was widely shared in the development of European companies, raised the possibility that the enormous economic power of American MNCs might thwart the policy-making processes of the European countries. According to him and other authors such as Wilkins (1977), the success of American MNCs during the two decades following the second world war was largely due to their technological and managerial capabilities to develop new products and technologies and exploit those innovations on a worldwide basis through a unique organizational system.

23. In Chapter 1, we briefly reviewed some of the key globalizing forces that have gathered increasing momentum during the last two decades. These forces, and their implications for multinational management have been described by many authors from diverse perspectives. Besides Levitt (1983) and Porter (1986), they include Kogut (1984, 1985), and Prahalad and Doz (1987).

CHAPTER 4

1. The concept of the transnational that we present in this chapter has many features that have been highlighted by other authors. The concept closest to our view, and the one that has substantially influenced our approach and interpretations, is in the seminal work of Perlmutter (1969). He developed a typology of different multinational mentalities or cognitive orientations toward international business and this typology remains as valid today as it was when proposed over two decades ago. He classified multinationals as ethnocentric, polycentric, and geocentric: The first refers to an approach of home country dominance that is central to the centralized lab model we have described; the second describes companies that treat each subsidiary on a country-by-country basis, similar to our model of the decentralized federation; and the third identifies companies that develop a cosmopolitan and integrative style—an approach that is similar to the organizational form we describe as the transnational.

   Similarly, the heterarchy model of MNCs proposed by Hedlund (1986), the multifocal organization described by Prahalad and Doz (1987), and the horizontal organizational form suggested by White and Poynter (1989) identify many of the environmental and organizational forces that are driving multinational companies to develop modern complex organizational capabilities and highlight some of the features of what we describe as the transnational. These models differ significantly in their levels of specificity but share the overreaching conclusion that organizational capability is increasingly the key constraint for effective worldwide operations.

2. For a more theory-grounded discussion of these dilemmas, see Ghoshal (1986).

3. This approach to configuration of assets and resources is consistent with work of Kogut (1985a) and Porter (1986) who differentiated the activities of the MNC into different value-generating activities—the so-called value-added chain—and proposed different strategic logics for the configuration of each of the activities.

4. The distinction among pooled, sequential, and reciprocal interdependencies has been made by Thompson (1967). For each type of interdependencies he proposed an appropriate coordination mechanism: rules, plans, and mutual adjustment, respectively.

5. For an excellent conceptualization of networks as a distinctive organizational form, see Aldrich and Whetten (1981).

6. Our use of "integrated" parallels Kanter's (1983) description of the "integrative" organization.

7. This conception of requisite differentiation follows from Ashby's (1956) law of requisite variety: "only variety can kill variety."

8. The theoretical underpinnings of our conception of differentiation may be traced to

Blau and Schoenherr (1971), Lawrence and Lorsch (1967), and Lawrence and Dyer (1983).

9. Lawrence and Dyer (1983) integrated these two previously separate logics for differentiation—the environmental contingency perspective (Lawrence and Lorsch, 1967) and the resource dependency perspective (Pfeffer and Salancik, 1978; Aldrich, 1979).

10. The concept of organizational learning has been discussed by various organizational theorists such as Cyert and March (1963), March and Olsen (1976), Argyris and Schon (1978), Duncan and Weiss (1979), and Hedberg (1981). There are considerable differences, however, in their conceptualization of organizational learning. In a comprehensive review of this literature Fiol and Lyles (1985) distinguished between learning as the development of insights and change in knowledge states on the one hand and structural and organizational adaptive outcomes on the other. Our own conception is intended to capture both strands. Our focus, though, is on innovation processes within the organization as this is perhaps the most important part of the broader concept of organizational learning.

11. This point has been highlighted by Vernon (1979).

12. This concept is in keeping with Lawrence and Lorsch (1967), who, in addition to need for requisite differentiation, stressed the importance of appropriate integration devices for improved organization performance.

13. The matrix organizational structure (Davis and Lawrence, 1977) evolved as a response to the needs to balance project/product and functional inputs but it required mechanisms of mutual adjustment to resolve the conflicts that it inevitably engendered. This is a topic to which we shall return in Chapter 8.

14. This conception of the transnational recognizes that organizations are also political arenas (Cyert and March, 1963; Pettigrew, 1973; Pfeffer, 1981; and Mintzberg, 1983) and the importance of the dominant coalition in the organization (Thompson, 1967).

15. These dominant coalitions are consistent with the predictions of the previous research on the determinants of intraorganizational power. The view that power accrues to the organizational subunit that handles critical contingencies was discovered in a field study of two French bureaucracies by Crozier (1964), theoretically formalized by Hickson et al. (1971), and empirically established by Hickson et al. (1971) and Hinings et al. (1974).

16. The difficulties of achieving this balanced approach for managing the distribution of power and influence in organizations are discussed in Bacharach and Lawler (1981).

17. The idea that the allocation of administrative resource be considered akin to a constrained maximization problem in economics has been suggested by Caves (1982), who admonished organization theorists for paying little attention to the costs/benefits of different administrative mechanisms. Important exceptions among organization theorists are Thompson (1967) and Ouchi (1977, 1980).

18. The use of centralization, formalization, and socialization as means of coordination and control has been discussed by many authors including Pugh et al. (1968, 1969), Blau and Schoenherr (1971), Child (1972, 1973), and Ouchi (1977, 1980). In the specific context of the multinational corporation, the process implications of these mechanisms were described by Bartlett (1979) in a model that distinguished "substantive decision management," "temporary coalition management," and "decision context management" as alternative management process modes in MNCs. See also the contributions by various scholars in a volume edited by Otterbeck (1981).

19. Nonaka (1972) pointed out that the interpenetration of market and hierarchical coordination was an important feature of Japanese organizations.

20. This is perhaps one of the most enduring insights in management theory and was the central theme in the works of both Barnard (1938) and Selznick (1959).

21. Compelling evidence for the importance of enlightened human resource management programs for corporate performance has been provided by Kanter (1983), based on a survey of the HRM practices of several major American corporations.

CHAPTER 5

1. Organizations may respond to crises in many different ways. Starbuck et al. (1978) and Starbuck (1983) argue that organizations primarily try to avoid coming to grips

with a crisis because of the vested interests of the dominant coalition in preserving the status quo. However, as Lewin pointed out (1951), crises may also trigger the "unfreezing" of an organization, and such unfreezing can result in fairly dramatic changes (Miller and Friesen, 1984).

2. Matsushita's sales loss due to the yen appreciation as estimated by Yamaichi Securities.

3. See Kogut (1985a) for an excellent managerial overview.

4. See Hout, Porter, and Rudden (1982) and Ghemawat and Spence (1986) for a discussion of the industrial economics perspective.

5. See Buckley and Casson (1976) and Rugman (1979) for the international management view.

6. See Kogut (1984, 1985a) and Porter (1986) for discussions of strategic logics that may be adopted in the international configuration of the value-added chain.

7. The dangers posed by volatility in the economic environment to such "ideally configured" operations were pointed out by Mascarenhas (1982), Kogut (1985b), and Ghoshal (1986).

8. For a more detailed discussion of the pitfalls of such perpetual corporate restructuring, see Bartlett (1982, 1983).

9. This incremental approach to change is proposed by Lindblom (1959) and Quinn (1980).

10. See Gold (1982) and Piore and Sabel (1984) for a more detailed discussion of the benefits and implications of flexible manufacturing.

11. From a speech by van der Klugt, "Penetrating Global Markets: High Technology Companies" presented at the conference "Going Global," sponsored by The Economist Conference Unit, London, June 1985.

12. Vernon (1979, 1980) was one of the earliest researchers to emphasize the importance of global scanning as an important source of competitive advantage.

13. See Kogut (1985a).

14. See Kogut (1985b) for a description of how an MNC can create options to turn the uncertainties of an increasingly volatile global economy to its own advantage. Multiple sourcing, production shifting to benefit from changing factor costs and exchange rates, and arbitrage to exploit imperfections in capital and information markets are, according to Kogut, some of the hallmarks of a superior global strategy.

15. See Lessard and Lightstone (1986) for a more detailed discussion of the financial and operational implications of volatile exchange rates in the context of global competition.

16. This is the crux of "flexible specialization," the system of production that Piore and Sabel (1984) argue will replace the previous system of mass production.

17. The crucial importance of global R&D for shaping successful international product policies has been stressed by Terpstra (1977).

18. See Kanter (1983).

19. Reciprocal interdependence (Thompson, 1967) creates conditions that require mutual adjustment and allows for the institutionalization of coordination based on the norm of generalized reciprocity (Powell, 1987).

CHAPTER 6

1. For a more detailed discussion of the problems of shaping a global product organization, see Davidson and Haspeslagh (1982).

2. This framework is derived from the well-known differentiation-integration concepts developed by Lawrence and Lorsch (1967) and was first applied to the analysis of MNC tasks by Prahalad (1976).

3. Most academic research on the topic has also been grounded on this assumption that the nature of the headquarters-subsidiary relation is similar for all the subsidiaries of a multinational. This assumption is manifest in many ways. Findings from data acquired from the subsidiaries of many different MNCs located in one national environment have been used to draw general conclusions regarding the extent of centralization in MNCs (Hulbert and Brandt, 1980). Contingency arguments, such as the need for a fit between the structure of the MNC and different aspects of its environ-

mental context such as the information-processing requirements (Egelhoff, 1982); task environment (Kagono, 1981); or product diversity (Daniels et al., 1985) have been based on measures of contingency and the formal structure of the MNC as a whole. Even studies that have focused on the contingent effects of different subsidiary characteristics on the structure of the MNC, while the contingency variables such as size, age, and so forth, have been measured separately for each subsidiary, use a single MNC level measure for structural properties like centralization (Gates and Egelhoff, 1984).

4. See Wilkins (1974) and Chandler (1986) for a discussion of the emergence and historical development of such multinational enterprises.

5. See Dyas and Thanheiser (1976), Wilkins (1977), and Yoshino (1976).

6. Leveraging differences in factor prices was the basic motivation behind many of the early calls for organizing a worldwide business. See for example, Clee and di Scipio (1959) and Clee and Sachtjen (1964).

7. The strong influence that different cognitive orientations can have on the actions, structures, and processes of organizations has been pointed out by Weick (1969, 1979).

8. This mentality is consistent with Levitt's (1983) rather strong views on the homogenization of global tastes and markets.

9. Perhaps this manager was influenced by Ohmae's (1985) use of the same metaphor.

10. The family metaphor was most explicitly used by Franko (1976) when he characterized the relationship between HQ and subsidiaries in European MNCs as resembling a mother-daughter relationship. This metaphor was used to draw attention to both the equal treatment of different subsidiaries, and the hierarchical status of the HQ—"mother"—and the subsidiaries—"daughters." A further development of the nature of this relationship may be found in Dyas and Thanheiser (1976).

11. The relation between the form of control and the emotional well-being and motivation of organizational members has been studied more broadly by Ouchi (1977).

12. See Bartlett, "Dominion Engineering Works," Harvard Business School case #9-383-185, and Bartlett, "Note on the Paper Machinery Industry," Harvard Business School case #5-383-191.

13. For a more detailed discussion of the various economies of scope that a multinational may exploit, see Ghoshal (1987).

14. See Christensen, "Bic Pen Corp.," Harvard Business School cases #9-374-305, #9-374-306.

15. The distinct advantages of the multinational in terms of its worldwide learning capacity have also been pointed out by Terpstra (1977) and Ronstadt (1977).

16. The sequential nature of the foreign direct-investment process has been described by Kogut (1983). Over time, this can easily lead to a configuration of resources that are unaligned with the MNC's current strategic environment. Moreover, these resource distributions are often very sticky and cannot be easily changed (Zeitz, 1980). A vivid example of this problem is provided by Stopford and Turner (1985) in their discussion of British multinationals and their skewed distribution of resources in Commonwealth nations.

17. For a more detailed discussion of these strategic roles, see Bartlett and Ghoshal (1986).

18. Rugman and Poynter (1982) observed a similar phenomenon in the trend toward assigning mature national subsidiaries worldwide responsibility for products with worldwide markets.

19. The importance of having a presence in all three major economic axes—the United States, Europe, and East Asia—has also been stressed by Ohmae (1985).

20. The reasons for this less-than-satisfactory diffusion of information have been highlighted by Westney (1987). In her view, the primary obstacles are (1) the unclear and often conflicting strategic agendas for the foreign R&D subsidiary; (2) the difficulty of having an effective research unit that is divorced from manufacturing and marketing; and (3) the difficulty of penetrating the local social, business, and research networks, especially in Japan.

21. International expansion by acquisition is a highly favored strategic choice these days.

The jury is still out on whether such a strategy has the intended positive outcome. It does appear clear, though, that for an acquisition to be successful, careful attention has to be given to the process by which its integration into the parent organization is implemented (Jemison and Sitkin, 1986).

22. The use of strategic alliances for global reach has burgeoned in recent years. For a review, see Kogut (1988), Contractor and Lorange (1987), and Horwitch (forthcoming).

23. Haspeslagh (1982) eloquently discusses the uses and limits of such portfolio planning techniques.

CHAPTER 7

1. This argument is implicit in the Product Cycle Theory proposed by Vernon (1966). It has been stated more explicitly in the internationalization and appropriability theories of foreign direct investment: see Buckley and Casson (1976), Calvet (1981), and Rugman (1979).

2. See Levitt (1983) for an interesting, if somewhat provocative, discussion of these two mentalities.

3. The not-invented-here (NIH) syndrome refers to the resistance of managers to ideas or solutions that have been generated elsewhere, and not by them. For a discussion and elaboration of this syndrome, see Allen (1977).

4. Full details of the development process are provided in Bartlett, "Procter & Gamble Europe: Vizir Launch," Harvard Business School case #9-384-139.

5. Westney and Sakakibara (1985) observed a similar system of internal quasi-markets governing the interface between R&D and operating units in a number of other Japanese companies.

6. See Westney and Sakakibara (1985) for a more detailed discussion of these transitions in the careers of research personnel in Japanese companies, and for a comparison of American and Japanese practices in this regard.

7. The organizational form we describe as the decentralized federation shares many common features with the mother-daughter organization that Franko (1976) describes as representative of many large European multinationals. Hedlund (1981) showed that national subsidiaries of such companies typically develop strong and entrepreneurial local management teams and accumulate relatively high levels of local resources—two attributes we feel are key to the ability of such companies to foster local innovations.

8. See Van Maanen and Schein (1979) for a rich and theory-grounded discussion on how such differences in socialization processes and career systems can influence managers' attitudes toward change and innovation.

9. See Bartlett and Yoshihara (1988) for a discussion of the problems of subsidiary management involvement in the decision-making processes of Japanese companies.

10. Much of the earlier research on organizational innovation has been focused on innovations that are conceived, created, and implemented within individual subunits of large and multiunit organizations. Burns and Stalker (1961), for example, state this explicitly: "The twenty concerns which were subject of these studies were not all separately constituted business companies . . . [some of them] were small parts of the parent organization. . . . This is why we have used 'concern' as a generic term." Other researchers have similarly observed a district sales office of General Electric, or a department in the headquarters of 3M, or a divisional data processing office of Polaroid, but not the overall configuration of any one of these companies. Therefore, the studies have focused on what we call local innovations. And most of them have identified internal integration, local slack, and decentralized authority as key factors that facilitate such innovations in organizations that have been variously described as "organic," "integrative," or simply "excellent" (see, for example, Burns and Stalker, 1961; Peters and Waterman, 1982; Kanter, 1983). To this extent, our findings regarding the factors that make local innovations efficient fully conform to the conclusions reached by earlier researchers. A major point of departure in our study, however, is that we view such local innovations as one of many different processes

through which innovations may come about in complex organizations and suggest that the organizational factors that facilitate the different innovation processes are not only different, but may also be mutually contradictory.

11. The use of personnel transfers as an integration mechanism in multinational companies has been highlighted by many scholars, most notably by Edstrom and Galbraith (1977).

12. See Kanter (1983).

CHAPTER 8

1. The difficulty of balancing the different political interests within an organization has been the subject of considerable scholarship in organization theory (e.g., Cyert and March, 1963; Zaleznick, 1970; Pettigrew, 1973; Wildavsky, 1979; Pfeffer, 1981; and Mintzberg, 1983). More recently, attention has been called to the additional problem of balancing differences in the "thought worlds" of organizational members that derive from differences in the local subcultures to which they belong (Douglas, 1986). For instance, Dougherty (1987) in a study of new-product development noted the very different conception that marketing, engineering, and manufacturing managers had of the activity. She further found that, in many cases, the failure of new-product development projects could be attributed to the difficulty of integrating these disparate thought worlds.

2. The importance of control over information as a key source of intraorganizational power was pointed out by Pettigrew (1972).

3. This is a classic example of the differences in "thought worlds" discussed in Note 1 above.

4. In addition to field interviews with company managers, the history of Ericsson's organizational development draws on Altman and Olsson (1977) and Meurling and Jeans (1985).

5. Building in redundancy and elements of misfit is the central prescription for a self-designing organization in Hedberg et al. (1976).

6. The importance of requisite ambiguity for a self-adaptive organization has been argued by March and Olsen (1976).

7. The use of such supplemental channels and forums by MNCs has been widespread and effective. For a more detailed discussion, see Bartlett (1983).

8. See Nystrom et al. (1976) for the importance of setting up organizational processes that do not necessarily have a well-defined, a priori objective, but create influence and information channels that can be used flexibly in a variety of contexts.

9. The quest for describing the features of a self-balancing (e.g., Wildavsky, 1972; Landau, 1973); self-adapting (e.g., Hedberg et al., 1976); and self-reflective organization (e.g., Argyris and Schon, 1978), has engaged organizational theorists for a long time.

CHAPTER 9

1. The role of headquarters management in establishing control over worldwide operations and the means by which it is done have been richly described by Doz and Prahalad (1981, 1984) and Prahalad and Doz (1981).

2. Centralization has been the variable of greatest interest in the research on the structure of HQ-subsidiary relations. An excellent contribution and review of the findings of this research may be found in Gates and Egelhoff (1984).

3. The use of centralization as a primary form of coordination and control in Japanese MNCs has been documented by Kagono (1981) and its limitations discussed by Bartlett and Yoshihara (1988).

4. Formalization may be interpreted as a set of routines and standard operating procedures (Nelson and Winter, 1982) and has been studied in this sense as an increasingly common approach used by European MNCs to coordinate headquarters-subsidiary relations by Hedlund (1981).

5. As quoted in the rather unflattering account of ITT by Sampson (1973).

6. See Schisgall (1981).

7. "The Procter Way" is a perfect example of Nelson and Winter's (1982) discussion of "routines."
8. Socialization is the process by which organization members arrive at domain consensus and shared values (Van Maanen, 1978; Van Maanen and Schein, 1979). Its value as a control and coordination mechanism has been discussed in Ouchi (1980). Jaeger (1983) has documented its use as a coordination mechanism in Japanese MNCs.
9. Edstrom and Galbraith (1977) first drew attention to the role of rotation and transfer of personnel as a strategy for coordination and control in the MNC.
10. In a presentation to students in the Management of International Business course at the Harvard Business School, April 1985.
11. The relative costs and benefits of different coordination and control mechanisms have been discussed by Thompson (1967) and Ouchi (1980). The importance of incorporating such a calculus in organizational analysis has been emphasized by Caves (1980), who argues that, as with any economic resource, control and coordination resources are also scarce. Hence, organizational design prescriptions must also follow the standard rigors of constrained maximization.
12. See Murray (1981) for a collection of essays on the transfer pricing problems in MNCs. For a more general treatment of the organizational issues surrounding transfer pricing see Eccles (1985).
13. Existing research on information processing in worldwide companies (e.g., Egelhoff, 1982) considers the information-processing problem as one of handling environmental or task contingencies. As we have stated, our conception includes in addition, information creation, information transfer, and learning.
14. However, as pointed out by Mascarenhas (1984), volatility in the global environment requires that formalization be supplemented with informal communication channels. For similar reasons Lessard and Lightstone (1986) have pointed out that formalization has to be richer than simple operating procedures and must include rehearsed strategic decision rules so that the options for flexibility and arbitrage that exist in an MNC (Kogut, 1985b) can actually be exercised.
15. These findings are reported in Ghoshal and Nohria (1987).
16. These multidimensional coordinative mechanisms are more like structural Gestalts (Khandwalla, 1977) that reflect the various trade-offs among the mechanisms and yet have an internal consistency suited to the particular context.

CHAPTER 10

1. March and Olsen (1976) are exemplar of the several theorists who have conceived of organizations more generally to be an arena of interaction for multiple political factions. The model of the organization they propose is labeled *organized anarchy*. This conception of the organization as a political economy of multiple interest groups is also associated with Benson (1975).
2. This is one of the most enduring prescriptions in the management of complex organizations, its origins being the works of Barnard (1938) and Selznick (1957).
3. Organizational mentality is also at the forefront of the recent cognitivist turn in organization theory. See Sims et al. (1986) for an excellent collection of some recent papers on this theme.
4. Similar features were found by Westley and Mintzberg (1988) to be central to the strategic vision articulated by Iacocca and Levesque.
5. The willingness to maintain a consistent proactive commitment—precisely the two step forward one step back samba step—proposed by Maljers is also the recommendation of White and Poynter (1984), who have argued that this should be the strategy of an MNC subsidiary if it is to maintain a viable bargaining status vis-à-vis the host country government.
6. Full details of this case are contained in the series of cases (A to D) on the company: See Bartlett and Yoshino, "Corning Glass Works, International," Harvard Business School cases #9-381-160 to #9-381-164.
7. See Tung (1982) for evidence of the failure of expatriate managers in foreign settings.
8. Kunda (1987) in a brilliant study of "Tech"—a disguised name for a prominent U.S.

minicomputer manufacturing firm—clearly describes the central role played by training and development in creating high-commitment cultures in organizations.

9. The importance of company-specific development programs as a socialization and change agent is discussed by Tichy (1983).

10. The methods used for spiritual training at Matsushita bear close resemblance to those described by Kunda (see Note 8 above).

11. These tacit, implicit sets of beliefs are what Schein (1985) defines as corporate culture.

12. The importance of the rotation and transfer of managers in the MNC as a strategy for integration and control was advanced by Edstrom and Galbraith (1977).

13. See Wildavsky (1979) for a classic statement of the problems of turf battles.

14. The strategy of using special forums with broad mandates that bring together different interest groups as a strategy of co-optation is also documented in Selznick's (1949) classic study of the evolution of a large public development agency—the Tennessee Valley Authority.

CHAPTER 11

1. For an illustration of how the volatility and dynamism of the international environment can affect purely national companies, see Lessard and Lightstone (1986).

2. See Powell (1987) and Eccles and Crane (1987) for theoretical discussions and interesting illustrations of the challenges of managing such networks or "hybrid organizations."

3. Even the early research on the evolution of MNC structure (e.g., Stopford and Wells, 1972) saw the global matrix as the ultimate stage. A more detailed discussion of the merits of this form may be found in a recent book by Prahalad and Doz (1987).

4. The use of metaphorical images that capture various facets of organizational life is the subject of a delightful book by Morgan (1986).

5. See Egelhoff (1982) for a model of the MNC as an information-processing system.

6. Field studies of organizations such as Dalton's Men Who Manage clearly reveal that informal interaction patterns may actually be more reflective of an organization's structure than its formal relationships.

7. For a detailed description of the "functional analog" system, see Bartlett and Yoshino, "Corning Glass Works, International (C1)," Harvard Business School case #9-381-163.

8. See Deal and Kennedy (1982).

9. There is an extensive organization development (OD) literature that is primarily concerned with the dynamics of organizational change and that supports the argument that changes in organizational structures or processes must be accompanied by enabling changes in the cognitive and effective orientation of individuals. Some of the important works in this tradition are those by Bennis (1966), Beckhard (1969), Beckhard and Harris (1977), Beyer and Trice (1978), Beer (1980), and Tichy (1983). A fascinating case study that describes the application of several of the principles advocated by this research tradition is Pettigrew's (1985) study of the reawakening of Imperial Chemicals Industries, p.l.c.

10. This point is emphasized by Miller and Friesen (1984). While they admit that evolutionary or incremental processes of change are more often effective transition strategies, they argue that in certain situations revolutionary or quantum change may be a more effective approach.

11. For a discussion of government policies that promote national champions see Poynter (1985) and Doz (1986).

12. For a review of the role of strategic alliances in modern strategy see Contractor and Lorange (1987) and Horwitch (forthcoming). The importance of international alliances that allow MNCs to develop a sensitivity in the three major economic axes—North America, Europe, and the Far East—is discussed by Ohmae (1985).

13. See the article "Corporate Couples" in Business Week (July 21, 1986) on the falling out of several prominent alliances. The reasons for such failures have been described by Hamel and Prahalad (1988).

14. See Note 9 above for a list of some of the previous research that can help guide such change processes.

APPENDIX

1. See Bartlett, 1979.
2. See Bartlett, "Compania Telefonia Mexicana (CTM): ATI in Mexico," Harvard Business School case #9-387-115. For reasons of confidentiality, the actual identity of the company has been disguised.
3. The history of EMI's development of the CT scanner is described in Bartlett, "EMI and the CT Scanner (A)," Harvard Business School case #9-383-194. The strategic and organizational difficulties of the company in managing this business are described in Bartlett, "EMI and the CT Scanner (B)," Harvard Business School case #9-383-195.
4. See Bartlett, "Merloni Group," Harvard Business School case #9-383-152.
5. See Bartlett, "Ideal Standard France: Pat Peterson," Harvard Business School case #9-382-139.
6. See Bartlett, "Conex do Brasil," Harvard Business School case #9-385-257.
7. See Bartlett, "Kentucky Fried Chicken (Japan) Limited," Harvard Business School case #9-387-043.
8. See Bartlett, "Dominion Engineering Works," Harvard Business School case #9-383-185, for a detailed description of why and how this company failed to respond to the new opportunities that were created, to a large extent, by its own technological innovations. For a broader discussion of the paper machinery industry and the strategies that were adopted by other companies, such as Voith, see Bartlett, "Note on the Paper Machinery Industry," Harvard Business School case #5-383-191.
9. See Bartlett, "Caterpillar Tractor Company," Harvard Business School case #9-385-276, and Bartlett, "Komatsu Limited," Harvard Business School case #9-385-277.
10. See Bartlett and Yoshino, "Corning Glass Works, International," series (A) to (D), Harvard Business School cases #9-381-160 to #9-381-164.
11. For a discussion on coarse grained and fined grained methodologies, see Harrigan (1983).
12. See Prahalad (1976) and Prahalad and Doz (1987).
13. We mailed a total of 82, 74, and 34 questionnaires to the different subsidiaries of Philips, Matsushita, and NEC, respectively. Given our qualification criteria, 71 (87%), 69 (93%), and 33 (97%) responses could be used, respectively.
14. The term "innovation" was defined in the questionnaire as any product, manufacturing process, or administrative system that was new for the subsidiary. The issue of "new for whom?" has been debated extensively in the literature on definition of innovations and, given the objectives of our study, we agree with those who argue that anything new to the adopting unit qualifies as an innovation, even if it is not new to the world as such. For an extensive discussion on this issue, see Zaltman et al. (1973).
15. See Allen (1977).
16. See Van Maanen and Schein (1979).
17. In the headquarters-level survey to be described later, the corporate managers were asked to rate directly the extents to which each subsidiary shared the parent's goals and values. The high-rank correlations between the subsidiary ranks calculated on the basis of the headquarters and subsidiary-level responses (see Table A.3) provides some support for this indirect system of measuring the variable at the subsidiary level.
18. Documented, among others, by Edstrom and Galbraith (1977).
19. See Young, Hood, and Hamill (1985) for both theoretical arguments and empirical evidence on the role of executive travel in developing cultural integration in worldwide companies.
20. These decision situations were adopted from the instrument developed and used by De Bodinat (1976).
21. Following the suggestions of De Bodinat (1976), we differentiated between local autonomy for strategic and operational decisions, and measured the former on the basis of relative influence exercised on the (1) introduction of a new product; (2) modification of production process; (3) restructuring of the subsidiary organization involving creation or abolition of departments, and the latter on the basis of relative

influence exercised on the other three decision situations. However, the measures of strategic and operational autonomy obtained were highly correlated for all three companies (see Ghoshal, 1986). Therefore, we dropped this distinction and adopted a single measure of autonomy.

22. See Ghoshal (1986) and Ghoshal and Bartlett (1988).
23. See Ghoshal (1986) and Ghoshal and Nohria (1987).
24. See Stopford (1983).
25. For more detailed analysis of sample response patterns, nonresponse bias, and measurement procedure, see Ghoshal (1986) and Ghoshal and Nohria (1987).
26. For an excellent review of the debate, see Downey and Ireland (1979).
27. We had pre-tested the headquarters-level questionnaire with ten senior managers who were participating in an executive education program at MIT's Sloan School of Management. Each manager had considerable experience of working at the headquarters of large multinational companies and the collective opinion of the group was that corporate managers could not have a reliable basis to estimate these attributes for the company's different national operations. Similar views were also expressed by corporate managers of Philips, NEC, and Matsushita when we consulted them regarding the designs of the questionnaires.
28. See Milligan and Cooper (1985).
29. For a theoretical analysis of the clustering procedure we used, see Everitt (1980).
30. See Burgelman (1984).
31. While we have compared the findings across the different methodologies, it is necessary to note that technical differences caused by the differences in measurement systems led to differences in the subsidiary context that are compared specially in Table A.12. This issue has been discussed in detail in Ghoshal (1986).
32. See Ghoshal and Bartlett (1988).

BIBLIOGRAPHY

Abegglen, J. C. The Japanese Organization: Aspects of Its Social Organization. New York: Free Press, 1958.

Aguilar, F. J. Scanning the Business Environment. New York: Macmillan, 1967.

Aldrich, H. E. Organizations and Environments. Englewood Cliffs, NJ: Prentice-Hall, 1979.

Aldrich, H. E., and D. A. Whetten. "Organization-sets, Action-sets, and Networks: Making the Most of Simplicity." In Handbook of Organizational Design, edited by P. C. Nystrom and W. H. Starbuck. London: Oxford University Press, 1981, pp. 385–408.

Allen, T. J. Managing the Flow of Technology. Cambridge, MA: MIT Press, 1977.

Allison, G. T. Essence of Decision: Explaining the Cuban Missile Crisis. Boston: Little, Brown, 1971.

Altman, A., and U. Olsson. LM Ericsson: 100 Years. Stockholm: Interbook Publishing AB, 1977.

Andrews, K. The Concept of Strategy. Homewood, IL: Irwin, 1980.

Argyris, C., and D. Schon. Organizational Learning: A Theory of Action Perspective. Reading, MA: Addison-Wesley, 1978.

Ashby, W. R. Introduction to Cybernetics. London: Chapman and Hall, 1956.

Bacharach, S. B., and M. Aiken. "Structural and Process Constraints on Influence in Organizations: A Level Specific Analysis." Administrative Science Quarterly, Vol. 21 (1976): 623–642.

Bacharach, S. B., and E. J. Lawler. Power and Politics in Organizations. San Francisco: Jossey-Bass, 1981.

Bain, J. Industrial Organization. New York: Wiley, 1959.

Baliga, B. R., and A. M. Jaeger. "Multinational Corporations: Control Systems and Delegation Issues." Journal of International Business Studies, Fall (1984): 25–40.

Barnard, C. I. The Functions of the Executive. 30th Anniversary Edition. Cambridge, MA: Harvard University Press, 1968.

Bartlett, C. A. Harvard Business School cases: "Compania Telefonica Mexicana (CTM): ATI in Mexico," #9-387-115; "EMI and the CT Scanner (A)," #9-383-194; "EMI and the CT Scanner (B)," #9-383-195; "Merloni Group," #9-383-152; "Ideal Standard France: Pat Peterson," #9-382-139; "Kentucky Fried Chicken (Japan) Limited," #9-387-043; "Conex do Brasil," #9-385-257; "Dominion Engineering Works," #9-383-185; "Note on the Paper Machinery Industry," #5-383-191; "Caterpillar Tractor Company," #9-385-276; "Komatsu Limited," #9-385-277; "Corning Glass Works, International," #9-381-160 to #9-381-164; "Procter & Gamble Europe: Vizir Launch," #9-384-139.

———. Multinational Structural Evolution: The Changing Decision Environment in International Divisions. Unpublished doctoral dissertation. Boston: Harvard Business School, 1979.

———. "Multinational Structural Change: Evolution Versus Reorganization," in The Management of Headquarters-Subsidiary Relationships in Multinational Corporations, edited by L. Otterbeck. Aldershot, UK: Gower Publishing, 1981, pp. 121–145.

———. "How Multinational Organizations Evolve." Journal of Business Strategy, Vol. 3, No. 1 (Summer 1982): 20–32.

———. "MNCs: Get Off the Reorganization Merry-Go-Round." Harvard Business Review (March–April 1983): 138–146.

————. "Building and Managing the Transnational: The New Organizational Challenge." In *Competition in Global Industries*, edited by M. E. Porter. Boston: Harvard Business School Press, 1986, pp. 367–401.

Bartlett, C. A., and S. Ghoshal. "Tap Your Subsidiaries for Global Reach." *Harvard Business Review* (November–December 1986): 87–94.

————. "Managing Across Borders: New Strategic Requirements." *Sloan Management Review* (Summer 1987): 7–17.

————. "Managing Across Borders: New Organizational Responses." *Sloan Management Review* (Fall 1987): 45–53.

Bartlett, C. A., and H. Yoshihara. "New Challenges for Japanese Multinationals: Is Organization Adaptation Their Achilles' Heel?" *Human Resource Management*, Vol. 27, No. 1 (Spring 1988): 19–43.

Baumol, W. J., J. C. Panzer, and R. D. Willig. *Contestable Markets and the Theory of Industry Structure*. New York: Harcourt Brace Jovanovich, 1982.

Beckhard, R. *Organization Development: Strategies and Goals*. Reading, MA: Addison-Wesley, 1969.

Beckhard, R., and T. Harris. *Organizational Transitions*. Reading, MA: Addison-Wesley, 1977.

Beer, M. *Organization Change and Development: A Systems View*. Santa Monica, CA: Goodyear, 1980.

Behrman, J. N., and W. A. Fischer. *Overseas R&D Activities of Transnational Corporations*. Cambridge, MA: Oelgeschlager, Gunn, & Hain, 1980.

Bennis, W. *Changing Organizations*. New York: McGraw-Hill, 1966.

Bennis, W., and B. Nanus. *Leaders: The Strategies for Taking Charge*. New York: Harper & Row, 1985.

Benson, J. K. "The Interorganizational Network as a Political Economy." *Administrative Science Quarterly*, Vol. 20 (1975): 229–249.

Beyer, J. M., and H. Trice. *Implementing Change*. New York: Free Press, 1978.

Blau, J., and R. A. Schoenherr. *The Structure of Organizations*. New York: Basic Books, 1971.

Blau, P. M. "A Formal Theory of Differentiation in Organizations." *American Sociological Review*, Vol. 35 (1970): 201–218.

Bower, J. *Managing the Resource Allocation Process*. Boston: Division of Research, Harvard Business School, 1970.

Brandt, K., and J. M. Hulbert. "Patterns of Communications in the Multinational Corporation: An Empirical Study." *Journal of International Business Studies*, Vol. 7, No. 1 (Spring 1976): 57–64.

Buckley, P. J., and M. Casson. *The Future of the Multinational Enterprise*. London: Macmillan, 1976.

————. *The Economic Theory of the Multinational Enterprise*. New York: St. Martins, 1985.

Burgelman, R. A. "Strategy Making and Evolutionary Theory: Toward a Capability Based Perception." Research paper 755, Stanford University, 1984.

Burgelman, R. A., and L. R. Sayles. *Inside Corporate Innovation: Strategy, Structure and Managerial Skills*. New York: Free Press, 1986.

Burns, T., and G. M. Stalker. *The Management of Innovation*. London: Tavistock, 1961.

Buzzell, R. D. "Can You Standardize Multinational Marketing?" *Harvard Business Review* (November–December 1968): 102–113.

Calvet, L. "A Synthesis of Foreign Direct Investment Theories and Theories of the Multinational Firm." *Journal of International Business Studies* (Spring–Summer 1981): 43–59.

Caves, R. E. "Industrial Organization, Corporate Strategy and Structure." *Journal of Economic Literature*, Vol. 18 (March 1980): 64–92.

————. *Multinational Enterprise and Economic Analysis*. Cambridge: Cambridge University Press, 1982.

Chandler, A. D. *Strategy and Structure: Chapters in the History of American Industrial Enterprise*. Cambridge, MA: MIT Press, 1962.

————. *The Visible Hand: The Managerial Revolution in American Business*. Cambridge, MA: Harvard University Press, 1977.

————. "The Evolution of Modern Global Competition." In *Competition in Global Industries*, edited by M. E. Porter. Boston: Harvard Business School Press, 1986, pp. 405–448.

Child, J. "Organization Structure and Strategies of Control: A Replication of the Aston Study." *Administrative Science Quarterly*, Vol. 17 (1972): 163–177.

————. "Strategies of Control and Organizational Behavior." *Administrative Science Quarterly*, Vol. 18 (1973): 1–17.

Chorafas, D. N. *Developing the International Executive*. New York: American Management Association, 1969.

Clark, B. R. "The Organizational Saga in Higher Education." *Administrative Science Quarterly*, Vol. 17 (1972): 1–25.

Clee, G. H., and A. di Scipio. "Creating a World Enterprise." *Harvard Business Review* (November–December 1959): 77–89.

Clee, G. H., and W. M. Sachtjen. "Organizing a Worldwide Business." *Harvard Business Review* (November–December 1964): 55–67.

Contractor, F. J., and P. Lorange (eds.). *Cooperative Strategies in International Business*. Cambridge, MA: Ballinger, 1987.

Cook, K. S. "Exchange and Power in Networks of Interorganizational Relations." *Sociological Quarterly*, Vol. 18 (1977): 62–68.

Cray, D. "Control and Coordination in Multinational Corporations." *Journal of International Business Studies* (Fall 1984): 58–98.

Crozier, M. *The Bureaucratic Phenomenon*. Chicago: University of Chicago Press, 1964.

Cutcher-Gershenfeld, J. *The Collective Governance of Industrial Relations*. Unpublished doctoral dissertation. Cambridge, MA: MIT Sloan School of Management, 1988.

Cyert, R., and J. March. *A Behavioral Theory of the Firm*. Englewood Cliffs, NJ: Prentice-Hall, 1963.

Dalton, M. *Men Who Manage*. New York: Wiley, 1959.

Daniels, J. D., R. A. Pitts, and M. J. Tretter. "Strategy and Structure of U.S. Multinationals: An Exploratory Study." *Academy of Management Journal*, Vol. 27 (1984): 292–307.

————. "Organizing for Dual Strategies of Product Diversity and International Expansion." *Strategic Management Journal*, Vol. 6 (1985): 223–237.

Davidson, W. H., and P. Haspeslagh. "Shaping a Global Product Organization." *Harvard Business Review* (July–August 1982): 125–132.

Davis, S. M., and P. R. Lawrence. *Matrix*. Reading, MA: Addison-Wesley, 1977.

Deal, T. E., and A. A. Kennedy. *Corporate Cultures: the Rites and Rituals of Corporate Life*. Reading, MA: Addison-Wesley, 1982.

De Bodinat, H. *Influence in the Multinational Enterprise: The Case of Manufacturing*. Unpublished doctoral dissertation. Boston: Harvard Business School, 1976.

DiMaggio, P., and W. Powell. "The Iron Cage Revisited: Institutional Isomorphism and Collective Rationality in Organizational Fields." *American Sociological Review*, Vol. 48 (1983): 147–160.

Dore, R. P. *British Factory—Japanese Factory*. Berkeley: University of California Press, 1973.

Dougherty, D. *Introducing New Products: The Myth of the "Mouse in Search of the Better Mouse-Trap."* Unpublished doctoral dissertation. Cambridge, MA: MIT Sloan School of Management, 1987.

Douglas, M. *How Institutions Think*. Syracuse: Syracuse University Press, 1986.

Downey, H. K., and R. D. Ireland. "Quantitative Versus Qualitative: Environmental Assessment in Organizational Studies." *Administrative Science Quarterly*, Vol. 24 (1979): 630–637.

Doz, Y. "National Policies and Multinational Management." Unpublished doctoral dissertation. Boston: Harvard Business School, 1976.

————. "Managing Manufacturing Rationalization within Multinational Corporations." *Columbia Journal of World Business* (Fall 1978): 82–93.

————. *Government Control and Multinational Strategic Management*. New York: Praeger, 1979.

————. "Government Policies and Global Industries." In *Competition in Global Industries*, edited by M. E. Porter. Boston: Harvard Business School Press 1986, pp. 225–266.

————. *Strategic Management in Multinational Companies.* Oxford: Pergamon Press, 1986.

Doz, Y., C. A. Bartlett, and C. K. Prahalad. "Global Competitive Pressures v. Host Country Demands: Managing Tensions in Multinational Corporations." *California Management Review,* Vol. 23, No. 3 (Spring 1981): 63–74.

Doz, Y., and C. K. Prahalad. "Headquarters Influence and Strategic Control in MNCs." *Sloan Management Review* (Fall 1981): 15–29.

————. "Patterns of Strategic Control in Multinational Corporations." *Journal of International Business Studies* (Fall 1984): 55–72.

Drucker, P. F. *Innovation and Entrepreneurship.* New York: Harper & Row, 1985.

Duncan, R. B., and A. Weiss. "Organizational Learning: Implications for Organizational Design." In *Research in Organizational Behavior,* Vol. 1, edited by B. Staw. Greenwich, CT: JAI Press, 1979, pp. 75–123.

Dutton, J., and S. Jackson. "Categorizing Strategic Issues: Links to Organizational Action." *Academy of Management Review,* Vol. 12 (1987): 76–90.

Dyas, G. P., and H. T. Thanheiser. *The Emerging European Enterprise: Strategy and Structure in French and German Industry.* London: Macmillan, 1976.

Eccles, R. G. *The Transfer Pricing Problem: A Theory for Practice.* Lexington, MA: Lexington Books, 1985.

Eccles, R. G., and D. B. Crane. "Managing Through Networks in Investment Banking." *California Management Review,* Vol. 30, No. 1 (Fall 1987): 176–195.

Edstrom, A., and J. R. Galbraith. "Transfer of Managers as a Coordination and Control Strategy in Multinational Organizations." *Administrative Science Quarterly,* Vol. 22 (June 1977): 248–263.

Edstrom, A., and P. Lorange. "Matching Strategy and Human Resources in Multinational Corporations." *Journal of International Business Studies* (Fall 1984): 73–83.

Egelhoff, W. G. "Strategy and Structure in Multinational Corporations: An Information-Processing Approach." *Administrative Science Quarterly,* Vol. 27 (1982): 435–458.

Evans, J. S. *Strategic Flexibility in Business.* Report No. 678. Palo Alto, CA: SRI International, 1982.

Everitt, B. *Cluster Analysis,* 2nd ed. New York: Wiley, 1980.

Fayerweather, J. "Four Winning Strategies for the International Corporation." *The Journal of Business Strategy* (Fall 1981): 25–36.

Fieldhouse, D. K. *Unilever Overseas: The Anatomy of a Multinational.* London: Croom Helm, 1978.

Fiol, M. C., and M. A. Lyles. "Organizational Learning." *Academy of Management Review,* Vol. 10, No. 4 (1985): 803–813.

Fischer, D. H. *Historian's Fallacies.* New York: Harper & Row, 1970.

Flaherty, T. M. "Coordinating International Manufacturing and Technology." In *Competition in Global Industries,* edited by M. E. Porter. Boston: Harvard Business School Press, 1986, pp. 83–109.

Foster, R. *Innovation: The Attacker's Advantage.* New York: Summit Books, 1985.

Fouraker, L. E., and J. M. Stopford. "Organization Structure and Multinational Strategy." *Administrative Science Quarterly* (June 1968): 57–70.

Franko, L. G. *The European Multinationals.* Greenwich, CT: Greylock, 1976.

Freeman, C. *The Economics of Industrial Innovation.* Cambridge, MA: MIT Press, 1982.

Fusfeld, H. I., and C. S. Haklisch. "Co-operative R&D for Competitors." *Harvard Business Review* (November–December 1985): 60–76.

Gabel, L. (ed.). *Product Standardization as a Tool of Competitive Strategy.* New York: North-Holland, 1987.

Galbraith, J. *Designing Complex Organizations.* Reading, MA: Addison-Wesley, 1973.

Garnier, G. H. "Context and Decision Making Autonomy in the Foreign Affiliates of U.S. National Corporations." *Academy of Management Journal,* Vol. 25, No. 4 (1982): 893–908.

Gates, S. R., and W. G. Egelhoff. "Centralization in Parent Headquarters-Subsidiary Relationships." Paper presented at the Annual Meeting of the Academy of Management, Boston, 1984.

Ghemawat, P., and M. A. Spence. "Modeling Global Competition." In *Competition in*

Global Industries, edited by M. E. Porter. Boston: Harvard Business School Press, 1986, pp. 61–79.

Ghoshal, S. *Environmental Scanning: An Individual and Organizational Level Analysis.* Unpublished doctoral dissertation. Cambridge, MA: MIT Sloan School of Management, 1985.

———. *The Innovative Multinational: A Differentiated Network of Organizational Roles and Management Processes.* Unpublished doctoral dissertation. Boston: Harvard Business School, 1986.

———. "Global Strategy: An Organizing Framework." *Strategic Management Journal* (September–October 1987): 425–440.

Ghoshal S., and C. A. Bartlett. "Creation, Adoption, and Diffusion of Innovations by Subsidiaries of Multinational Corporations." *Journal of International Business Studies* (Fall 1988): 365–388.

———. "Matsushita Electric Industries LTD." Harvard Business School case #9-388-144.

Ghoshal, S., and N. Nohria. "Multinational Corporations as Differentiated Networks." Working paper 87/13. Fontainebleau, France: INSEAD, 1987.

Gold, B. "Robotics, Programmable Automation, and International Competitiveness." *IEEE Transactions and Engineering Management* (November 1982): 135–146.

Gruber, W. M., S. Mehta, and R. Vernon. "The R&D Factor in International Investment of U.S. Industries." *Journal of Political Economy* (February 1967): 20–37.

Hall, R. H. *Organizations: Structure and Process.* Englewood Cliffs, NJ: Prentice-Hall, 1972.

Hamel, G., and C. K. Prahalad. "Do You Really Have a Global Strategy?" *Harvard Business Review* (July–August 1985): 139–148.

———. "Strategic Alliances: Success or Surrender." Mimeo. London Business School, 1988.

Hannan, M., and J. Freeman. "The Population Ecology of Organizations." *American Journal of Sociology*, Vol. 82 (1977): 929–964.

———. "Structural Inertia and Organizational Change." *American Sociological Review*, Vol. 49 (1984): 149–164.

Harrigan, K. R. "Innovation Within Overseas Subsidiaries." *The Journal of Business Strategy*, Vol. 4, No. 4 (Spring 1984): 47–55.

———. "Research Methodologies for Contingency Approaches to Business Strategy." *Academy of Management Review*, Vol. 8, No. 3 (1983): 398–405.

Haspeslagh, P. "Portfolio Planning: Uses and Limits." *Harvard Business Review* (January–February 1982): 58–73.

Hedberg, B. L. T. "How Organizations Learn and Unlearn?" In *Handbook of Organizational Design*, edited by P. C. Nystrom and W. H. Starbuck. Vol. 1. London: Oxford University Press, 1981, pp. 3–27.

Hedberg, B. L. T., P. C. Nystrom, and W. H. Starbuck. "Camping on Seesaws: Prescriptions for a Self-Designing Organization." *Administrative Science Quarterly*, Vol. 21 (March 1976): 41–65.

Hedlund, G. "Autonomy of Subsidiaries and Formalization of Headquarters-Subsidiary Relations in Swedish MNCs." In *The Management of Headquarters-Subsidiary Relationships in Multinational Corporations*, edited by L. Otterbeck. Aldershot, UK: Gower Publishing, 1981, pp. 25–78.

———. "The Hypermodern MNC: A Heterarchy?" *Human Resource Management* (Spring 1986): 9–35.

Hickson, D. J., C. R. Hinings, C. A. Lee, R. E. Schneck, and J. M. Pennings. "A Strategic Contingencies' Theory of Intraorganizational Power." *Administrative Science Quarterly*, Vol. 16 (1971): 216–229.

Hinings, C. R., D. J. Hickson, J. M. Pennings, and R. E. Schneck. "Structural Conditions of Intraorganizational Power." *Administrative Science Quarterly*, Vol. 19 (1974): 22–44.

Hofstede, G. "National Culture in Four Dimensions." *International Studies of Management and Organizations*, Vol. 13 (1983): 97–118.

Horwitch, M. *Post-Modern Management: Its Emergence and Meaning for Strategy.* New York: Free Press, forthcoming.

Hout, T., M. E. Porter, and E. Rudden. "How Global Companies Win Out." *Harvard Business Review* (September–October 1982): 98–108.

Hrebeniak, L. G., W. F. Joyce, and C. C. Snow. "Strategy, Structure, and Performance: Past and Future Research." In *Strategy, Organization Design, and Human Resource Management*, edited by C. C. Snow. Greenwich, CT: JAI Press, forthcoming.

Hulbert, J. M., and W. K. Brandt. *Managing the Multinational Subsidiary*. New York: Holt, Rinehart and Winston, 1980.

Itami, H. *Mobilizing Invisible Assets*. Cambridge, MA: Harvard University Press, 1987.

Jacobs, D. "Dependence and Vulnerability: An Exchange Approach to the Control of Organizations." *Administrative Science Quarterly*, Vol. 19 (1974): 45–59.

Jaeger, A. M. "The Transfer of Organizational Culture Overseas: An Approach to Control in the Multinational Corporation." *Journal of International Business Studies* (Fall 1983): 91–114.

Jaeger, A. M., and B. R. Baliga. "Control Systems and Strategic Adaptation: Lessons from the Japanese Experience." *Strategic Management Journal*, Vol. 6 (1985): 115–134.

Jemison, D. B., and S. B. Sitkin. "Corporate Acquisitions: A Process Prospective." *Academy of Management Review*, Vol. 11, No. 1 (January 1986): 145–163.

Kagono, T. "Structural Design of Headquarters-Division Relationships and Economic Performance: An Analysis of Japanese Firms." In *The Management of Headquarters-Subsidiary Relationships in Multinational Corporations*, edited by L. Otterbeck. Aldershot, UK: Gower Publishing, 1981, pp. 147–185.

Kanter, R. M. *The Change Masters*. New York: Simon and Schuster, 1983.

Keegan, W. J. *Multinational Marketing Management*, 2d ed. Englewood Cliffs, NJ: Prentice-Hall, 1980.

Khandwalla, P. M. *The Design of Organizations*. New York: Harcourt Brace Jovanovich, 1977.

Kiechel, W. "Playing the Global Game." *Fortune*, November 16, 1981.

Killough, J. "Improving Payoffs from Transnational Advertising." *Harvard Business Review* (July–August 1978): 102–110.

Kimberly, J. R. "Imitation, Innovation and Institutionalization in the Creative Process." In *The Organizational Life Cycle*, edited by J. R. Kimberly and R. H. Miles. San Francisco: Jossey-Bass, 1980.

Knox, A. M. *Coming Clean: A Postscript after Retirement from Unilever*. London: Heinemann, 1976.

Kogut, B. "Foreign Direct Investment as a Sequential Process." In *The Multinational Corporation in the 1980s*, edited by C. P. Kindelberger and D. B. Audretsch. Cambridge, MA: MIT Press, 1983, pp. 38–56.

———. "Normative Observations on the International Value-Added Chain and Strategic Groups." *Journal of International Business Studies*. (Fall 1984): 151–168.

———. "Designing Global Strategies: Comparative and Competitive Value-Added Chains." *Sloan Management Review* (Summer 1985): 15–28.

———. "Designing Global Strategies: Profiting from Operating Flexibility. *Sloan Management Review* (Fall 1985): 27–38.

———. "Joint Ventures: Theoretical and Empirical Perspectives." *Strategic Management Journal*, Vol. 9, No. 4 (1988): 319–332.

Kotter, J. P. *The Leadership Factor*. New York: Free Press, 1988.

Krugman, P. Review of Bruce Scott and George Lodge (eds.), "U.S. Competitiveness in the World Economy." *Journal of Economic Literature*, Vol. 24 (March 1986): 110–111.

Kunda, G. *Engineering Culture: Culture and Control in a High-Tech Organization*. Unpublished doctoral dissertation. Boston: Harvard Business School, 1987.

Landau, M. "On the Concept of a Self-Correcting Organization. *Public Administrative Review* (1973): 533–542.

Laurant, A. "The Cross-Cultural Puzzle of International Human Resource Management." *Human Resource Management* (Spring 1986): 91–102.

Lawrence, P. R., and D. Dyer. *Renewing American Industry*. New York: Free Press, 1983.

Lawrence, P. R., and J. W. Lorsch. *Organization and Environment*. Boston: Division of Research, Harvard Business School, 1967.

Lehmann, J. P. *The Roots of Modern Japan*. London: Macmillan, 1981.

Lessard, D., and J. Lightstone. "Volatile Exchange Rates Can Put Operations at Risk." *Harvard Business Review* (July–August 1986): 107–114.

Lessard, D., and N. Nohria. "Rediscovering Expert Functions in the MNC: The Emergent Matrix." In *Management of the Multinational Corporation*, edited by C. Bartlett, Y. Doz, and G. Hedlund. London: Routledge (forthcoming).

Levitt, T. "The Globalization of Markets." *Harvard Business Review* (May–June 1983): 92–102.

Lewin, K. *Field Theory in Social Science*. New York: Harper & Row, 1951.

Lindblom, C. E. "The Science of Muddling Through." *Public Administration Review* (1959): 79–88.

Lorange, P., M. S. Scott Morton, and S. Ghoshal. *Strategic Control*. St. Paul, MN: West, 1986.

March, J. G., and J. P. Olsen. *Ambiguity and Choice in Organizations*. Bergen, Norway: Universitetsforlaget, 1976.

March, J. G., and H. A. Simon. *Organizations*. New York: Wiley, 1958.

Mascarenhas, B. "Coordination of Manufacturing Interdependence in MNCs." *Journal of International Business Studies* (Winter 1984): 91–106.

Merton, R. K. "The Role-Set: Problems in Sociological Theory." *British Journal of Sociology*, Vol. 8 (1957): 106–120.

Meurling, J., and Jeans, R. *A Switch in Time*. Chicago: Telephony Publishing, 1985.

Meyer, J. W., and B. Rowan. "Institutionalized Organizations: Formal Structure as Myth and Ceremony." *American Journal of Sociology*, Vol. 83 (1977): 340–363.

Miller, D. "The Genesis of Configuration." *Academy of Management Review*, Vol. 12 (1987): 686–701.

Miller, D., and P. H. Freisen. *Organizations: A Quantum View*. Englewood Cliffs, NJ: Prentice-Hall, 1984.

Milligan, G. W., and M. C. Cooper. "An Examination of Procedures for Determining the Number of Clusters in a Data Set." *Psychometrica*, Vol. 50 (1985): 159–179.

Mintzberg, H. *The Structuring of Organizations: A Synthesis of the Research*. Englewood Cliffs, NJ: Prentice-Hall, 1979.

———. *Power In and Around Organizations*. Englewood Cliffs, NJ: Prentice-Hall, 1983.

Mohr, L. "Determinants of Innovation in Organizations." *American Political Science Review*, Vol. 63 (1969): 111–126.

Morgan, G. *Images of Organization*. Newbury Park, CA: Sage, 1986.

Murray, R. (ed.). *Multinationals Beyond the Market: Intra-Firm Trade and Control of Transfer Pricing*. New York: Halstead Press, 1981.

Negandhi, A. R., and R. Baliga. "Internal Functioning of American, German and Japanese Multinational Corporations." In *The Management of Headquarters-Subsidiary Relationships in Multinational Corporations*, edited by L. Otterbeck. Aldershot, UK: Gower Publishing, 1981, pp. 107–120.

Nelson, S., and S. Winter. *An Evolutionary Theory of Economic Changes*. Cambridge, MA: Harvard University Press, 1982.

Nonaka, I. *Organization and Market: Exploratory Study of Centralization vs. Decentralization*. Unpublished Ph.D. dissertation. Berkeley, CA: Graduate School of Business Administration, UC Berkeley, 1972.

Normann, R. "Organizational Innovativeness: Product Variation and Reorientation." *Administrative Science Quarterly*, Vol. 16 (1971): 203–215.

Nystrom, P. C., B. L. T. Hedberg, and W. H. Starbuck. "Interacting Processes and Organization Designs." In *The Management of Organization Design*, edited by R. H. Kilmann, L. R. Pondy, and D. P. Slevin, Vol. 1. New York: Elsevier North-Holland, 1976, pp. 209–230.

Ohmae, K. *Triad Power*. New York: Free Press, 1985.

Otterbeck, L. (ed.). *The Management of Headquarters-Subsidiary Relationships in Multinational Corporations*. Aldershot, UK: Gower Publishing, 1981.

Ouchi, W. G. "The Relationship Between Organizational Structure and Organizational Control." *Administrative Science Quarterly*, Vol. 22 (March 1977): 95–113.

———. "Markets, Bureaucracies, and Clans." *Administrative Science Quarterly*, Vol. 25 (1980): 129–144.

Ouchi, W. G., and J. B. Johnson. "Types of Organizational Control and Their Relationships to Emotional Well Being." *Administrative Science Quarterly*, Vol. 23 (June 1978): 293–317.

Owen, N. "Scale Economies in the EEC: An Approach Based on Intra EEC Trade." *European Economic Review* (February 1976): 143–163.

Pascale, R. T. "Communication and Decision-Making Across Cultures: Japanese and American Comparisons." *Administrative Science Quarterly* Vol. 23, No. 1 (1978): 91–110.

Perlmutter, H. V. "The Tortuous Evolution of the Multinational Corporation." *Columbia Journal of World Business* (January–February 1969): 9–18.

Perlmutter, H. V., and D. A. Heenan. "Cooperate to Compete Globally." *Harvard Business Review* (March–April, 1986): 136–152.

Perrow, C. B. "The Bureaucratic Paradox: The Efficient Organization Centralizes in Order to Decentralize." *Organizational Dynamics*, Vol. 5 (1977): 2–14.

Peters, T. J., and R. H. Waterman. *In Search of Excellence*. New York: Harper & Row, 1982.

Pettigrew, A. M. "Information Control as a Power Resource." *Sociology*, Vol. 6 (1972): 187–204.

———. *The Politics of Organizational Decision-Making*. London: Tavistock, 1973.

———. *The Awakening Giant: Continuity and Change in ICI*. Oxford: Basil Blackwell, 1985.

Pfeffer, J. *Power in Organizations*. Boston: Pitman, 1981.

———. *Organizations and Organization Theory*. Boston: Pitman, 1982.

Pfeffer, J., and G. R. Salancik. *The External Control of Organizations: A Resource Dependence Perspective*. New York: Harper & Row, 1978.

Picard, J. "Organizational Structures and Integrative Devices in European Multinational Corporations." *Columbia Journal of World Business* (Spring 1980): 30–35.

Piore, M. "Corporate Reform in American Manufacturing and the Challenge to Economic Theory." Working paper. Cambridge, MA: MIT Sloan School of Management, 1987.

Piore, M., and C. Sabel. *The Second Industrial Divide*. New York: Basic Books, 1984.

Poole, J. "SKF Reintegrates Internationally." *Multinational Business*, No. 4 (1976): 1–7.

Porter, M. E. *Competitive Strategy*. New York: Free Press, 1980.

———. "The Contributions of Industrial Organization to Strategic Management." *Academy of Management Review*, Vol. 6 (1981): 609–620.

———. *Competitive Advantage*. New York: Free Press, 1985.

———. "Competition in Global Industries: A Conceptual Framework." In *Competition in Global Industries*, edited by M. E. Porter. Boston: Harvard Business School Press, 1986, pp. 15–60.

———. "Changing Patterns of International Competition." *California Management Review*, Vol. 28, No. 2 (1986): 9–40.

Powell, W. "How the Past Informs the Present: The Uses and Liabilities of Organizational Memory." Working paper. Stanford, CA: Stanford Center for Advanced Study in the Behavioral Sciences, 1987.

———. "Hybrid Organizational Arrangements." *California Management Review* (Fall 1987): 67–87.

Poynter, T. A. *International Enterprises and Government Intervention*. London: Croom Helm, 1985.

Prahalad, C. K. *The Strategic Process in a Multinational Corporation*. Unpublished doctoral dissertation. Boston: Harvard Business School, 1976.

Prahalad, C. K., and Y. Doz. "An Approach to Strategic Control in MNCs." *Sloan Management Review* (Summer 1981): 5–13.

———. *The Multinational Mission: Balancing Local Demands and Global Vision*. New York: Free Press, 1987.

Provan, K. "The Federation as an Interorganizational Linkage Network." *Academy of Management Review*, Vol. 8 (1983): 79–89.

Pugh, D. S., D. J. Hickson, and C. R. Hinings. "The Context of Organization Structure." *Administrative Science Quarterly*, Vol. 14 (1969): 91–114.

Pugh, D. S., D. J. Hickson, C. R. Hinings, and C. Turner. "Dimensions of Organization Structure." *Administrative Science Quarterly*, Vol. 13 (1968): 65–105.

Quelch, J. A., and E. J. Hoff. "Customizing Global Marketing." *Harvard Business Review* (May–June 1986): 59–68.

Quinn, J. B. *Strategies for Change: Logical Incrementalism.* Homewood, IL: Irwin, 1980.

Reader, W. J. *Fifty Years of Unilever.* London: Heinemann, 1980.

Rohlen, T. P. *For Harmony and Strength: Japanese White Collar Organization in Anthropological Perspective.* Berkeley: University of California Press, 1974.

Ronstadt, R. C. *Research and Development Abroad by U.S. Multinationals.* New York: Praeger, 1977.

Ronstadt, R. C., and R. J. Kramer. "Getting the Most Out of Innovation Abroad." *Harvard Business Review* (March–April 1982): 94–99.

Rugman, A. M. *International Diversification and the Multinational Enterprise.* Lexington, MA: Lexington Books, 1979.

Rugman, A. M., and T. A. Poynter. "World Product Mandates: How Will MNCs Respond?" *Business Quarterly* (October 1982): 54–61.

Rumelt, R. P. *Strategy, Structure, and Economic Performance.* Boston: Division of Research, Harvard Business School, 1974.

Sampson, A. *The Sovereign State of ITT.* New York: Stein and Day, 1973.

Schein, E. H. *Organizational Culture and Leadership.* San Francisco: Jossey-Bass, 1985.

Scherer, F. M., E. Kaufer, and R. D. Murphy. *The Economics of Multiplant Operation: An International Comparisons Study.* Cambridge, MA: Harvard University Press, 1975.

Schisgall, O. *Eyes on Tomorrow: The Evolution of Procter & Gamble.* Chicago: J. G. Ferguson Publishing, 1981.

Schoenberg, R. J. *Geneen.* New York: Warner, 1985.

Scott, B., and G. Lodge (eds.). *U.S. Competitiveness in the World Economy.* Boston: Harvard Business School Press, 1986.

Selznick, P. *TVA and the Grass Roots.* Berkeley: University of California Press, 1949.

———. *Leadership in Administration: A Sociological Interpretation.* New York: Harper & Row, 1959.

Servan-Schreiber, J. J. *The American Challenge.* New York: Atheneum, 1968.

Shimada, H., and J. P. MacDuffie. "Industrial Relations and 'Humanware': Japanese Investment in Automobile Manufacturing in the U.S." Working paper. Cambridge, MA: MIT Sloan School of Management, 1987.

Sims, H. P., Jr., D. A. Gioia, and Associates. *The Thinking Organization: Dynamics of Organizational Social Cognition.* San Francisco: Jossey-Bass, 1986.

Snow, C. C., and L. G. Hrebeniak. "Strategy, Distinctive Competence, and Organizational Performance." *Administrative Science Quarterly*, Vol. 25 (1980): 317–336.

Starbuck, W. H. "Organizations as Action Generators." *American Sociological Review*, Vol. 48 (1983): 91–102.

Starbuck, W. H., H. Greve, and B. L. T. Hedberg. "Responding to Crises." *Journal of Business Administration*, Vol. 9 (1978): 111–137.

Stinchcombe, A. "Social Structure and Organizations." In *Handbook of Organizations*, edited by J. March. Chicago: Rand McNally, 1965, pp. 142–193.

Stopford, J. M. *World Directory of Multinational Enterprises.* Detroit, MI: Gale Research Company, 1983.

Stopford, J. M., and L. Turner. *Britain and the Multinationals.* London: Wiley, 1985.

Stopford, J. M., and L. T. Wells, Jr. *Managing the Multinational Enterprise.* New York: Basic Books, 1972.

Takeuchi, H., and I. Nonaka. "The New Product Development Game." *Harvard Business Review* (January–February 1986): 137–146.

Takeuchi, H., and M. E. Porter. "Three Roles of International Marketing in Global Strategy." In *Competition in Global Industries*, edited by M. E. Porter. Boston: Harvard Business School Press, 1986, pp. 111–146.

Teece, D. J. "Transaction Cost Economics and the Multinational Enterprise." *Journal of Economic Behavior and Organization*, Vol. 7 (1986): 21–45.

——— (ed.). *The Competitive Challenge.* Cambridge, MA: Ballinger, 1987.

Terpstra, V. "International Product Policy: The Role of Foreign R & D." *Columbia Journal of World Business* (Winter 1977): 24–32.

Thompson, J. D. *Organizations in Action.* New York: McGraw-Hill, 1967.

Tichy, N. M. *Managing Strategic Change.* New York: Wiley, 1983.

Tsurumi, Y. The Japanese Are Coming. Cambridge, MA: Ballinger, 1976.

Tung, R. "Selection and Training of Personnel for Overseas Assignments." Columbia Journal of World Business, Vol. 16, No. 1 (1982): 68–78.

Tushman, M. L. "Special Boundary Role in the Innovation Process." Administrative Science Quarterly, Vol. 22 (1977): 587–605.

Van Maanen, J. "People Processing: Strategies of Organizational Socialization." Organizational Dynamics, Vol. 7 (1978): 19–36.

Van Maanen, J., and E. Schein. "Toward a Theory of Organizational Socialization." In Research in Organizational Behavior, edited by B. M. Staw, Vol. 1. Greenwich, CT: JAI Press, 1979, pp. 209–264.

Venkatraman, N. "The Concept of Fit in Strategy Research: Towards Verbal and Statistical Correspondence." Working paper. Cambridge, MA: MIT Sloan School of Management, 1987.

Vernon, R. "International Investment and International Trade in the Product Cycle." Quarterly Journal of Economics, Vol. 80 (1966): 190–207.

———. Sovereignty at Bay. New York: Basic Books, 1971.

———. Storm Over the Multinationals. Cambridge, MA: Harvard University Press, 1977.

———. "The Product Cycle Hypothesis in a New International Environment." Oxford Bulletin of Economics and Statistics, Vol. 41 (November 1979): 255–267.

———. "Gone Are the Cash Cows of Yesteryear." Harvard Business Review (November–December 1980): 150–155.

Watson, C. M. "Counter-competition Abroad to Protect Home Markets." Harvard Business Review (January–February 1982): 40–46.

Weick, K. E. The Social Psychology of Organizing, 2d ed. Reading, MA: Addison-Wesley, 1969.

———. "Educational Organizations as Loosely Coupled Systems." Administrative Science Quarterly, Vol. 21 (1976): 1–19.

———. "Cognitive Processes in Organizations." In Research in Organizational Behavior, Vol. 1, edited by B. M. Staw. Greenwich, CT: JAI Press, 1979, pp. 41–74.

Wells, L. T., Jr. The Product Life Cycle and International Trade. Boston: Division of Research, Harvard Business School, 1972.

Westley, F., and H. Mintzberg. "Strategic Vision: Levesque and Iacocca." Working paper. Montreal: McGill University, 1988.

Westney, E. D. Imitation and Innovation. Cambridge, MA: Harvard University Press, 1987.

Westney, E. D., and K. Sakakibara. "The Role of Japan-Based R&D in Global Technology Strategy." Technology in Society, Vol. 7 (1985): 315–330.

White, R., and T. A. Poynter. "Strategies for Foreign-Owned Subsidiaries in Canada." Business Quarterly (Summer 1984): 59–69.

———. "Organizing for Worldwide Advantage." In Management of the Global Corporation, edited by C. Bartlett, Y. Doz, and G. Hedlund. London: Routledge (forthcoming).

Wildavsky, A. B. "The Self-Evaluating Organization." Public Administration Review (1972): 509–520.

———. The Politics of the Budgetary Process, 3d ed. Boston: Little, Brown, 1979.

Wilkins, M. The Emergence of Multinational Enterprise: American Business Abroad from the Colonial Era to 1914. Cambridge, MA: Harvard University Press, 1974.

———. The Maturing of Multinational Enterprise: American Business Abroad from 1914 to 1970. Cambridge, MA: Harvard University Press, 1977.

Williamson, O. E. The Economic Institutions of Capitalism. New York: Free Press, 1985.

Wilson, C. H. The History of Unilever: A Study in Economic Growth and Social Change. London: Cassell, 1970.

Yates, J. Control Through Communications: The Genesis of Internal Communications in American Firms: 1895–1920. Book manuscript. Cambridge, MA: MIT Sloan School of Management.

Yoshino, M. Y. Japan's Managerial System. Cambridge, MA: MIT Press, 1968.

———. Japan's Multinational Enterprises. Cambridge, MA: Harvard University Press, 1976.

Yoshino, M. Y., and T. B. Lifson. The Invisible Link: Japan's Sogo Sosha and the Organization of Trade. Cambridge, MA: MIT Press, 1986.

Young, S., N. Hood, and J. Hamill. "Decision Making in Foreign-Owned Multinational Subsidiaries in the United Kingdom." Working paper 35. Geneva: *International Labour Office*, 1985.

Youseff, S. M. "Contextural Factors Influencing the Control Strategy of Multinational Corporations." *Academy of Management Review* (March 1975): 136–143.

Zaleznik, A. "Power and Politics in Organizational Life." *Harvard Business Review* (May–June 1970): 47–60.

Zaltman, G., R. Duncan, and J. Holbek. *Innovation and Organization*. New York: Wiley, 1973.

Zeitz, G. "Interorganizational Dialectics." *Administrative Science Quarterly*, Vol. 25 (1980): 72–88.

ABOUT THE AUTHORS

Christopher A. Bartlett is a professor of general management at the Harvard Business School, where he is also chairman of the International Senior Management program.

Sumantra Ghoshal is an associate professor who teaches business policy and international management at the European Institute of Business Administration (INSEAD) in Fontainebleau, France.

INDEX

204-214